Baedeker

D0626333

Algarve

SIGHTSEEING HIGHLIGHTS ✷ ✷

The Algarve is a region with uniquely beautiful landscape, delightful towns and sleepy villages. There are some highlights which absolutely must be seen. We have collected these here so you know what not to miss under any circumstances!

Cabo de São Vicente
The southwestern tip of Europe

2 ✷✷ Cabo de São Vicente
The extreme south-western tip of Portugal and of Europe has always inspired people. Not least to fantasize about what might be beyond the horizon.
► page 231

3 ✷✷ Costa Vicentina
Certainly one of Europe's most impressive coastlines. Wide sandy coves alternate with high cliffs where sparse vegetation battles against the wind.
► page 176

4 ✷✷ Faro
The capital of the Algarve is a popular venue for shopping; its pretty historic town centre is worth seeing.
► page 183

1 ✷✷ Algar Seco
Bizarre rock formations near Carvoeiro: wind and weather have created a most unusual landscape, which can be explored by hiking.
► page 170

7 Serra de Monchique
5 Fóia
3 Costa Vicentina
8 Silves
© Baedeker
1 Algar Seco
6 Ponta da Piedade
2 Cabo de São Vicente
4 Faro

Ponta da Piedade

Here the most unusual rock formations jut out of the water: arches, tors, crags, whole caves open up. The best way to explore the rock world is by boat.

5 ✱✱ **Fóia**

The drive to the highest peak in the Algarve is worthwhile because of the wonderful view: you can see almost all of the Algarve from here!
▶ **page 239**

6 ✱✱ **Ponta da Piedade**

Superb rocky landscape with rocky points, tors, natural arches and towers – all of it best seen by boat
▶ **page 204**

7 ✱✱ **Serra de Monchique**

This mountain range, a quiet world best explored on foot, is located in the western Algarve. The Romans were already attracted by the hot springs there.
▶ **page 237**

8 ✱✱ **Silves**

The old capital city of the Moors seems relatively provincial today. But it has an attractive, relaxed atmosphere and a few interesting sights.
▶ **page 243**

Costa Vicentina

There is always wind on the west coast.

BAEDEKER'S BEST TIPS

Of all the Baedeker tips in this book, here are some especially interesting and useful ones right away. Experience and enjoy the Algarve at its most beautiful!

⚠ Cafe Se7e
Absolutely the right eatery for football fans ▶ page 64

⚠ Taste cataplana
A culinary must for Algarve visitors! ▶ page 88

⚠ Summer means festivals
Travel to the Algarve in the high season and experience top-class international and Portuguese musicians. ▶ page 84

⚠ Health spa
Relaxation in a refined old ambience: the Romans already appreciated the warm springs in the Serra de Monchique. ▶ page 94

⚠ Forum Algarve
Shopping heaven – you can buy more or less anything here. ▶ page 114

⚠ Train ride through the eastern Algarve
By train from Faro towards the Spanish border – a route that leads through beautiful landscape and almost always along water ▶ page 130

⚠ Pretty hot stuff
Restaurants in and around Guia serve a spicy specialty: chicken in piri-piri sauce. ▶ page 150

⚠ Relaxing river trip
An enjoyable boat trip on the Guadiana in the extreme eastern Algarve ▶ page 152

⚠ Hike the lagoons
Fishermen, shell collectors and bird-watching: two routes through the Ria Formosa ▶ page 159

Magnificent views
Fabulous views on the Costa Vicentina from the path near Carrapateira

Surfing
Learn it here: riding the waves at Praia do Amado

🚹 May Day in Alte
If you're in the Algarve on 1 May, go to Alte! ▶ **page 160**

🚹 Pottery in Olaria
A vast selection of typical Algarve ceramics in a large pottery near Porches ▶ **page 168**

🚹 Surfing
For everyone who has always wanted to ride the waves: there are surfing schools at Praia do Amado. ▶ **page 178**

🚹 Superb views
On the Costa Vicentina: take the tour along a track right above the sea. ▶ **page 179**

🚹 Wine-tasting
Taste the rich red wines of the Algarve here. ▶ **page 194**

🚹 Mild summer nights in Olhão
Hardly anyone holidays in Olhão. But the summer nights are just as beautiful here as elsewhere. ▶ **page 214**

🚹 Marisqueira Filho
This popular restaurant is located right in the middle of the flat lagoon landscape. ▶ **page 260**

Try cataplana
Mussels, fish or meat cooked with paprika, onions and potatoes

Sunbathing cove in the
Rocky Algarve near Lagos
► page 79

BACKGROUND

PRACTICALITIES

PRICE CATEGORIES
Hotels
Luxury: double room from €180/£155
Mid-range: double room €70 – 170/
£60 – 145
Budget: double room up to €70/£60

Restaurants
Expensive: over €25/£21
Moderate: €10 – 25/£8.50 – 21
Inexpensive: under €10/£8.50
(for a main course)

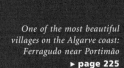

One of the most beautiful villages on the Algarve coast: Ferragudo near Portimão
▶ **page 225**

TOURS

SIGHTS FROM A to Z

Background

SUN, SEA AND DREAMY COVES,
PICTURESQUE ROCKY COASTS
AND MILES-LONG BEACHES –
THE ALGARVE IS JUSTLY FAMOUS
FOR THESE. THIS HOLIDAY PARADISE ALSO
HAS A PICTURESQUE, RURAL HINTERLAND.

UNDER THE SOUTHERN PORTUGUESE SUN

Broad slopes with cork oaks, fig and carob trees, yellow-blooming mimosa shrubs, lush almond and peach orchards, red poppy meadows – and everywhere the chirping of cicadas and the sweet smell of orange blossoms. Spring in the Algarve is one of the most beautiful things that a European who is tired of winter can dream of!

But the Algarve is one of Europe's most popular travel destinations, not just in spring. What with 3000 hours of sunshine annually this region entices visitors all year long. The so-called Rocky Algarve, or Windward Coast, with its beaches and sandy coves between picturesque cliffs made it famous. But the Sandy Algarve, or Leeward Coast, in the east is wonderful – flat beaches and dunes stretch for miles along the coast; small islands ideal for swimming lie off the coast of the lagoon system, which is paradise for birds. On the west coast the Atlantic Ocean pounds with all its might a partly deserted coast: pure nature!

Paradise Lost?

In the past decades the Algarvios have been confronted with the fact that such blessings of nature also have disadvantages. Holiday resorts

Fishing villages
White houses, blue sky and boats rocking gently in the water

were built almost everywhere along the coast. In many places the building clearly went too far – that cannot be overlooked. Construction did not even come to a halt at designated nature preservation areas. Large parts of the coast are internationally owned, and what was once a paradise was quickly lost. Many Portuguese today refuse to set foot in their southernmost region.

Surprisingly, only a few miles from the concrete blocks built for tourists, an unexpected magic, not reflected in the tourist brochures, has managed to survive. Even along the coast there are still romantic coves which are all but deserted. The hinterland is a completely different Algarve, a quiet, gentle hilly garden landscape with small, sleepy villages – no sign of the glittery, noisy tourist mayhem here. And finally there are the mountains. Here the villages are light years

← *On the Costa Vicentina*

Hinterland
Rural scenes: simple cottages, lovingly tended and always appealing

Fish market
Fresh fish is available in the Algarve everywhere: sold in the markets in the morning, served in restaurants at noon or in the evening.

Almond blossoms
While much of Europe is still freezing, southern Portugal is transformed into a sea of almond blossoms.

Holidays!
The Algarve is a paradise for children: sun, sand, sea – splashing, swimming, playing on the beach …

Algarve villages
with white-washed houses and little churches – often an unexpected treasure

Coastal landscape
Fabulous bays between cliffs – with a little luck there is even a secluded place during the high season.

away from the cities on the coast. The quiet mountain world is an invitation to picnics under tall trees with the culinary delights of the region, which can sometimes even be bought by the roadside: sausages, pine nuts, figs, almonds prepared all sorts of ways, aromatic honey and fresh goat's cheese.

Congenial Old Algarve Towns

Along with beaches and enchanted countryside, the charms of the Algarve include unique, in part historic small towns, all of which have their own character: beautiful Tavira with its houses reflected in the water, the »royal« border town Vila Real de Santo António on the Rio Guadiana laid out in right angles, Olhão with its cube houses and somewhat whimsical atmosphere, international Faro with its pretty historic centre, the old Arab capital Silves, Lagos – with a great past and friendly present. And fi-

nally there is the conglomeration of houses in Sagres, a place that now hardly shows any sign of its glorious past: in the 15th and 16th centuries this region at the south-western extremity of the European continent was the centre of an epochal event as Portugal gradually discovered the world on great ocean voyages. Almost all of these cities were founded in ancient times. Phoenicians, Celtiberians, Romans and Arabs already valued the location of the Algarve and left traces of their highly developed cultures there. The Arab have influenced southern Portugal especially, but hardly any architectural testimony to this remains.

Seafood
Algarve was made for food-lovers!

Classic Beach Holiday

But most people come to Portugal's south to relax and enjoy sun, sand and sea. And there's hardly a place more suitable! Nice accommodation is easy to find – the selection is huge. There are beaches for every taste. The only other things you need for a successful holiday are beach clothing and suntan cream; snacks are available at the beach bars. The best way to end the day is with a tasty fish dish and an ocean view.

Facts

The lush vegetation, uniquely beautiful coast and the climate are what make the southernmost province of Portugal so charming; they have drawn veritable floods of tourists for decades. The whole region profits from them, but has also been permanently changed by them – both the landscape and the people who live and work here.

Nature and Environment

The Algarve is extremely varied, something that can hardly be imagined from a look in the usual travel brochures. It is bordered by water on three sides: the Atlantic Ocean to the west and south, while the Guadiana River in the east forms the border to Spain. To the north two large mountain ranges isolate the region: the Serra de Monchique to the north-west and the Serra do Caldeirão to the north and north-east. The Algarve can be roughly divided into a narrow and in places very touristy coastal strip, the **Litoral**, the **Baroccal** foothills and the sparsely populated mountain regions with hardly any tourism, the **Serra**.

The coast alone has great variety, from steep cliffs to flat sandy beach with dunes. The slightly hilly hinterland begins north of the coastal strip. It is very green and lush, especially in winter and spring. In the central hinterland and to the east there is fertile and gentle garden landscape with orchards, almond, fig and olive trees. To the west the increased influence of the Atlantic makes the environment rougher; in the extreme west low shrubs and macchia characterize the view. In the mountains forests of eucalyptus, chestnut and stone oak trees, and higher up hardy rockroses, dominate.

> **? DID YOU KNOW …?**
>
> ■ The name Algarve comes from the time of the Arab rule. The Algarve was part of the Emirate of Córdoba and was located in the western part of the area dominated by Arabs at that time. Thus it was given the name »Al-Gharb« (= the West).
> After five centuries of Arab rule the name for this region developed into »O Algarve« after it was added to the Portuguese kingdom in the 12th century. The Arab origins are still reflected in the use of the article with the name: »the Algarve«.

West coast/ Costa Vicentina

Spectacular and legendary Cabo de São Vicente is the south-western tip of the European mainland. The European continent ends here – a broad rock plateau drops sharply to the Atlantic Ocean from a height of 60m/200ft. The cape, which is named after St Vincent, is at the southernmost end of the Costa Vicentina, which extends to Odeceixe in the north: rough coastal cliffs interrupted by large or small sandy coves. The cliffs rise to 150m/500ft above the sea. The Atlantic Ocean crashes ashore along this section of coastline, and breaks on large boulders or rolls in foamy waves across the beaches. The entire western coastline of the Algarve has been placed under nature protection since 1998 as part of the Parque Natural do Sudoeste Alentejano e Costa Vicentina – and is thus one of the most intact coastal regions in Europe.

← *The Algarve's assets: cliffs, beautiful sandy beaches and the ocean*

Ponta de Piedade – unique rock formations, a magnet for tourists in the summer

Rocky Algarve   The western section of the Algarve's southern coast from Cabo de São Vicente until just before Faro is also called the Rocky Algarve or the **Barlavento** (Windward Coast). There is a massive rocky cliff coastline here interspersed with small sand coves or alternatively longer beaches separated by picturesque rock formations. Numerous grottoes and caves, offshore rock formations and bizarre cliff formations are what give this region its character.

Sandy Algarve   The Sandy Algarve to the east stretches from around Vale do Lobo west of Faro to the mouth of the Guadiana River. This section of coastline is also called **Sotavento** (Leeward Coast) and is influenced by the Atlantic Ocean far less than the coast further west. Here there are miles-long, broad sandy beaches and also an extensive system of lagoons. The **lagoon region similar to tidal basins** is separated from the open sea by a 60km/35mi chain of islands, which with occasional gaps stretches from Praia de Faro to Manta Rota west of Tavira. Natural water channels and a few artificially constructed canals, like the ones near Tavira, Faro and Olhão, connect to the sea. The lagoon is becoming more and more silted up in the course of time. Natural waterways to the open sea also silt up or move eastwards. Because of the meagre amounts of fresh water that flow from the hinterland

and constant replenishment by the tides, the lagoon is very salty. The mixture of relatively warm, shallow water, soft clay soil and the high salt and oxygen content due to the frequent exchange of water in the lagoon make for a very unusual environment with a great variety of flora and fauna. For this reason the lagoon region of the Ria Formosa has been under nature protection since 1987.

The mountains in the north of the Algarve divide it from central **Serra** Portugal and form a protective barrier. They keep cold weather from the north away and make for North African climatic conditions in the southern foothills and coastal region of the Algarve. The extensive **Serra do Caldeirão** rises to 589m/1944ft. The highest peaks can be found in the **Serra de Monchique**: Fóia with its 902m/2977ft and Picota Peak with its 773m/2551ft. The mountain regions mainly consist of clay shale and sandstone, the latter being used often for building in the Algarve. In the Serra de Monchique there are hot springs caused by volcanic activity; they are often used for medicinal purposes. Many small rivers from the mountains of the Algarve hinterland flow southwards to the coast. They provide a more or less adequate amount of water after the rainy winter and spring months. The water is stored in several large reservoirs.

? DID YOU KNOW ...?

■ Only 65km/40mi south-west of the Algarve the ocean floor drops off about 4000m/13,200ft. The Gorringe Bank, an undersea mountain range about 5000m/16,500ft high, is located 250km/150mi south-west of the Algarve coast. The Eurasian and African continental plates meet here, which causes frequent tectonic shifts. The epicentre of the horrific earthquake of 1755, which decimated the entire Algarve coast, was in the Gorringe Bank.

The Guadiana, which forms the border to neighbouring Andalusia **Guadiana** to the east, is the Algarve's most important river. Its name is derived from the Arabic Uadi Ana (Ana's river). Its source is in Spain in La Mancha and it is 830km/500mi long. In Roman times the Guadiana was navigable until beyond Mértola. Today only small boats can travel the last 48km/30mi between Pomarão and Vila Real de Santo António. It is between 100 and 500m (330 and 1650ft) wide, and has an average depth of just 5m/16ft.

Climate

With **3000 hours of sunshine** annually the Algarve can claim to have some of the most stable weather conditions on earth, and in Europe to be the region with by far the most sunshine. The coast is protected from cooler weather by the mountains to the north and thus has a climate similar to North Africa's. In addition to the many hours of sunshine, there is also the warm and dry Mediterranean in-

Nothing but nature: Costa Vicentina with its bracing Atlantic climate

fluence, which counteracts that of the Atlantic and leads to mild temperatures in the winter.

Temperatures The warmest months are June, July, August and September. In this season the daily temperatures rise to 28°C/80°F. But since there is always a light breeze from the sea, it is almost never too hot. In the winter, on the other hand, it never gets really cold; the temperatures rarely go below 10°C/50°F. Cabo de São Vicente has the lowest temperature fluctuation on the Iberian peninsula, at 6.2°C/11°F.

However, a warm jacket is indispensable, since even in summer the evenings can get windy and cool. As it is never very cold in the winter, houses often have no heating and can get uncomfortably cool at this time of year.

The temperatures of the Atlantic Ocean are generally below those of the Mediterranean Sea: In the summer the water temperature can rise to 22°C/71°F, but in the winter is only 15°C/59°F. In the western Algarve the water temperatures can be a bit cooler than in the east, where the influence of the Atlantic decreases and that of the Mediterranean increases.

Precipitation The average precipitation lies between 350 and 600mm (14 and 24in). There is generally more rain in the Algarve hinterland than along the coast. November usually has the most rainfall.

Plants and Animals

Plant lovers should come to the Algarve early in the spring. In December everything that looked brown and burnt turns green again. In January and February the almond trees are the first plants to blossom. **Flora**

In the Algarve hinterland the Serra de Monchique has an especially great variety of plants, but a diverse flora is also to be found in the undeveloped areas along the coast. The areas Ria Formosa and the Costa Vicentina, which are under nature protection, are especially interesting. In these regions a variety of flora and fauna were able to develop relatively undisturbed on large, continuous areas.

Many exotic plants from all over the world also flourish in the Algarve. The discoverers of the 15th and 16th centuries brought back many plants from overseas which now flourish in Portugal. In the centuries before that the Romans and the Arabs introduced plants from the entire Mediterranean region to southern Portugal.

The most typical tree of the Algarve is the **almond tree** (*Prunus dulcis*; in Portuguese *amendoeira*), whose white and light pink blossoms announce spring in the Algarve in January and which dominates the landscape with its light green leaves. It blossoms between mid-January and late February. Its almond fruits (*amendoas*) can be seen right after the blossoming; they reach their full size by April and can be

Almonds – one of the trademarks of Algarve flora

THE SNOW OF THE ALGARVE

Imagine the Algarve without almonds. No snow-white sea of blossoms in January or February. No falling petals blown about by the breeze. No almonds for sale in the markets. No sweet, no salty, no roasted, no candied almonds. And no marzipan delicacies.

But this was the situation in the Algarve before a certain Arab emir fell in love with the Swedish woman named Gilda. She packed everything up and moved to be with him in the sunny Al-Gharb. They married and are said to have been very happy. But something depressed the Swedish woman in the first winter already. During the second winter she was silent and unapproachable, and in the third she became very sad.

Emir with imagination

She stared at the lush green surroundings of the castle for hours without saying a word. The emir asked her maid for help. The maid already knew what the problem was: her mistress missed the **snow of her homeland**. Her homesickness for the north got worse with each winter. The lovesick emir was shocked, but proved to be extraordinarily clever: he had **thousands of almond trees** brought in secret from his homeland. One ship after another landed and delivered *Prunus amygdalus* seedlings. They were planted quickly without the homesick Gilda noticing. The plan was a complete success: the next winter, when thousands of almond trees blossomed, the emir led his Swedish bride onto the castle walls. There was an endless sea of almond blossoms.

»This is the **snow of Al-Gharb**,« the generous emir said proudly. And his astonished Swedish bride? She is said to have been overjoyed at the sight of the **snow white, softly falling blossoms**.

harvested in July and August. Afterwards the leaves become dry and unattractive, but the trees do not lose their leaves until winter.

Knotty, slow-growing **olive trees** (Olea europaea) are very common in the Algarve as in the whole Mediterranean region. Olive trees can live to be 2000 years old. They were brought to Portugal by the Arabs. This tree has been cultivated since ancient times and used to be seen as a sign of wealth. They blossom in May and June. The long, dry summer is vital for the ripening of the olives (Portuguese: azeitonas). They turn from green to black as they ripen. The harvest starts in November and continues until March. Oil is produced from them.

The **carob tree** (Ceratonia siliqua) is also a characteristic feature of the Algarve landscape and there have been efforts for some time to cultivate it systematically. The many hours of sunshine make for ideal conditions in the Algarve. Carob trees grow large brown pods that are very nutritious and can be used for animal feed .

The **strawberry tree** (Arbutus unedo), which is common to the Algarve, is a member of the heather family. It only grows to be 2–3m/ 7–10ft tall and has leathery leaves. It is often found growing along the side of the roads. It gets its name from its fruits, which resemble strawberries in colour and shape. It is used to produce *medronho*, a clear spirit.

A special characteristic of **orange trees** (Citrus sinensis) is that they blossom and have fruits at the same time, between February and June. The fruits begin to grow during these months already. The small white blossoms have an unbelievably aromatic scent, which can cover the entire eastern Algarve under the right weather conditions, since this is where most of the orange plantations are situated. The oranges are harvested from December to March and sometimes even into the summer.

Lemon trees (Citrus limonium) are cultivated somewhat less than oranges. They have larger leaves than oranges and their blossoms have pink tips.

Characteristics of **fig trees** (Ficus carica) are that their leaves grow at the same time as the blossoms and that they have five »fingers«. The green and dark violet figs ripen in August; their pulp is edible.

The thorny **pomegranate tree** (Punica granatum) is native to the eastern Mediterranean region. It has red blossoms between May and September. Pomegranates have a hard, leathery skin that contains many seeds covered with the fruit pulp. Because of the many seeds, the pomegranate is considered to be a symbol of fertility. They are harvested in October and November.

The **loquat** (Mespilus japonica) has only been cultivated in the Algarve and Portugal for about 200 years. Its plum-sized deep yellow fruits (nêsperas) have large brown stones and a pleasant sour taste; they ripen in April, latest in May.

The **cork oak** (Quercus suber) is important for Portugal's economy, since it is the world's leading producer of cork. Cork oaks form a layer of dead cells around their trunks to prevent the loss of water and even out temperature changes. The 3cm/1.2in layer of cork can be peeled off and processed. The cork is peeled off when the tree is more than 20 years old. The cork grows back and can only be removed again after nine years. The last number of the year when the cork was last removed is carved into the peeled trunk. For example, the number seven means that the tree was last peeled in 2007 and cannot be peeled again until 2016.

Like the cork oak, the **holm oak** (*Quercus ilex*) is an evergreen tree. It can be recognized by its dark green, leathery leaves which have a white, fuzzy shimmer on the underside. Holm oaks sometimes grow as areas of continuous woodland. If they grow in an open area they can form very large crowns.

The **eucalyptus** (*Eucalyptus globulus*), which is common in the mountainous regions, was imported from Australia. Since there is a completely different ecological system in Portugal than in Australia, eucalyptus trees are responsible for the desertification of large areas of land because their long roots can draw water from very deep underground. They grow unusually quickly and need large amounts of water. Since they are cultivated for the manufacture of paper, the desertification of huge areas is imminent. An area that has been dried out by eucalyptus trees takes 60 years to recover its former ecological balance after they have been cut down.

Orange groves in the hinterland: in spring a captivating aroma wafts across the land.

Oranges – sweet, fresh and juicy

In gardens and along the roadside the **Judas tree** (*Ceris siliquastrum*) can often be seen; in April it is covered with pretty pink blossoms and begins to grow its heart-shaped leaves. Later in the year it can be recognized by its long pods. Judas is supposed to have hanged himself on such a tree.

Acacia dealbata, which is locally called **mimosa**, is also very pretty. In February and March it produces countless yellow blossoms. Its leaves are something special: they are finely feathered and draw together when touched.

The **jacaranda** (*Jacaranda mimosifolia*), which has beautiful violet-blue blossoms from May until early July but no leaves at first, originally came from Brazil. In Portugal it is often used to line streets or in parks.

The very decorative **stone pine** or **umbrella pine** (*Pinus pinea*) stands out because of its broad crown. It can be found in small woods or more often standing alone, in which case the crowns are pronounced. The seeds in the large pine cones are edible and taste like hazelnuts.

The **araucaria** (*Araucaria excelsa*) or Norfolk Island pine originated in New Caledonia. It can be found often in parks in Portugal. It can be recognized by its shape: Its needles are layered like so many small brushes.

Of the palm trees, the **Canary Island date palm** (*Phoenix jubaea canariensis*) can be found frequently in the Algarve. It originated in the Canary Islands and spread through the entire Mediterranean region from there. It is known by its small yellow-orange fruits, which grow

Flamingos are common in the swampy areas of the Ria Formosa and near Castro Marim.

in long bunches between the palm fronds; they are not edible.

The **agave** (*Agavae americana*), which is now a permanent resident of Portugal and the Mediterranean region, was brought to Europe during the time of the discovery of the Americas. The flower stalks, which grow as tall as trees, are characteristic. After it has bloomed the flower and leaves die, but the roots remain and new plants grow from them.

Among the shrubs in the Algarve the **gum rockrose** (*Cistus ladanifer*) can be seen especially often. In the higher elevations between late March and June whole seas of white-yellow flowers on low shrubs can be seen. The flowers look wrinkled and the leaves appear sticky.

Fauna While the habitat for animals has been destroyed along the coast for the most part by the spread of construction, the mountains and nature reserves maintain relatively good conditions, even for some rare animals. A quite large variety of species can be observed here.

Birds that can be found, especially in protected areas, include the heron, osprey, sandpiper, oystercatcher, kingfisher and plover. Storks come all the way into the cities to nest there. The swamps near Castro Marim, which are under nature protection, are known for their many flamingos. There are azure-winged magpies in the woods and rufous bush robins in the orchards of the Algarve hinterland. The cliffs are nesting grounds for the European roller and the bee-eater.

Of the 200,000 species of **butterflies** known in the world, about

1600 live in Portugal. In the Algarve only about 300 species have been counted, including the saturna, oak egger, death's-head hawkmoth, red admiral, blues, hummingbird hawkmoth, swallowtail, scarce swallowtail and common brimstone. The Algarve is not very conducive to butterflies. Much of it is too heavily populated and the protected areas are close to the sea where butterflies find little to eat. Butterflies hardly come to the Algarve from northern regions, where there is a great variety of species; they are kept out by the mountains in the Alentejo and in the northern Algarve.

Mammals are found in the Algarve largely as domesticated farm animals, mainly donkeys, goats, sheep. The few species of wild animals live in the mountains: wild boar, deer and foxes.

The most common **reptiles** are lizards, which can often be seen sunning themselves on walls. They disappear quickly as soon as something moves nearby. The common gecko has special suction pads on its prominent toes and can thus climb up and down smooth walls.

The chameleon prefers to remain unseen.

In the protected areas there are chameleons which can change their colour to fit their surroundings and the time of day as protection against their enemies. Snakes, some of which are poisonous, also live in the Algarve.

Along the Algarve coast various kinds of **seashells** can be found. On the sandy beaches of the east coast there is much less variety than on the western coast, which offers diverse habitats with limestone cliffs and rocky beaches. Venus clams, mussels, cockles, trigoniidae, sword razors, oysters and rock snails are most common.

Environmental Problems · Nature Conservancy

The effects of tourism present an unusually large problem in the Algarve. In the 1950s the coast was as good as undeveloped. In the following decades large parts of the coastal strip were covered with con-

Tourism takes its toll

The swampy areas around Castro Marim are a nature reserve; they are home to many rare plants and animals.

crete or asphalt, destroying the natural habitat of numerous plants and animals and changing the appearance of the landscape within a very short period of time.

Environmental awareness
There was no real environmental awareness in Portugal for a long time. The effects of tourism, among other things, changed this when people suddenly realized that they could not take an unblemished environment for granted. Joining the EU in 1986 was also a turning point, since on the one hand it made funds for industrial complexes and road building available, while on the other hand the EU expected new environmental legislation to be followed. In 1987 the first basic environmental law was passed in Portugal. In 1989 a national office for the environment, in 1990 a ministry for the environment was established. Several non-governmental **environmental protection organizations** have taken on the job of raising public awareness for environmental issues. The best known and largest of these are Amigos da Terra, APEA (Associação Portuguesa dos Engenheiros do Ambiente), GEOTA (Grupo de Estudos de Ordenamento do Território e Ambiente), QUERCUS (oak – Associação Nacional de Conservação da Natureza) and LPN (Liga para a Protecção da Natureza), which was founded as long ago as 1948. An important local environmental organization in the Algarve is Almargem with offices in Loulé; Almargem initiated the hiking trail Via Algarviana through the hinterland.

Nature reserves
Signs of rising environmental awareness are not least 16 nature reserves of various sizes. The most important are **Costa Vicentina** in the western Algarve, which was placed under protection in 1988 as the Parque Natural do Sudoeste Alentejano e Costa Vicentina, and the **lagoon region of the Ria Formosa** west and east of Faro. It has had the status of a nature reserve since 1987. Already in 1975 the **swamps near Castro Marim** were protected as Reserva Natural do Sapal de Castro Marim.

One environmental problem relevant to the Algarve is that of water supply. In many years there is hardly any rain even in the winter and spring. There are acute **water shortages** regularly in the whole region. There were droughts from 1981 to 1984 and 1992 to 1996; the other years had enough rain in the winter months to fill the reservoirs and the underground water tables. The winter of 2000–2001 was especially rainy, supposedly the wettest in the past 500 years. Most of the fields were flooded and crops could not be planted. By contrast the year 2005 was extremely dry; reservoirs dried up and crops failed. There was talk of rationing drinking water; politicians quarrelled about how to use water and churches said special prayers for rain. 20,000 people in Portugal had to get their water from tank trucks. Even the hotels asked guests to save water.

Water supply

But along with extended drought, factors such as a **worn-out water system** or inefficient use of water also led to water shortages. The **price of water** is still very low in Portugal and leads to waste. Sometimes water is diverted around the water meters, too. Apart from agriculture and consumption in the cities, water is also used for the numerous golf courses in the region, where the greens and fairways are watered mostly with ground water. Mainly by building **reservoirs**, the Portuguese government is trying to provide for a regular supply of water. In the Algarve alone there are four large reservoirs, and the region has meanwhile begun to get water from the Barragem de Alqueva, the largest reservoir in Europe, which dams up the Guadiana River in the Alentejo near Alqueva and Moura.

In recent decades there have been regular forest and wild fires in the Algarve. The **Serra de Monchique** was affected several times. Along with the region's extreme dryness in years with little rainfall and some open burning of waste, the practice of cultivating monocultures – mainly purely pine forests – is another reason for the increased danger of forest fires. Sometimes fires are started deliberately in order to gain open land for crops that grow quickly, like eucalyptus. Moreover, lack of foresight and thoughtlessness cause forest fires. In forests that are not cared for by the owners and are abandoned, fires spread especially quickly. Normally it takes about two years for shrubbery to start growing back after a wild fire, and trees take many more years.

Forest fires

Near Monchique burnt wood is collected and used to produce cellulose and **biomass fuel**. The latter

i Common fire hazards

- Extinguish cigarettes carefully. Do not throw cigarette butts or burning matches away carelessly. Do not throw them out of a moving car.
- Light camping gas cookers, candles, campfires only under strictest supervision
- Do not leave empty bottles or glass shards laying on open ground; pick up glass shards and dispose of them
- Do not expose lighters or combustible material to direct sunlight or heat
- Do not park vehicles with catalytic converters on areas of dry vegetation
- In case of fire call tel. 112

is a cheap ecological source of energy – since it produces relatively little carbon dioxide – and is used to generate electricity near Monchique.

Coastal erosion A problem specific to the coast is erosion. The unique rock cliffs west of Faro are crumbling: in many places there are signs to warn visitors against going too close to the cliffs. Whole sections of beach have had to be closed as a safety measure. For the same reason buildings on top of the cliffs have been closed, for example the small hotel and restaurant above Praia de Beliche near Cabo de São Vicente.

Population · Politics · Economy

Statistics Portugal has about 10 million inhabitants. About 395,000 of these live in the Algarve, which constitutes about 5% of Portugal's area. In comparison, more than 2 million people live in the Lisbon metropolitan area. The Algarve's average population density is 70–75 inhabitants per sq km (approx. 180 inhabitants per sq mi). The most sparsely populated regions have less than 20 inhabitants per sq km (50 per sq mi) and include the areas in the north-east of the Algarve between Salir and Alcoutim, in the west between Aljezur and Vila do Bispo and in the mountains east of Monchique. In contrast the entire coast east of Luz near Lagos has a very high population density of more than 100 inhabitants per sq km (260 per sq mi). The only exception are the regions west of Faro and east of Tavira.

? DID YOU KNOW ...?

■ The number of people living in the Algarve at least triples in the summer months when all hotel and guesthouse rooms, holiday flats and houses, and campgrounds are occupied?

Development The Algarve is one of the most **popular residential areas** in Portugal. Only Lisbon and the industrial region Setúbal were considered to be more attractive places to live and work in recent years. The population in the mountain regions has been declining steadily since 1930. The population of the coast increased until 1940, then began to decline, and increased again sharply from 1960.

Language The official language is Portuguese. There are no marked dialects, but the Portuguese that is spoken in the Algarve is different from standard Portuguese. The vowels are often different and the final syllables are dropped more frequently.

In general many expressions from **Arabic** have been preserved in Portuguese, as can be seen in the place names of the Algarve. Almost

all words that begin with the syllable *al-*, have Arabic origins, including the word »Algarve«, and the place names »Albufeira«, »Aljezur«, »Almancil«, »Alvor«, »Alcantarilha«, »Algoz«, »Alcaria«, »Alfanzina«, »Alporchinhos« or words like *almoço* (lunch) and *almofada* (pillow).

Religion The Portuguese population is 95% Roman Catholic, with the remaining 5% being Protestant, Muslim or Jewish. There is a separation of church and state in Portugal. The Catholic religion is practised in very different ways in various regions of Portugal. Catholicism plays a relatively small role in everyday life in the Algarve compared to the north of the country. However, the **feast days of the saints**, which are celebrated to honour the local patron saint, have a fixed place in the calendar in the Algarve.

Bearing the burden of pilgrimage in Loulé

Since 1974 great value has been attached to a **solid primary education** in Portugal. During the dictatorship in previous decades, the illiteracy rate in Portugal had been above the European average. In 1970 29% of all Portuguese over the age of 15 were illiterate; in 2001 only 5% of men and 10% of women were illiterate. Older people and women especially could not and cannot read or write. Nine years of schooling have been compulsory in Portugal since 1987 – before that it was only compulsory for six years, and until the mid-1960s only for four years. A university was founded in the Algarve, located in Faro, with a few branch campuses, for instance in Portimão.

Family and society The old **family structures** are beginning to dissolve in Portugal, especially in the Algarve. Until not too long ago families of several generations lived together in one house or apartment. Today young men and women are more likely to move out, which is of course a **consequence of tourism** and the job opportunities it brings. There are more core families now. Women have become more independent by

Small shops are the place to trade the latest news. This important aspect of social life was lost with the birth of modern hypermercados.

working outside the home, but they are often still responsible for the housework along with their job: there are still no signs of a trend towards equality in this respect.

The Algarve is an exception within Portugal, since it lives mainly from tourism. The advent of tourism brought on a general restructuring of society. As many people take jobs along the coast, the rural regions, especially the more remote ones, are deserted or populated only by old people. In these areas there is still much unemployment and poverty. The poorest region of the Algarve is the district Alcoutim in the north-east. Tourism has led to an especially clear **division in the population** in the Algarve, which is most apparent in divergent standards of living. Many young adults work in some branch of the tourist trade and have attained a certain level of affluence. Older Algarvios or the ones who work in fishing or agriculture have seen an already low standard of living reduced even further.

When the dictatorship was ended by the Carnation Revolution in 1974, Portugal got a socialist constitution, which identified the country as a democratic parliamentary republic. The socialist elements were weakened through a change in the constitution in 1982, and a re-privatization law in 1990 eliminated it completely. The last change

Political system

Facts and Figures *Algarve*

- ▶ The Algarve extends from the Atlantic Ocean in the west to the Guadiana, the river on the border to Spain in the east.
- ▶ Extent from east to west: *c* 135km/84mi
- ▶ Extent from north to south: 30km/18mi at the narrowest point, 50km/30mi at the widest point
- ▶ Coastline: approx. 200km/120mi

Administrative structure
- ▶ The area of the historic province Algarve corresponds to the administrative district of Faro
- ▶ Administrative and district capital is Faro
- ▶ The district (*distrito*) is divided into 16 counties (*concelhos*) and 77 communities (*freguesias*).

Population
- ▶ *c* 395,000
- ▶ Average population density: 70 – 75 per sq km/180 – 185 per sq mi
- ▶ Population density in central coastal region: 100 per sq km/259 per sq mi
- ▶ Population density in the most sparsely populated Algarve regions: 20 per sq km/52 per sq mi

Language
- ▶ Portuguese

Algarve
- ▶ The southernmost of Portugal's 11 historic provinces
- ▶ The south-western tip of the Iberian peninsula and of Europe

Area
- ▶ 4960 sq km/1915 sq mi, 5% of the area of Portugal

in the constitution took place in 2001. The state president is the head of state and is elected for a five-year term. A new parliament is elected every four years. The state president then nominates a prime minister according to the election results.

Political parties   The two largest parties are the **Partido Social Democrático (PSD)**, which was established in 1974, and the **Partido Socialista (PS)**. Both names are misleading. The PSD is not a social democratic party, but rather has a liberal conservative platform. The PS, which was established in 1973 by Mário Soares when he was in exile, is a social democratic party. Along with these two large parties, the following also have seats in the Portuguese parliament: the right-wing conservative Centro Democrático e Social – Partido Popular (CDS-PP), the Coligação Democrática Unitária (CDU; democratic unity coalition), a group consisting mainly of communists (PCP) and greens (PEV), and the Bloco de Esquerda (BE), a left-wing party of intellectuals and former communists, which has seats in the Portuguese and the European Parliament and opposes globalization and the European Union.

Economy

Between 1995 and 2003 investments in the Algarve grew by 13.4%, the national average for that period being 8.3%. The main source of income in the Algarve is currently **tourism**. The majority of the Algarve population works in the hotel and gastronomic business or the building industry. Other Algarvios continue to work in agriculture and fishing or fish processing. These two branches were the main source of income until the late 1960s, but since then have become much less important.

The region lives on tourism

Algarvian **industry** has never played a major role within Portugal. There is a small fish- and cork-processing industry. The most important industrial zones are located further north. Even the building materials industry, which profits from construction activity on the Algarve coast, is located in the north.

Industry

Portugal has changed greatly since its entry into the EU in 1986. New roads were built, in the Algarve too, and the infrastructure has improved. Huge shopping centres have replaced small shops. On the whole the cities look more modern. However, the country is still marked by great contrasts, as the southernmost province of Portugal shows. Modernization has passed by many inland regions. Portugal's disastrous financial situation will make the situation in the Algarve's hinterland – poverty, high unemployment and emigration to the cities – even worse.

European Union

Next to agriculture, fishing was the most important industry in the Algarve for a long time. **Tuna and sardine fishing** in particular have played an important role on the Algarve coast. Today about 30% of Portugal's fish are caught in the Algarve. The largest fishing ports are **Olhão** and **Portimão**. Vila Real de Santo António is one of the smaller fishing ports. Boats leave from Olhão for high-seas fishing off the coast of Africa and to catch **cod** in the Arctic Ocean. Some of Portugal's cod, the popular *bacalhau*, is imported from Norway. In the lagoon regions around Faro and Alvor and at the mouth of Rio Arade near Portimão there is some clam harvesting; mussels, scallops and oysters are raised in aquaculture off the island of Armona. The fishing industry was modernized in the 1950s, which included the intro-

Fishing

duction of trawlers for catching sardines. Meanwhile the Portuguese fishing fleet is antiquated and no longer competitive with other European fleets, especially the Spanish fleet. Fish quotas and EU compensation have also reduced the number of fishermen drastically. Those who are still fishing are forced to stay near the coast because their boats are poorly equipped, and only fish for sardines. One consequence of this is that enough sardines are caught to cover domestic demand, but other fish have to be imported and are more expensive.

The **fish-processing industry** has also experienced huge losses. In the mid-20th century there were still 200 fish factories in the Algarve, with 30 alone in Portimão. But the industry has hardly received subsidies since 1974 and many businesses have had to close. There are only four fish factories in the Algarve presently – in Portimão and Olhão. A new factory, opened in Olhão in 2011, processes clams and fish from the aquaculture near Armona.

Agriculture   In the Barrocal and the Serra a majority of the population made a living from agriculture in the past. The climate there makes up to four harvests a year possible. Since the late 1980s all of Portuguese

Fishing – hard work that doesn't bring much income any more

agriculture has been struggling with the **consequences of EU membership**; EU agricultural policy is mostly limited to abandonment premiums and early retirement regulations, for which the smallholders in the Algarve often cannot even fulfil the requirements. Agriculture along the coast has been given up because the land was sold for tourism purposes at a greater profit. Another problem is that well under 10% of the people working in agriculture are below the age of 35, but 25% are above the age of 65 – in the future agriculture may die out from sheer lack of personnel.

Fruit-growing

The production figures for the fig harvest are an example of the decline of agriculture. Between 1953 and 1962 the production was at 16,000 tons annually, while today it is only around 2000 tons. One of the reasons for this lies in the fact that fig trees were cut down to make larger citrus plantations. The **production of citrus fruits** grew proportionally from 16,000 tons annually between 1953 and 1962 to around 150,000 tons today. In general the production of figs, almonds, olives and carob has declined drastically – either the fruits are not harvested or the trees are not cared for, since hardly any labour is available in rural areas. In comparison to the 1950s olive oil production has declined by 75%. The production of **carob** has managed to remain stable, since recent research has discovered new industrial uses for the pods. While 40,000 tons were harvested annually in the 1950s, current annual harvests are still around 30,000 tons.
Wine-growing has also declined. In the past many Algarve farmers produced wine. Today wine-growing on small areas hardly pays anymore, but recently a small number of farmers have begun to specialize in wine-growing and now produce high-quality wines. In **fruit-growing** a positive trend can be observed, thanks to subsidies from Brussels. Old trees are being cut down and new ones planted, including new varieties that yield more and make cultivation more intensive and also more lucrative.

Vegetable-growing

Sweet potatoes, tomatoes, beans, cucumbers, paprika, lettuce and herbs are planted, often in greenhouses to intensify the effects of sunlight and to protect them from strong winds or downpours in the winter.

Forestry

The **processing of eucalyptus trees** is an important economic factor; whole hilltops in the Algarve are covered with young eucalyptus trees. The wood is used to produce cellulose. Because of relatively lax environmental regulations, the cellulose industry, which presents great environmental problems, has settled in Portugal – mainly around Tejo. The paper factories on the one hand and the cultivation of eucalyptus on the other have a negative effect on the environment. The trees grow quickly and draw great amounts of water from the ground, which dries out. The **cultivation of cork oaks** is playing less and less of a role in the economy. Even though Portugal remains the

Drying maize the traditional way: turning the cobs with a rake

world's leading producer of cork, processing has declined since cork is increasingly being replaced by synthetic materials.

Tourism The **most important economic sector** in the Algarve is without a doubt tourism. **Mass tourism**, as it has developed in the last decades of the 20th century along the Algarve coast, does not exist in the rest of Portugal. In the 1980s tourism in the Algarve grew by 15% every year. 50% of all holidaymakers in Portugal spend their holidays on the Algarve, compared with only about 25% in Lisbon and its surroundings, and the rest on the northern Atlantic coastline and on the islands that belong to Portugal.

In 2010 13.3 million overnight stays were registered, which against all previous forecasts was an increase of 2.6% over the previous year – but 2009 was also the worst year in 15 years. About 2 million holidaymakers come to the Algarve every year, a number that has declined in the past years. Since 2008 the number of British tourists, who normally make up 50% of the Algarve visitors, has fallen, as has the number of German visitors. Now the industry is turning to Portuguese and Spanish visitors. Many Spanish day-trippers visit cities in the eastern Algarve like Vila Real de Santo António and Tavira.

Tourism continues to expand in the Algarve. For some time there has been an emphasis on **quality and individual tourism**. Apartment complexes have been built on parts of the coast that were not yet developed, like Martinhal near Sagres. Golf tourism will continue to be promoted and yacht harbours are also being planned.

Transportation

The traffic routes to Spain were expanded by means of EU subsidies. The so-called Via do Infante is being built through the Algarve from Andalusia to Lisbon. The motorway runs parallel to the highly frequented N 125, which connects the coastal towns. Because of its distance from the towns the motorway will be used primarily by through traffic. The motorway is not yet finished in the western Algarve.

Car transport

The international airport in Faro was opened in 1965 and expanded considerably in 1989. In 1989 about 2.5 million passengers were processed here; in 1998 the number rose to 4.1 million passengers. Between 2001 and 2009 the airport was again expanded and completely modernized. Now it can handle up to 8 million passengers annually. In August 2008 alone almost 745,000 passengers took off and landed at Faro airport.

Air travel

History

The Algarve's isolated yet exposed location in south-western Europe has always determined its history. The region has had connections with North Africa for a long time – both friendly and warlike. Later the well-situated harbours were ideal for the voyages of exploration. And in the 20th century tourism came to the Algarve with its practically North African climate.

First Settlers: Celtiberians

from 2200 BC	Iberians settle the south of the Iberian peninsula
from 1000 BC	Phoenicians found trading posts on the Portuguese coast
from 700 BC	Celtic tribes arrive on the Iberian peninsula from the north
from 500 BC	Greeks trade on the Portuguese coast

After 2200 BC the Iberians arrived – as far as can be told from North Africa – on the Iberian peninsula and settled in the Algarve. Phoenicians only arrived more than 1000 years later. They were looking for amber and tin, travelling up and down the Portuguese coast, and established their first trading posts here.   **Iberians**

From about 700 BC Celtic tribes entered the Iberian peninsula from the north and in the course of the next centuries mingled with the Iberians to form the Celtiberians. About 30 or 40 Celtiberian tribes, the **Lusitanians**, formed the largest ethnic group in the Iberian peninsula. They built so-called *castros* or *citânias*, fortified settlements on elevations that were easy to defend. Around 500 BC Greek traders reached the Portuguese coast and founded trading posts.   **Celtic tribes**

Roman Lusitania

2nd century BC	Lusitania becomes part of the Roman province Hispania ulterior
27 BC	Hispania ulterior is divided into the two provinces Baetica and Lusitania
3rd century AD	Early Christianization of Lusitania
from 410	Alans and Vandals come to southern Portugal
418	Visigoths penetrate as far as the Algarve

Around 450 BC **Carthage** spread its sphere of influence from North Africa to include the Iberian peninsula. The conflict between Carthage and Rome was now also carried on here. In the late 3rd century   **Romans**

← *Portugal's caravels conquered the world's seas:*
  they sailed proudly under the cross of the Knights of Christ.

BC the **Romans** began to conquer the Iberian peninsula. During the Second Punic War (218–201 BC) they fought primarily against the Carthaginians but also tried to secure borders against the Celtiberians in the north and the Lusitanians in the west of Iberia. The peace accord of 201 BC, between Carthage and Rome, sealed Roman pre-eminence in Iberia. They divided the peninsula into the provinces of **Hispania ulterior** in the south-west and Hispania citerior in the north-east.

At the end of the Celtiberian War (197–179 BC), in which Romans fought against Lusitanians, Lusitania became part of the province of Hispania ulterior.

The man with the armband The Lusitanians offered strong resistance to Roman occupation between 147 and 139 BC, inspired by the Lusitanian **Viriatus**, »the man with the armband«, whom the Portuguese later celebrated as a national hero in poetry and art. After his murder in 139 BC, Lusitanian resistance against Rome faded.

The birth of Lusitania In 45 BC, **Julius Caesar** became sole ruler of the Roman Empire and thus also over the province of Hispania ulterior. In 27 BC Augustus split Hispania ulterior into the two Roman provinces of Baetica, whose territory more or less matched present-day Andalusia, and **Lusitania**.

Lusitania encompassed all of the Algarve coast, and extended to the Douro in modern northern Portugal and eastwards into modern Spain. The Vulgar Latin that was spoken everywhere in the Roman Empire later developed into Portuguese.

Roman legacies Some **Roman buildings** survive in the Algarve; the bridges in Tavira and Silves date back to Roman times. North of Faro large baths and a water sanctuary were built. The cape at the south-western tip of the European mainland, Cabo de São Vicente, became a sacred site with the name Promontorium Sacrum because of its prominent position.

Extracting salt from sea water to conserve fish was already practiced by the Romans. Finally the Romans built a system of roads that is partially still in use today. The present N 125, the east-west connection along the Algarve coast, goes back to the Romans. An important Roman road runs from Faro via Tavira and Mértola to Beja. **Christianization** apparently started early in the province of Lusitania. The first Christian congregations are documented from the 3rd century AD.

Vandals, Alans and Visigoths During the Germanic migrations, Vandals and Alans came as far as southern Portugal. Visigoths penetrated into the Algarve and conquered Faro, where they established a bishop's see, built the first Christian church and practised a cult that emphasized worship of the Virgin Mary.

The Moors in Al-Gharb

from 711	Arabs and Moors conquer large parts of Iberia. Portugal falls to the Emirate of Córdoba, under the Moors the Algarve becomes the province of Al-Gharb with the capital city Silves (Xelb).
922	Vikings attempt to invade Xelb.
1035–1065	The Reconquista begins under Fernando I of Castile and León.
1139	Afonso Henriques defeats the Moors and is crowned as the first king of Portugal.
1189	The Arab capital Silves is conquered.
1250	The Algarve cities are incorporated into the kingdom of Portugal.

In 711 Arabs and Berber Moors from North Africa crossed the Straits of Gibraltar and stormed much of the Iberian peninsula. There was hardly any resistance to the invasion, as the Visigoth empire had become weak. **Roderick**, the last Visigoth king, was quickly defeated. With the exception of the northern mountain regions including Asturia, which remained Visigothic, the Moors occupied the entire Iberian peninsula in only five years. The territory of present-day Portugal also fell to the Arab **Emirate of Córdoba**, the later Caliphate of Córdoba. The capital of the Moorish province of Al-Gharb was **Xelb, today's Silves**. The Moors or Arabs brought a highly developed culture to the Iberian peninsula. They had extensive knowledge of the natural sciences, especially medicine, geography, seafaring and astronomy. They also installed a **system of irrigation** that is still in use in a similar form; the Algarve was cultivated successfully. Citrus, fig, almond and olive trees were introduced. Trade relations with Arab North Africa flourished. Al-Gharb was a wealthy region, Xelb a famous and wealthy city with a population of 40,000. Under Arab rule followers of different religions apparently lived together peacefully; the cities had Arab, Jewish and Christian quarters. In the south of the Iberian peninsula, Arab rule was not threatened for a period of 500 years. Only in the year 922 did **Vikings** try to invade the rich capital Xelb from the south over the Rio Arade. They were surrounded and repulsed at the mouth of the river.

The Algarve becomes Moorish

? DID YOU KNOW ...?

- The conquerors from North Africa were mainly Berbers. Arab armies coming from the east invaded north-west Africa; there they encountered the Berbers, who resisted the invasion of their land with all their might. After being conquered and converted to Islam, they were used to conquer the Iberian peninsula. The Romans had called the Berbers from the Atlas Mountains *mauri*, so they were called *moros* or *mouros* on the Iberian Peninsula.

»Noras« came to Portugal with the Moors.
These ox-powered wells were adopted by the Portuguese; some still exist today.

Reconquista During the rule of King Fernando I of Castile and León (1035 – 1065) the Reconquista began, the **reconquest** of the territory occupied by the Arabs. Between 1112 and 1385 – starting from León-Castile – large parts of the Arab kingdom were gradually conquered by Christian troops. In the first half of the 12th century the Portuguese state formed. After a victory over the Moors near Ourique in the Alentejo, Afonso Henriques had himself crowned as **Afonso I**, the **first king of Portugal**, and thus completed the separation from León-Castile. As a consequence Portugal time and again had to resist Castilian claims. Afonso I was able to re-conquer Lisbon thanks to help from German, Flemish and British crusaders. His successors expanded the kingdom to the south. Under Sancho I parts of the west Algarve were conquered with the help of famous crusaders like Frederick Barbarossa and Richard the Lionheart. In 1189 **Silves** was conquered. A **bishop's seat** was established in the city, with a Flemish priest as the first bishop. In 1191 the Arabs were able to re-conquer the cities that they lost in the Algarve with the help of Seville and Córdoba.

Between 1240 and 1249, during the rules of Sancho II and Afonso III, the Arabs were finally defeated in the whole of the Algarve. This ended the Reconquista there. Time and again there were conflicts with neighbouring Castile. Under Portuguese rule, trading relations with North Africa ended, and the entire region was completely re-structured economically, culturally and religiously. Jews and Arabs were driven out or enslaved. Only a few Arab artists and craftsmen, **mudéjars**, were allowed remain in the country. The Arab agricultural system was adopted. The Portuguese also profited from the Arabs' scientific knowledge during the subsequent era. In 1250 the towns of the Algarve were annexed to the kingdom of Portugal. Portugal became the first country on the European continent to achieve a territorial expansion which has survived almost unchanged to this day. In 1319 Dinis I made Castro Marim in the extreme east of the Algarve the seat of the **Knights of Christ**, who played a major part in Portugal's »Golden Age« in the following years.

The Algarve is part of Portugal

The Rise and Fall of a World Power

1385–1580	The Aviz dynasty: great voyages of discovery and conquest and Portugal's Golden Age
1444	Slaves are sold for the first time in Lagos
1485–1521	Manuel I: Portugal at the height of its economic and cultural flowering
1521–57	Decline sets in under João III
1578	Young King Sebastião is killed in the Battle of Al-cácer Quibir in Morocco
1580–1640	Spanish Interregnum

The **Avis Dynasty** began with João I. In the 200 years of their rule – from 1385 to 1580 – Portugal became the **leading sea and colonial power** in Europe. The most important voyages of discovery and conquest took place in this time, and as a consequence Portugal was able to amass unbelievable wealth. Along with Lisbon the Algarve was an important centre of activity; Lagos became the most leading port in the Algarve. **Henry the Navigator**, a son of João I, was named **Grand Master of the Order of the Knights of Christ** (1418), which put enormous financial means at his disposal. It is reported that he es-

Age of Exploration

tablished a kind of centre of knowledge near Sagres, where geographical and nautical information were gathered. In the docks of Lagos a new kind of ship was built, the **caravel**, apparently based on construction plans from Sagres. The caravel was far superior to past sailing ships in manoeuvrability and seaworthiness. Sagres was not suitable as a port because there was no hinterland, which is why the voyages of exploration that Henry organized all departed from Lagos. First the Madeira island group was discovered (or re-discovered) and

Portuguese Voyages of Discovery

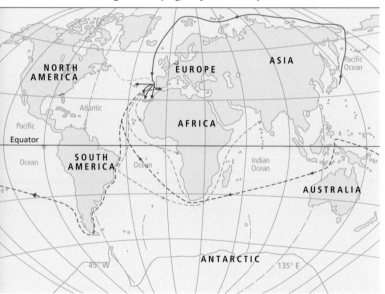

→ Scientific centre at Sagres Capture of Ceuta 1415; Madeira 1419; Azores 1427; Gil Eanes rounds Cape Bojador 1434.

- ‑ ➤ Sea route to India:
Álvaro Fernandez and Diniz Diaz discover the mouth of the Senegal River in 1444. Diogo Cão reaches the mouth of the Congo River in 1492. Bartolomeu Dias rounds the Cape of Good Hope in 1488. Pedro Álvares Cabral reaches Brazil in 1500. Starting out in 1497 from Belém near Lisbon, Vasco da Gama sails aound the Cape of Good Hope, reaches Mozambique in south-east Africa in 1498 and in the same year reaches India (Calicut).

- ‑ ➤ Gaspar Corte Real reaches Newfoundland in 1501.

- ‑ ➤ In 1519, in the service of the Spanish, Fernão de Magelhães sails from Sanlúcar de Barrameda across the southern Atlantic, passes through the Strait of Magellan at the southern tip of South America in the Pacific Ocean in 1520, and is killed in 1522 on Mactan in the Philippines in a battle with the indigenous people there. One of his ships returns to Europe across the Indian and southern Atlantic Oceans to become the first to sail around the world.

→ In 1660, David Melgueiro sets out on a Dutch ship from Japan and sails north around Asia and northern Europe to Portugal.

colonized (up to 1423), followed by the Azores (1427). Later the ships of Henry the Navigator advanced ever further along the coast of West Africa. They reached Cape Verde, the Gambia and finally also Guinea. A desire for adventure was one reason for these trips across the oceans, but economic interests were more important. Among other things alternatives to the Arab-controlled land routes to the **spice countries** in Asia were sought. Moreover, fighting Islam was an important motive for Henry's seafaring endeavours, which laid the foundation for Portugal's rise to be a mighty colonial power.

After the discovery of the mouth of the Senegal River, black African slaves were sold at auction for the first time in Lagos during the reign of Afonso V in 1444. The **slave trade** became a main source of income along with the spice trade. It was only banned by law in the 19th century (▶Baedeker Special, p.204).

Beginning of the slave trade

Manuel I (1485–1521) founded the **Portuguese trading empire** with posts in East India, East Asia, South Africa and Brazil. The country experienced its »Golden Age« under his rule. Lisbon developed into the centre of global trade. The crown, nobility and merchants attained unimaginable wealth, but the extraordinary colonial expansion overstretched the capacities of the Portuguese people, so that the population declined rapidly within a short period of time. At this time the Algarve had a population of only about 54,000 people.
In 1497 **Vasco da Gama** departed from Belém, Lisbon's port, rounded the Cape of Good Hope and was the first European to reach India via the sea route. Belém had meanwhile displaced the Algarve ports as the most important point of departure and return for long-distance voyages.

The »fortunate king«

Under João III (1521–57) Portuguese colonial power in the Far East fell apart – the economic decline began. In 1540 the **Inquisition** was introduced. Jews, Jewish converts, atheists, witches and Christians who did not fit the Inquisitors' view of society or who drew attention to themselves through their lifestyle or opinions were persecuted. The Inquisition was only abolished in 1820.

Start of decline

In 1578 young King **Dom Sebastião** started from Lagos, which had been made the capital of the Algarve in the previous year, on a crusade against Morocco. In the devastating battle of Alcácer Quibir, in which great numbers of Portuguese soldiers were killed, the young king also fell.

The »longed-for king«

Since there was no heir to the throne, the Avis dynasty died out. The Spanish king **Philip II**, a grandson of Manuel I, claimed the Portuguese throne and occupied Portugal by force. During the Spanish Interregnum from 1580 to 1640 Portugal lost some of its colonies in South-East Asia and South America. Spanish financing of its colonial

Spanish Interregnum

The Victoria, a ship in Magellan's fleet, was the first to sail around the world.

wars included taxing the Portuguese population. In 1640 a rebellion of the Portuguese nobility led to the longed-for independence from Spain.

1640–1910: Bragança Dynasty

1706–50	Portugal increasingly declines under the wasteful rule of João V
1755	A severe earthquake rocks the land
1807	Napoleonic troops occupy Portugal
1832–34	Liberal Wars between Liberals and Absolutists
1908	Carlos I and his heir Luís Filipe are murdered in Lisbon

The Bragança dynasty was inaugurated by the Duke of Bragança, who had himself crowned as King João IV; he had taken part in the rebellion against Spain. The country became even poorer during this era and did not succeed in building up its own economy.

The period after 1640 was marked by the **Restoration Wars** between Spain and Portugal. The border towns along the Guadiana were the sites of many battles. Military help was requested from England, which sealed English hegemony in Portugal. In 1668 Spain recognized Portugal's independence conclusively. During the reign of **João V** (1706–1750) Portugal continued to decline due to the extravagant lifestyle of the king, despite the discovery of the **Brazilian gold mines**. This made Portugal financially dependent on England.

Under **José I** (1750–77) **enlightened absolutism** reached its climax in Portugal. José's prime minister Marquês de Pombal introduced numerous reforms in the spirit of the Enlightenment and mercantilism. During José's rule a natural catastrophe took place that shocked all of Europe: on 1 November 1755 a devastating **earthquake** rocked the Algarve coast and the Portuguese mainland. The capital Lisbon was almost completely destroyed. There was great destruction also in all towns of the Algarve – in Monchique in the mountains there was also great damage. The coastal towns were flooded by a 20m/65ft tidal wave. Many harbours and river mouths were blocked up. In the course of the following year more small earthquakes followed, the last of them on 20 August 1756. José I had the ruined centre of Lisbon completely rebuilt under the direction of the Marquês de Pombal and according to the Marquês' ideas about urban planning. Pombal was active in the Algarve as well: in 1774 he had the planned city of **Vila Real de Santo António** on the Guadiana built on the lines of his reconstruction of Lisbon. After the death of José I almost all of the Marquês de Pombal's reforms were rescinded in 1777 under Maria I. Enlightened ideas were quashed with the help of the **Inquisition**. Meanwhile **Faro** had replaced Lagos in 1756 as **capital of the Algarve**. At this time Portugal's southernmost province had 85,000 inhabitants.

The 19th century began violently: as a traditional ally of the English, Portugal was occupied by Napoleon – England's greatest enemy – in 1807. The **royal family** fled to **Brazil**. In the Algarve there was massive resistance to the occupation. While the Portuguese succeeded in liberating themselves in 1811, the later king João VI had no thought of returning to Portugal from Brazil as yet. In Lisbon, meanwhile, things were happening: the Cortes convened in 1821 and devised a liberal constitution that demanded a **constitutional monarchy**. This constitution was confirmed by João VI after his return – the era of absolutism was over.

Napoleon and consequences

João VI died in 1826 without the succession having been settled. Under his sons, the liberal **Pedro** and the reactionary **Miguel**, conflicts broke out that led to confrontations between liberals and absolutists in all of Portugal and reached their peak in the so-called **Liberal Wars** (1832–34). Miguel annulled the liberal constitution, had himself crowned and persecuted the liberals. Thereupon supporters of the liberal Pedro fought against reactionary monarchists who supported Miguel's regime. In the Algarve a monarchist guerrilla troop terrorized the region under the notorious Remexido. Albufeira was besieged in 1833 and burned. The supporters of Miguel were defeated in 1834 and Miguel was sent into exile.

Industrialization Industrialization began relatively late in Portugal and only developed slowly. In the Algarve fish-processing and the cork industry played a major role. In 1889 the railway line from Lisbon to Faro was opened. At this point the population of the Algarve had grown to 230,000.

End of the monarchy The end of the monarchy loomed at the beginning of the 20th century. In 1908, King Carlos I and the heir to his throne, Luís Filipe were assassinated in Lisbon. Several unsuccessful uprisings were caused by the royal family's inability to solve economic problems. In 1910 a revolution by civilians and the military in Lisbon was finally successful. The last king of the Bragança dynasty, Manuel II, abdicated and fled to Great Britain.

Republic, Dictatorship and Present

1910	The republic is proclaimed
1933	Salazar proclaims the »Estado Novo«
1969	An earthquake destroys countless houses in the Algarve
1974	The dictatorship is ended by the Carnation Revolution
2004	Portugal hosts the European Football Championship

Republic and dictatorship A republic was declared on 5 October 1910. The following years were characterized by domestic political problems and countless changes of government. In 1926, the military took power in a coup and dissolved the democratic system just as it was beginning to become stable. **General Carmona** proclaimed the Second Republic and brought **António de Oliveira Salazar**, previously minister of finance and founder of the fascist União Nacional party, into his government as prime minister. In 1933 the dictatorial »**Estado Novo**« (New State) was established, which oriented itself towards National Socialist Germany and fascist Italy. During World War II Portugal remained neutral but severed diplomatic ties to Germany on 6 May 1943.
In 1969 many houses were destroyed by an earthquake in the Algarve.

Resistance to the dictatorship increased. The regime's restrictions on the Portuguese population as well as the senselessness and expense of the colonial wars in Africa became more and more obvious. On **25 April 1974** the Carnation Revolution began in Lisbon, a military coup that was supported by large sectors of the population and finally toppled the dictatorship. At first a socialist constitution was passed, but there were several changes in government and numerous different coalition governments. The basic direction of policy was generally pro-Western.

Carnation Revolution

After Portugal joined the EU in 1986 the political situation stabilized and the economy began to improve. From 1987 the Liberal Conservatives were in power for eight years, followed by the Socialists, and from April 2002 a conservative coalition government of PSD and CDS-PP under José Manuel Durão Barroso (PSD) was in power; he became president of the EU commission in 2004. He was followed in office by José Sócrates (PS). After Sócrates resigned in connection with the country's catastrophic economic situation, early elections in June 2011 brought another PSD and CDS-PP coalition government. The election results in the Algarve reflected the national results: 37% of the vote went to the PSD, just under 23% to the PS. The economist **Pedro Passos Coelho** became the new prime minister with the aim of modernizing the country from the ground up. The **president** is **Anibal Cavaco Silva (PSD)**, who has been in office since 2006 and was re-elected in 2011.

Political and economic development

The population of the Algarve is presently about 370,000. Every year the Algarve suffers from large **forest fires**. Large areas of the Serra de Monchique burned in recent years. In 2003 and 2004 disastrous conflagrations swept across the province, but in 2005 the Algarve, unlike other parts of Portugal, was spared for the most part. In 2004 Portugal hosted the **European Football Championship**, which failed to give the tourist industry the expected boost. However, the Algarve continues to invest in **tourism**. In 2008 the hiking trail Via Algarviana was opened – a sign that natural tourism is being promoted.

Algarve today

Art and Culture

The legacy of the Moors is conspicuous by their absence, bearing in mind that they lived for half a millennium in southern Portugal and left many signs of their culture in neighbouring Andalusia. What remains are typical Portuguese churches and chapels with tiles, gold-leaf work and the Manueline style. And a few characteristic Algarvian elements.

Art History

Artistic Heritage

The Algarve has little to offer in terms of art history. Like the Portuguese capital, the Algarve coast was heavily damaged by the **earthquake in 1755**. Many buildings were completely destroyed or heavily damaged so that few original structures from earlier years have been preserved. Until the middle of the 13th century the Algarve's development was similar to neighbouring Andalusia. In 1250 the Algarve was annexed to the kingdom of Portugal, and from then on the two cultures developed separately. Unlike in Andalusia, there are only a few traces of the 500-year long **Moorish period** left in the Algarve. The influences of the Moors are to be found in areas of life and work such as language or agriculture more than in the architectural legacy.

But the Algarve is also different from the northern regions of Portugal, where Christian churches were built much earlier, in the Romanesque style, after only a short Moorish presence. By contrast the **first Christian churches** in the Algarve were not built until the 13th century, and in the **early Gothic style**. The stone that is used for some churches and fortresses in the Algarve stands out. Some of it is red sandstone from the Serra de Monchique, and some is yellow sandstone right from the coast.

Romans and Moors

The most important witnesses to the Roman period can be seen in **Milreu** near Faro. Remains of a Roman patrician villa, baths and a water sanctuary have been found there. Near Vilamoura Roman mosaics were found, and on the grounds of the Quinta de Marim near Olhão **Roman salt works** were discovered. The bridges in Tavira and Silves are of Roman origin but were renovated later. **Roman relics**

Almost all fortresses in the Algarve go back to Moorish days, but remains can only be seen in the inner courtyard of the fort on Silves. Among the **few remains of Moorish architecture** are also the wall remnants of a fort in Salir. The archaeological museum in Silves displays a cistern and a few smaller finds from the Moorish period. **Legacy of the Moors**

13th to 16th Centuries

The oldest church in the Algarve is near the village of Raposeira. It is a well-preserved **early Gothic chapel** from the 13th century. Only parts of the formerly Gothic structures of the cathedrals in Silves and **Oldest Christian church**

← *A common sight in the south of Portugal: blue and white tile paintings*

Fish mosaics in Milreu: a Roman water sanctuary was excavated here.

Faro survived the earthquake. In Silves the main doors, the former choir and the crossing are easy to recognize, while in Faro the bell tower remains.

Manueline style

Manueline style, which is named after Manuel I, is a purely **Portuguese style of ornamentation** that was developed in the early 16th century. At this time the discoveries and conquests overseas caused the country to **flourish culturally and economically**, as can be seen in the architecture and other areas. The Manueline style developed in the transition between the Gothic period and the Renaissance. The buildings have elements typical of the European late Gothic or the early Renaissance period, but the ornamentation reflected current national events. Thus certain **motifs recurred** regularly: the cross of the Knights of Christ, the crown and the »M« for Manuel as signs of the initiators of the conquests, ropes, caravels, anchors and armillary spheres – a nautical instrument – as symbols for seafaring, as well as stylized coral, shells and tropical plants, leaves and flowers to show the contact with far-off lands. Influences from other cultures rarely found their way into this architecture, of which the Torre de Belém in Lisbon is a particularly beautiful example. The most important **architects of this period** were Diogo de Boytaca, Diogo de Francisco de Arruda and João de Castilho.

There are no important buildings in the Algarve, as there are in Lisbon, Batalha or Tomar, where the Manueline style was developed to the full. Since the Manueline style was closely tied to the overseas discoveries, it was used most frequently in places or in regions that were directly connected with the Portuguese history of seafaring and conquest. Thus there are many small churches in the Algarve with elements of the Manueline style. The portals, and sometimes also the arches between the nave and the choir, have Manueline decorations. Beautiful examples of Manueline ornamentation can be seen on and in the churches of Alvor, Alte, Monchique, Luz de Tavira, Estômbar and Odiáxere. There is a Manueline roadside cross in Silves.

Renaissance architecture generally played only a small role in Portugal. Since work was carried out in Manueline style for a long time, stylistic development was delayed. By the middle of the 16th century far less finance was available for large building projects, and at the end of the Golden Age there was little reason to build prestigious structures. In the Algarve only a few churches

Manueline decorated columns

have preserved **rare Renaissance elements**. These are mostly doorways, as in Tavira on the Igreja da Misericórdia, in Faro on the Igreja de São Pedro, in Mexilhoeira Grande or in Castro Marim on the little Igreja da Misericórdia in the castle courtyard.

Baroque

In the late 17th century the long-sought **gold mines** of Brazil were finally found, and money was available again. Under the wasteful king João V many churches and palaces were built in Portugal in the early 18th century, or existing churches were furnished with Baroque altars or chapels. In the Algarve there are quite a few churches with Baroque decoration. A purely Baroque church is the Igreja do Carmo in Faro. The Baroque **Igreja de São Lourenço in Almancil** with its azulejo walls and the **Igreja de Santo António in Lagos** with its talha dourada decorations have become famous.

Azulejos

Azulejos, ceramic tiles, can be found everywhere in Portugal; they were used to decorate chapels, churches, palaces, railway stations or entire façades of houses. Azulejos – the word is derived from Arabic *az-zuleycha* (mosaic tile) – come from Arabia. They were imported from southern Spain in the early 16th century. Azulejos were produced as **relief tiles** by the Moors. The colouring was put in small depressions and then the tiles were fired. Green, blue, black, reddish brown and white were the characteristic colours of the time.

After the Moors were driven out of southern Spain, the tiles were produced in Portugal. By means of the **majolica process**, which was developed in Italy, large flat tiles could now be painted. The fired ceramic tiles were given a white tin glaze and then painted with metal oxide colours. In the 17th century a native Portuguese style developed, influenced by Chinese porcelain painting of the Ming dynasty and by tile production in Delft. Whole tile carpets in blue, white and green were created. **Clearly defined patterns** like the »Ponta de Diamante«, a stylized cut diamond pattern, were used. Finally ever larger **Baroque tile paintings** dominated in the 18th century. Church walls, inner and outer palace walls, imposing stairways, fountains and benches were decorated with these tile paintings. An excellent example of this is the entire Baroque interior of Igreja de São Lourenço in Almancil.

In the early 19th century, when Portugal was shaken by civil war, azulejo production all but came to a standstill. It was only revived in the middle of the century. **As in Brazil** tiles were now used to decorate private homes, shops and public buildings both inside and out. The practical aspects of façade coverings became more important, and large surfaces of wall painting became less common. Art Nouveau brought another revival, and then interest declined sharply. In the past decades the Portuguese azulejo tradition was revived and modern and old-style motifs were used to decorate public areas.

Talha dourada

Talha dourada is a Portuguese Baroque specialty consisting of **wood carvings covered with fine gold leaf**, used to decorate church interiors. The wood was mainly oak and the gold came from Brazil. Talha dourada is basically an ostentatious show of wealth, which the country could enjoy after the discovery of the Brazilian gold mines. At first paintings were framed in talha dourada; later pulpits and high altars were decorated with it and the decoration was sometimes continued all the way to the walls. In the Algarve the Igreja do Carmo in Faro is decorated with talha dourada, and the most famous example is the Igreja de Santo António in Lagos.

18th and 19th Centuries

Almost all of the buildings in the Algarve, whether homes, public buildings or churches, were built after 1755, i.e. **after the earthquake**. They were either reconstructed or built completely new.

The bishop of the Algarve at that time, Francisco Gomes do Avelar, promoted the rebuilding of many churches in the late 18th century. The Italian architect Francisco Xavier Fabri, who designed many buildings for Lisbon as well, was brought to the Algarve and given charge of the building projects. Among the new structures in the period after the earthquake, the **Rococo palace in Estói** deserves special mention.

Something unique happened in Portugal in the late 18th century in civic planning. The earthquake of 1755 caused great damage, and whole cities were completely destroyed. The lower quarter of the Portuguese capital Lisbon was rebuilt afterwards according to principles deriving from the philosophy of the minister **Marquês de Pombal** (▶ Famous People). Pombal was the most important advocate of enlightened absolutism

Extravagant gold decoration: »talha dourada«

in Portugal. He had the lower quarter rebuilt in an ordered, rational and functional chequerboard pattern, and followed the same principle when the city of **Vila Real de Santo António** in the Algarve was built from scratch on a greenfield site.

20th Century

The 20th century had a decisive influence on the Algarve. Tourist projects have been built here since the 1960s, and high-rises appeared in the late 1970s. The motorway bridge near Portimão across Rio Arade is a remarkable construction from the early 1990s.

Mosaic pavement

In all of Portugal there are squares and pavements with beautiful black and white mosaic pavement. After the 1755 earthquake some-one had the idea of using the rubble from homes, palaces and churches to make small tesserae for paving the sidewalks. Special pat-terns or motifs were often created with painstaking work. The arti-sans who do this are called *calceteiros*. Once a common trade in Por-tugal, there are now only very few *calceteiros*, who work for very low wages. These mosaics can be admired in the centres of Faro, Lagos, Albufeira and Portimão. The most beautiful one can be seen on the Praça do Marquês de Pombal in Vila Real de Santo António, where in 1879 a starburst pattern was created.

Windmills

Windmills are rare relics of the past in the Algarve. Once these whitewashed, round and slightly conical mills were a characteristic of Algarve landscape. They had small **triangular sails**, often with small **ceramic jars** hanging from them so that when the windmill turned it would produce a whistling sound to tell the miller how strong the wind was. The most beautiful ones among the very few left in the Algarve are near São Brás de Alportel, in Odeceixe and in Odiáxere.

Açoteias

Açoteias can be seen mainly in Olhão and neighbouring Fuzeta. Cube-shaped one- to three-storey fishermen's houses that were built here all have **flat roofs or roof terraces**, which are called *açoteias*. These are used to dry laundry, fish, fruits, nets and other fishing im-plements, sometimes also for sitting outdoors. Many *açoteias* lead to *mirantes*, small lookout towers where fishermen's wives would watch for their husbands returning from the sea.

Chaminés

Trademarks of the Algarve are the *chaminés*, chimneys. **Algarvian chimneys** serve not only to draw away smoke, but are obviously works of art in their own right. Observant travellers will see how many different kinds there are: round or square, hip-roofed or with pointed towers, like small bird houses or short minarets. The pat-terns of holes in the sides are unique, too. *Chaminés* used to be made by hand and each one is unique. Today they are also mass produced.

Painting and sculpture

There is hardly any 20th-century painting or sculpture of historical value in the Algarve. In the Museu Municipal in Faro a few unre-markable Portuguese paintings from the 19th and 20th centuries are on display. Some galleries and arts centres exhibit works by contem-porary artists.

The sculpture depicting King Dom Sebastião on Praça Gil Eanes in Lagos should be mentioned first as an example of modern sculpture. The city of Lagos has placed various works by contemporary sculp-

One of the few remaining windmills stands in Odeceixe. The miller knew how strong the wind was from the noise it made blowing over the clay pots tied to the ropes.

tors around the city; the one of the lost and longed-for king is by far the best-known. It is the work of **João Cutileiro** , one of the most famous Portuguese sculptors of the 20th century. He created the figure of Dom Sebastião in the early 1970s. It portrays not a ruler but a young man in a suit of armour with an almost naïve expression. It has become an emblem of the city and a popular subject for personal photos and for street artists.

Folklore

The best way to get to know Portuguese folklore is one of the many *festas* that take place all year round. Folk festivals of all kinds, but especially festivals for patron saints, are venues for local music and dance groups, which play and dance to music typical of the region wearing costumes of that region. In the Algarve most of these events are tailored to tourism and it takes a little luck to find festivals where real local traditional music and dancing is performed.

Festas

Typical instruments of Portuguese folklore are guitars, sometimes the *viola de arame* with metal strings, clay pipes (*pipas*), bagpipes (*gaitas de foles*) and especially a square tambourine with drum skins on both sides (*adufe*).

Dances fall into two categories: *danças*, which are created for a special event, and *bailes*, which are commonly known in a certain area. In the Algarve the *corridinho* is especially popular. It is a quick polka, accompanied by guitar, accordion and meanwhile also fifes, mandolins and castanets.

← *Dom Sebastião, »longed for« by the Portuguese and recreated by João Cutileiro, has many imitators.*

Famous People

Seafarers especially made a name for themselves in the history of the Algarve with its 200km/120mi of coastline. But other people are also connected to Portugal's southernmost coast: a saint after whom Portugal's most famous cape is named; a writer who described life in the Algarve in a novel; and a football star who has a bar here.

Martin Behaim (1459 – 1507)

Martin Behaim was significantly involved in the scientific prepara- **Created the**
tions for the exploration of the world's oceans. He was born in 1459, **oldest preserved**
the son of a wealthy cloth merchant in Nuremberg. He went to Flan- **globe**
ders at the age of 17 as a textile merchant. When he returned a short
while later because of financial problems he got into trouble with the
authorities. In order to escape punishment he fled to Portugal. In
Lisbon he claimed in 1484 to be a student of the mathematician and
scientist Regiomontanus, an astronomer who worked in Nuremberg
calculating the positions of the planets. The Portuguese court under
João II admitted Behaim to the **»junta of astronomers and mathematicians«** who gave the Portuguese seafarers the latest theoretical
knowledge. In 1486 Behaim was probably a member of the expedi-
tionary crew of Diogo Cão, who sailed along the coast of West Africa
as far as today's Namibia.

Behaim advanced in Portugal to be an authority as a geographer, but
it is unclear what his accomplishments exactly were. He exchanged
information with Magelhães and was also in contact with Christopher Columbus. In 1491 he returned to Nuremberg and a year later
created a globe that went down in history as the **oldest preserved
globe of the earth**. The globe shows the Indian Ocean as an inland
sea and Japan as further to the east than it really is. America, which
Christopher Columbus had just reached, is missing completely. In
1493 Behaim went back to Portugal. He died of the plague on 8
August 1507.

João de Deus (1830 – 1896)

Many kindergartens and streets in Portugal are named after João de **Educationist and**
Deus. He came from São Bartolomeu de Messines and grew up in **poet**
modest circumstances as the son of a shop owner in the Algarve. As
he studied for ten years at the law faculty in Coimbra, he was already
30 years old when he found temporary work in the Alentejo as a
journalist. In 1868 he became member of parliament for Silves
county, but resigned soon after as he did not feel equal to the job
and thought that his political work would not change anything.

Flores de Campo, his **first volume of poetry**, was published in 1869.
Meanwhile João de Deus lived in Lisbon and became part of the literary scene that met at the famous Café Martinho. He was appreciated as a poet whose work was marked by sincere emotions. His last
anthology, *Campo de Flores*, which was published in 1893, contains
his best poems. João de Deus' satirical poetry was less well known.
From 1877 he studied various **methods of education** and developed
a model close to the Montessori method that was adopted by many

← *Henry the Navigator, one of the pioneers
of Portugal's Golden Age*

kindergartens in Portugal. While he was highly praised by some, he also had to prevail against intense antagonism.

Bartolomeu Dias (c 1450 – 1500)

Knight of Christ and seafarer As a member of the order of Knights of Christ, Bartolomeu Dias played an important role in the 15th-century Portuguese voyages of discovery and conquest. He gained fame as the first European who **sailed around the southernmost point of Africa**.

The Portuguese king had commanded him to find the sea route to India, so Dias set sail in 1487 from Portimão. He rounded the cape in 1488 but did not realize this because he was battling a heavy storm. Only on the return trip did it become clear to him that he had sailed around the southern tip of Africa. He called the cape **Cabo Tormentoso** (stormy cape). But João II gave it a more optimistic name: Cabo da Boa Esperança (Cape of Good Hope). The name also expressed the confidence that the voyage around the cape was a milestone in discovering the sea route to India.

Bartolomeu Dias took part in other important ventures in the following years. When Vasco da Gama set out in July 1497 for India, Bartolomeu Dias accompanied the fleet as far as Cabo Verde in West Africa. In 1500 he sailed in his own ship with the fleet that discovered Brazil under the leadership of Pedro Álvares Cabral. As they sailed around the southern point of Africa, a storm blew up at the Cape of Good Hope. Bartolomeu Dias' ship came in distress – he was killed right next to the cape that he had discovered.

Gil Eanes (born c1400)

Sailed around Cape Bojador Gil Eanes came from Lagos, but his dates of birth and death are not known for sure. He made a name for himself by sailing around Cape Bojador in 1434. In the Middle Ages it was assumed that beyond these West African foothills there was a churning, boiling sea, in which lived monsters that swallowed boats. Henry the Navigator claimed, based on his research, that the ocean beyond Cape Bojador was no different from the ocean off the coast of Portugal. Gil Eanes became convinced and dared to sail into the unknown. After his successful return he set sail for a second time and landed about 300km/180mi further south along the West African coast. In 1444 he took part in an armed expedition to Lanzarote. Gil Eanes is considered to have prepared the way with his pioneering feats for the first discoveries and conquests on the coast of West Africa and for the voyages around Africa.

Luís Figo (born 1972)

Football idol Among the many famous people and stars worldwide who come to the Algarve to relax or who have moved here, Figo is one of the few

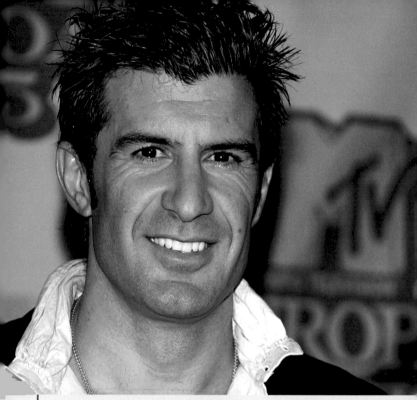

Luis Figo – the idol of all Portuguese football fans

who can claim to be playing a home game. Luís Filipe Madeira Caeiro Figo was born in Almada, south of Lisbon, on 4 November 1972, and grew up in a faceless working-class quarter. He played football from a young age, albeit for a pretty disastrous suburban team called Pastilhas. Yet it was there that he was discovered. Aged 12 he came to the youth team of Sporting Lisbon, and he made his debut with the professional team there aged 17, in 1990. He remained with Sporting for five years before going to Barcelona and then joining Real Madrid, from where he moved on to Inter Milan in 2005. Europe crowned him Footballer of the Year in the year 2000, and in 2001 he was named **World Footballer of the Year**. He played for the Portuguese national team from 1991 to 2006. Figo broke off a psychology degree for his football career. In addition to his mother tongue, he speaks fluent Spanish and English, as well as some Swedish – he is married to a Swede. A plain bar in the harbour of Vilamoura, which was opened in 1979 by Paulo China, was the favourite bar during family holidays of the young, unknown and quite shy Luís Figo – an unusual place in the otherwise quite posh Vila-

> ! **Baedeker** TIP
>
> **Café Se7e**
> Figo's bar in the marina of Vilamoura, named after the number on his shirt, is a kind of memorial to Figo's career, with pictures and souvenirs from his time as football player. Other sports celebrities show up here too. Tel. 289313943

moura. But this bar had at least a whiff of the world of the rich and famous, and sometimes famous footballers of that time could be seen here from afar, since stars like Eusébio also came to the **marina of Vilamoura**. Meanwhile Figo has opened his own bar with Paulo China – an immigrant from Mozambique and owner of several popular Algarve bars.

João II (1455 – 1495)

First Renaissance king

João II went down in history under the name John the Perfect, because he unerringly guided the development of the country at the time of the voyages of discovery and exploration and prepared Portugal's role as one of the leading sea and trade powers. The king from the Avis dynasty died in 1495 in the Algarve.

While his father Afonso V, whom he succeeded in 1481, was still firmly in the Middle Ages in his thinking and way of ruling, João II showed himself to be open to the ideas of the **Renaissance**. The young king ruled strictly, and the nobility and clergy had to submit to his will. João II **promoted his country's voyages of discovery**. Under his rule Portugal began to develop into an important sea power. He founded the »junta of astronomers and mathematicians« so that the explorers would have the necessary theoretical knowledge. During his reign the mouth of the Congo River was discovered and the Cape of Good Hope was circumnavigated. But **Christopher Columbus'** discovery of America, which was financed by the Spanish crown, also took place during his reign and has been a bitter pill for Portugal to swallow until today. At that time Portugal was preoccupied with finding a sea route to India. Columbus had also approached João II persistently with his repeated suggestions for a route to the spice islands. The king had his convention of astronomers examine Columbus' plans. They came to the conclusion that the western route proposed by the man from Genoa could not lead to India and Japan, or would take much longer than an eastern route. When Columbus then discovered the American continent more or less by accident in 1492, Portugal was left out.

Another tragedy in the life of John the Perfect was the early death of his son and heir to the throne, Afonso, who was killed in a **riding accident** on the banks of the Tejo near Santarém. In 1495 João II travelled to the Algarve for a **curative stay** in the Algarve near Monchique. He died a short time later at the age of 40 in Alvor near Portimão. He was buried in the cathedral of Silves but his remains were later taken to Batalha.

Lídia Jorge (born 1946)

Lídia Jorge, who comes from the small Algarvian town of Boliqueime **Author** near Albufeira, is among the best-known authors in Portugal. She grew up as an only child. At the age of nine years she was sent to secondary school in Faro and for the first time was confronted with city life. After finishing her schooling Lídia Jorge went to Lisbon to study Romance languages. During the colonial wars she spent some years in the former Portuguese colonies Mozambique and Angola. Back in Portugal she worked in a secondary school and later taught literature at the University of Lisbon.

Lídia Jorge describes life in remote Algarve villages

Since the publication of her novels *O Dia dos Prodígios*, *O Cais das Merendas*, *Notícia da Cidade* and *A Costa dos Murmúrios* in the 1980s, Lídia Jorge has maintained a firm place in Portuguese contemporary literature. Her subject is the **political and social situation in Portugal** after the Carnation Revolution, and the changes or the stagnation that can be seen in the country since 1974. In *O Dia dos Prodígios* (*The Day of the Prodigies*, 1980) she describes life in sleepy Vilamaninhos, an imaginary Algarvian village where the residents wait for big changes after the Carnation Revolution. Many of the characters and events in this novel have their roots in Jorge's childhood. Her most recent book was published in 2005 *Milene*. She has received many international prizes, most recently the first »Albatross«, a newly created international prize for literature, in spring 2006.

Marquês de Pombal (1699 – 1782)

Sebastião José de Carvalho e Mello Marquês de Pombal, **the pioneer** **Statesman and** **of enlightened absolutism in Portugal**, expressed his world view in **reformer** the complete rebuilding of the Vila Real de Santo António near the mouth of the Guadiana River. José I made him foreign minister in 1750 and as prime minister in 1756. He saw his most important responsibilities in restructuring the state finances, educational reform,

O NAVEGADOR – THE NAVIGATOR

Henry, born in 1394 as the third son of King João I, was later given the name »the Navigator« by history, even though he himself never took part in a long sea voyage. Large monuments were erected on the 500th anniversary of his death in 1960. But who was this Henry, who was glorified in the 19th century?

This much is certain: Dom Henrique O Navegador, Henry the Navigator, was a central figure in the Portuguese large-scale plans to circumnavigate the world; he was thirsty for knowledge, one of the most important figures of the early Portuguese era of discovery and conquest. Henry was born on 4 March 1394 in Porto. He gained respect early by **conquering Ceuta in Morocco**; at that time his fame spread through all of Europe. His father gave him responsibility for defending and administering Ceuta. He zealously collected stories and **reports by Arab traders** who had sailed along the African coast or made trading trips across the African mainland. He wanted to know what these regions looked like to the last detail. It gradually dawned on him that there could be no sea monsters south of Cabo Bojador in the *mar tenebroso*, the sea of darkness, who would attack the sailors. The ocean obviously did not become saltier, thicker, stiffer and hotter, as was told in Portugal. The idea that ships would be sucked into a whirlpool beyond the south Moroccan cape and fall off the end of the world also seemed odd to him.

Algarve – seafaring centre

The Portuguese rulers supported Henry's seafaring ambitions. In October 1443 he was given the sole right to carry out all sea voyages south of Cape Bojador. Only a few days later the **region of Sagres** was given to him. However only from 1457 onwards did he spend most of his time in Sagres. Henry was very reclusive, wore simple clothing, and was deeply pious, if the court biographer Zurara is to be believed. According to various contemporary reports, the crown prince wanted to carry out an ambitious harbour project in Sagres, but there is no evidence that this is really true. Still, it is assumed that Henry gathered **seafarers, geographers, navigators, astronomers and cartographers** together in Sagres on the southwestern edge of Portugal and tried to combine their knowledge to make it useful for practical seamanship. At that time the Algarve was undoubtedly the centre of Portuguese seafaring. The research must have been well organized and very effective. The **caravel**, a new type of ship for which Arab and northern European models were used, was not the least of the results. It proved to be especially stable, mobile and manoeuvrable.

Research about the Navigator

For a long time Henry's enterprises were portrayed as unselfish; only recent research has revealed that **personal business interests** played an additional or even a major a role. Henry the Navigator was apparently partner in a trading enterprise in Lagos, which in his time had a monopoly on all new goods that were brought to Portugal from Africa. He already had the monopoly on tuna fishing. In the end it became known that Prince Henry financed his research not only with money from the Knights of Christ, of whom he was made Grand Master at the age of 24, but to no small degree from **tax revenue** from the poor people of the Algarve. And finally research has shown that the heir to the throne pursued his goals vigorously, and went so far as not even saving his own brother, who was captured by Arabs and was to have been traded for Ceuta.

Henry and the consequences

However, with ideas that were unconventional in his day, and despite the fact that his crossing to Ceuta was the only sea voyage he ever undertook, Henry the Navigator **distanced himself from the medieval thought of his time**. This is probably his actual undeniable accomplishment. Henry did not experience the consequences of his endeavours. He probably did not even dream that the world would be changed forever after his death. He died in 1460 – before the Portuguese even reached the equator.

the promotion of the economy and trades with the goal of breaking free from Britain's economic hegemony, as well abolishing the slave trade. But he showed himself to be ruthless in the choice of means he considered necessary to achieve his manifold ends. He passionately fought the Jesuits and minor nobles who stood in the way of his reforms with their excessive privileges. His services to the reconstruction of Lisbon after the devastating earthquake in the year 1755 were outstanding. Following a state-of-the-art approach to urban planning which he had developed for the **lower part of Lisbon**, he had the model city Vila Real de Santo António built in the Algarve on a chequerboard pattern in less than five months on the site of a town that had been destroyed by flooding. After the death of José I the marques fell out of favour. Pressure from his numerous enemies resulted in his banishment to Pombal, where he died only a year later.

Dom Sebastião (c1554 – 1578)

The »longed-for« king

It was less the actual person than the myth that has developed around Dom Sebastião that has in a strange way given the Portuguese king his significance. Dom Sebastião was born in 1554 shortly after his father's died in an accident, and thus inherited the throne after the death of his grandfather João III in 1557. Until he was 14 a brother of João III acted as regent. Then the young Dom Sebastião, who was known as »the longed-for« since his birth, began to rule personally. He is described as having been arrogant and fanatically religious. One of his main goals was to bring North Africa under Christian rule. In 1578 Dom Sebastião set out from Lagos to fulfil his mission. There was a terrible battle near **Alcácer Quibir** in which about 8000 soldiers were killed. No-one in Portugal wanted to believe that the young king had fallen in battle. For a long time people yearned for his return. »The longed for« did not reappear, however. Instead impersonators claimed to be the true king. Since then the character of Sebastião has been transformed in myth into the saviour that people wait for in hard times, the man whose coming will make everything better. Even the term **Sebastianism** was coined: it refers to the fatalistic passivity and waiting attitude that is supposed to be common in Portugal.

José Joaquim de Sousa Reis (d. 1838)

Fighter

As leader of a guerrilla troop in the Algarve, José Joaquim de Sousa Reis entered Portuguese history under the name **Remexido**. He came from Estômbar and lived for a long time in São Bartolomeu de Messines. He commanded a force during the reign of the absolutist king Miguel. In 1833 liberal troops occupied parts of the Algarve, and in the ensuing civil wars Remexido commanded the west Algarvian forces. In 1834 the so-called Liberal Wars ended, but the conflicts continued below the surface. In 1836 Remexido became active again. He invaded villages with a small band of soldiers and fought liberals. He caused a bloodbath in an infantry barracks during which a number soldiers were murdered. The **guerrilla troop of Remexido** hid in the inaccessible mountains and, not even special troops were able to put an end to his activities. In 1838 Remexido was found east of São Marcos da Serra and caught. He was condemned to death in Faro and shot by a firing squad in August 1838.

São Vicente (d. 304)

The cape at the southwestern tip of Portugal and thus Europe is named after São Vicente. Little is actually recorded about his life. His date of birth is unknown, but he was born in Saragossa. As a deacon there he was a close associate of Bishop Valerius. In 304 he was condemned to death; he is supposed to have been laid on a glowing hot grid. It is said that during his martyrdom the room glowed with light, a carpet of blood formed and angelic singing could be heard. He was buried in Valencia. About one hundred years later a cult formed around Vicente, who was later canonized. According to Portuguese tradition in the 8th century, an **unmanned dinghy with two crows and the remains** of St Vicente was washed ashore at Cabo de São Vicente, which was later named after him. The version in which Christians fled from Valencia when the Arabs invaded and took his remains appears more realistic. They landed at the cape, where they apparently built a chapel in his honour. A »crow's church« is mentioned in Arabic texts, and the cape itself is called the »Crow's Cape«. When Lisbon was retaken from the Arabs, St Vincent's bones were brought there, and today they are kept in the cathedral. São Vicente is honoured in Portugal as the **patron saint of seafarers and wine-growers**, as well as being the patron saint of Lisbon. On the city's coat of arms he is depicted in a boat accompanied by two crows. However, Portugal has to share the saint with Spain because he is honoured there as well: in Avila there is also a grave in a church dedicated to him.

Saint

Practicalities

THE BEST BOAT TRIPS OR
BEACHES, TIPS ON THE
LANGUAGE, WHAT TO
KNOW ABOUT PORTUGUESE COOKING,
DATES OF FESTIVALS AND EVENTS – IN SHORT:
EVERYTHING YOU NEED TO KNOW FOR A
SUCCESSFUL ALGARVE HOLIDAY.

Accommodation

Hotels

← *O Algar beach cave near Benagil, east of Carvoeiro*

On the Algarve coast there are more than enough hotels, including many large and very good ones. Hotels in Portugal are officially graded according to the star system, though there are frequently major differences in quality within one category. Luxury hotels are awarded five stars, basic hotels one. Similar categories apply to motels and apartment hotels as to hotels.

Guesthouses

Guesthouses (*pensão*, pl.: *pensões*), ranging from one to four stars, are also popular. Lower-category guesthouses are occasionally more reasonably priced and just as well furnished and equipped as hotels that have the same number of stars. A *residencial*, similar in price and comfort, is for the most part a smaller hotel or guesthouse. *Albergarias* correspond to guesthouses of the highest category.

Pousadas

Pousadas are state-owned hotels of a high standard located in **historic buildings** in places steeped in history or of **outstanding scenic beauty**. The interior decoration of the building is always very tasteful and appealing. Since most of them have only a few rooms, reservations should be made well in advance. In the Algarve there are three pousadas: in Sagres in a beautiful location above the sea, in Tavira in a former monastery and in Estói near Faro in an 18th-century palace. In southern Alentejo there is a pousada in Santa-Clara-a-Velha.

Turismo de Habitação

»Turismo de Habitação« establishments are exceptionally beautiful places to stay. Owners of old townhouses or small **country residences** offer travellers the chance to stay on their beautiful estates. Visitors sleep in rooms elegantly decorated with old furniture and can even share other spacious areas of the house. The houses receive public sponsorship, are registered with the central tourism department and must have a plaque at the entrance. In the Algarve there are however only a few establishments of this kind.

Accommodation in the country

Alongside the »Turismo de Habitação« there is also the »Turismo Rural«, which offers overnight stays in country homes or wineries, and the »Agroturismo«, which provides accommodation in farmhouses or outbuildings.

Private rooms

Probably the best-priced alternative is accommodation in private rooms (*quartos*), which is often offered in places frequented by tourists. The rooms are well-kept and simply furnished. Breakfast is usually included.

Prices

The prices for hotels and guesthouses may vary considerably depending on the season. The prices for single rooms are about 30% lower than for double rooms in both guesthouses and hotels.

USEFUL ADDRESSES FOR ACCOMMODATION

POUSADAS

▶ **Pousadas de Portugal**
Rua Soares de Passos 3
Alto de Santo Amaro
1300-314 Lisboa
Tel. 218 442 000
Tel. 218 442 001 (reservations)
www.pousadas.pt

TURISMO DE HABITAÇÃO
TURISMO RURAL

▶ **Solares de Portugal / Center**
Praça da República
4990-062 Ponte de Lima
Tel. 258 931 750 (reservations)
www.solaresdeportugal.pt
www.center.pt

ESTALAGENS

▶ **Estalagens de Portugal**
Campo Grande, 35 2º
1700-087 Lisboa
Tel. 213 565 319
Fax 213 565 399
www.estalagensdeportugal.com

CAMPING

▶ **Federação de Campismo e Montanhismo de Portugal**
Avenida Coronel Eduardo
Galhardo, 24 D
1170-105 Lisboa
Tel. 218 126 890/1
Fax 218 126 918
www.roteiro-campista.pt

▶ **Internet**
http://en.camping.info
Information on all camp sites in
the Algarve

YOUTH HOSTELS

▶ **Movijovem**
Rua Lúcio de Azevedo 27
1600-146 Lisboa
Tel. 217 232 100
Fax 217 232 101
Reservations for individual
travellers
Tel. 00 351 ? 707 20 30 30
www.juventude.gov.pt

Relax in luxury: not a problem in Vila Vita Parc resort!

Camping

There are both public and private camp sites in Portugal, which are allocated one to four stars. A passport or a **CampingCard** must be handed in for the duration of the stay; the latter can be obtained at www.campingcard.co.uk, and means a discount on participating sites. Most camp sites are open all the year round. Spending the night on roads, motorway service stations, in parks or on open land is prohibited in Portugal.

Youth hostels

In the Algarve there are six youth hostels (*pousadas de juventude*), some in beautiful locations. An international youth hostel pass is required, which is issued by the Youth Hostels Association. The youth hostels are located in Faro, Lagos, Portimão, Tavira, Alcoutim and Arrifana on the west coast.

Arrival · Before the Journey.

By plane

The Algarve's international airport is Aeroporto de Faro. All year round flights depart from London and many regional airports to Faro by a number of airlines, for example easyjet from Belfast, Glasgow, Bristol, Liverpool and Newcastle, and Ryanair from a number of Irish and British airports.

By car

By car, depending on the point of departure, there are various possible routes from the French-Spanish border to reach different destinations in the Algarve: Paris – Bordeaux – Hendaye/Irun – Burgos – Salamanca – Seville – Ayamonte – Algarve; or Paris – Bordeaux – Hendaye/Irun – Burgos – Salamanca – Vilar Formoso – Lisbon – Algarve. The more eastern route runs through Lyon – Perpignan – Le Perthus / La Junquera – Barcelona – Madrid – Seville – Algarve. The distance between London and Lisbon is roughly 2200km/1400mi. Considerable tolls must be taken into account as well as the petrol costs.

By train

By train from London, Portugal is best reached by taking the Eurostar from Waterloo International to Gare du Nord in Paris, negotiating urban Paris to get to Gare Montparnasse, then boarding a high-speed TGV from Paris to Irun on the Spanish border, and finally taking the Sud Express overnight to Lisbon. From Lisbon there are regional trains to Faro and there is regular train service along the Algarve coast. Alternatively, travellers can take Eurostar and then the overnight TALGO express train from Gare d'Austerlitz to Madrid, and then board the Lisboa Express; it is also possible to spend a day in Madrid and then take the Lusitania Trainhotel overnight to Lisbon. The travel time from London to Lisbon is at least 24 hours. The price of a normal train ticket is as high as that for a moderate flight. InterRail travellers may wish to choose more circuitous routes to avoid paying extra charges for fast trains.

USEFUL INFORMATION

AIRPORT

▶ **Aeroporto de Faro**
Tel. 00 351 – 289 800 801
www.ana.pt
The airport is located *c* 6km/3.5mi
from Faro; buses run to the centre
of town, albeit not very regularly
or often. Taxis are a good alternative (driving time *c* 15 min).

BUS AND COACH SERVICE

▶ **Faro Bus Station**
Avenida da República
Tel. 289 899 760

▶ **Eurolines Ltd.**
52 Grosvenor Gardens
London SW1W 0UA
Tel. 0870 514 3219
www.eurolines.com

AUTOMOBILE CLUB

▶ **Automóvel Club de Portugal**
Rua Rosa Araújo 24–26
P-1250-195 Lisboa
Tel. 213 180 100, www.acp.pt

▶ **Brisa**
Tel. 808 508 508, www.brisa.pt

Buses leave for Portugal daily from London's Victoria Coach Station, By bus or coach
travel by ferry across the English Channel, and arrive in Lisbon 37
hours later after stops at several places in France and Spain. There is
also a service to Faro, in southern Portugal, which takes two days.
Both routes are operated by Eurolines Ltd.

Arrival and Departure Regulations

For stays in Portugal of up to 90 days, a valid passport is sufficient Travel
for citizens of the UK, Republic of Ireland, USA, Canada, Australia documents
and New Zealand. Children must have their own passport or be entered in a parent's passport. A minor under the age of 18 travelling
to Portugal without a parent or guardian must either be met at the
airport or point of entry by a parent or guardian, or carry a letter of
authorization to travel from a parent or guardian. The letter should
name the adult responsible for the child during the stay.
It is required by law for foreign nationals to show some form of
identification if requested by the police or judicial authorities: this
normally means a passport. For those driving a car in Portugal, this
requirement is rigorously enforced; in addition, always carry your
driving licence and the car's registration certificate. The international
green insurance card, confirming third-party insurance, is required
in the event of damage. If the driver of the car is not the owner then
he or she must be able to present a notarized power of attorney
granted by the vehicle owner.

Those wishing to bring pets to Portugal will need a certificate of Pets
health issued by an official veterinary surgeon shortly before the

departure, as well as proof of anti-rabies inoculation administered at least 30 days but no more than twelve months before the date of travel. The inoculation date and the type of vaccine must be stated.

Customs regulations In the EU, which includes Portugal, the UK and Republic of Ireland, the movement of private goods is largely duty-free. Certain standard maximum quantities apply (e.g. 800 cigarettes, 10 litres of spirits and 90 litres of wine per traveller over 17 years of age).

Travellers over 17 years of age from non-EU countries such as the USA, Canada, Australia and New Zealand can import the following into Portugal: 200 cigarettes or 100 cigarillos or 50 cigars or 250g of loose tobacco; 2 litres wine and the same quantity of sparkling wine, or 1 litre of spirits exceeding 22% alcohol by volume, or 2 litres of spirits with less than 22% alcohol by volume. Adults can bring gifts worth up to €175; for minors below 15 years the limit is €90.

Beaches

Beaches for every taste The coastal landscape of the Algarve has great variety: from the largely untouched, empty beaches of the Costa Vicentina in the west to the picturesque sandy coves of the Windward Coast (Rocky Algarve) to the endlessly long beaches of the Leeward Coast (Sandy Algarve). The most beautiful beaches are described here from west to east.

Costa Vicentina

In the north-west Algarve from Odeceixe to Cabo de São Vicente in the south-west lies the Costa Vicentina, a section of coast that is under nature protection. It is marked by a very rough, windy climate, and the water temperature here is three to four degrees Celsius (five to seven degrees Fahrenheit) lower than further east along the Algarve. But the beaches are empty and in an impressive landscape. Anyone who like this kind of climate and natural surroundings is in the right place here, where the beaches are still an insider's tip. But the strong surf should not be underestimated: children should be taken to beaches further east. The beaches are described in detail in the section ►Sights from A to Z (Costa Vicentina).

Windward Coast

Small coves, which can get very crowded in the high season, dominate the Windward Coast (Rocky Algarve). The harsh influence of the Atlantic Ocean weakens further to the east.

Sagres Near **Beliche** there is a 500m/1,650ft-long beach. Its location between cliffs is breathtaking (access from the parking lot on the road

Praia do Amado on Costa Vicentina

between Sagres and Cabo de São Vicente). Near **Martinhal** there is a 750m/2,500ft-long beautiful sandy beach with dunes, which is suitable for children since it is protected by the harbour. **Zavial**: 200m/660ft-long beach of fine sand without rocks; little used.

The town is right on a 750m/2,500ft-long sandy beach that is surrounded by cliffs; suitable for surfing beginners. There are smaller sand, gravel and rocky coves west and east of Salema.

Salema

Holidaymakers in Burgau have to make do with a relatively small beach of 300m/1000ft below the town.

Burgau

In the high season be prepared for a lot of hubbub on the 200m/660ft-long Praia da Luz, which is scattered with rocks. Various kinds of water sports, including diving, several restaurants. The beach is well suited for children.

Luz

There are only small beaches right by Lagos, but there are picturesque coves between high cliffs nearby. The **Praia Dona Ana**, south of Lagos, is one of the picture-postcard coves of the Algarve and thus very busy in the summer. The expansive, shallow **Praia Porto de Mós**, like the Praia Caniaval, is one of the locals' favourite beaches. Praia

Lagos

Beach signs

- »*area concessionada*« = guarded beach
- »*praia não vigilada*« = unguarded beach
- red flag = bathing prohibited, even close to the beach
- yellow flag = swimming further out in the water prohibited
- green flag = all swimming allowed
- blue and white chequered flag = beach periodically unguarded
- »Blue Flag« = European seal of approval (complies with water quality, environmental protection, and safety norms)

do Pinha, Praia da Batata and Praia dos Estudantes are smaller beaches right next to Lagos. East of the Lagos marina lies **Meia Praia**, one of the longest beaches in this section of coastline with good diving and surfing opportunities, ideal for beach hikers. During the high season a small boat runs regularly between Lagos and Meia Praia.

Praia de Alvor and Praia dos Três Irmãos are the continuation of Meia Praia beyond the estuary and the jetties of **Alvor** – an expansive and broad sandy beach with a few pretty rocky coves to the east (near Prainha). There are restaurants and various sports opportunities.

Praia da Rocha There is a broad sandy beach with a few rocks right by the town; above the beach runs a road with tall apartment buildings; the beach is very full during the high season. There are many restaurants here, and the beach is also well suited for children and people who want to stroll.

Ferragudo Well-tended beach at the mouth of the Rio Arade; several small rocky coves are within walking distance. The skyline of Praia da Rocha opposite is a bit annoying, however, and the water here at the mouth of the river does not meet the usually excellent standards of the Algarve, according to an EU report. There is still plenty of activity, and water sports centres are a point of attraction as well. Further to the south two coves face the open sea.

Carvoeiro Small sandy cove with a few rocks at the town centre, hopelessly overcrowded in the summer. Further to the east there are several coves bordered by high cliffs. Among the most beautiful is **Praia da Marinha**.

Armação de Pêra From the town eastwards there is a 6km/3.5mi-long beach that is very broad in places. Even in the high season the beach is not too crowded – one disadvantage is the ugly row of high-rises from the town. Further to the east the beautiful **Praia da Galé** stretches for miles towards Albufeira.

Albufeira West of Albufeira lie some very pretty small coves (for example Praia de São Rafael, Praia da Coelha and Praia do Castelo); the nice municipal beach right by the town is overcrowded during the high season; further to the east near Oura there is less activity.

Longest beach in the area; it reaches as far as Vilamoura but is not very wide. Well suited for children, also great fun for surfers. The bright red cliffs are its trademark.

Good beach right by the town; suitable for children; above the beach is the road with apartment buildings; very touristy with various sports facilities.

Flat, fine-grained sand beach with some rocks, cliffs; various sports opportunities, good surfing conditions. The beach was recently elevated at great expense and labour so that it now lies 5m/16ft higher than before.

Long fabulous beach with dunes backed by a lagoon; bordered by a pine forest. Access via a wooden bridge. Considered to be a celebrity beach, windsurfing possible.

Leeward Coast (Sandy Algarve)

There are wonderful sandy beaches on the offshore lagoon islands around Faro – Ilha Deserta can be reached by boat from Faro; the

There are wonderful little coves between the cliffs near Lagos.

Dunes on Ilha de Tavira in the Sandy Algarve

mile-long Praia de Faro near the airport can be reached by car or bus. This beach is especially well visited on summer weekends since there are lots of weekend cottages nearby.

Olhão From Olhão regular boat connections to the offshore islands Culatra and Armona and their long flat beaches with dunes, ideal for children.

Tavira Ilha de Tavira with its miles-long sand beach, dunes and a small woods lies off Tavira. The beach is ideal for children. Ilha de Tavira can be reached from Tavira or from Quatro Águas by boat. West of Tavira near Santa Luzia (Pedras d'El Rei) there is a bridge from which a little train runs to the beach.

Cabanas / Cacela This offshore island can be reached by fishing boats from Cabanas; at low tide there is a place to cross on foot; very good, long and empty beach; the lagoon system ends near Manta Rota.

Monte Gordo West and east of Monte Gordo there is a miles-long light-coloured sandy beach with dunes; but the town itself is dominated by highrises.

Children in the Algarve

In general The Algarve coast is well suited for a holiday with older and younger children. Good weather can be expected even in autumn and spring, and the beaches can be enjoyed even in these seasons. In general bear in mind that the Atlantic Ocean is calmer and warmer in the eastern Algarve than in the west. In the east there are long sandy beaches; in the west on the otherwise rough **Praia da Bordeira** and the Praia da Amoreira there are shallow lagoons. Especially nice beaches are at Martinhal, Salema, Luz, Vilamoura (Praia da Falésia, Praia da Marinha), on **Ilha de Tavira**, on Culatra and Armona, near Monte Gordo as well as near the tourist centres Armação de Pêra and Quarteira. Many hotels and apartment complexes have a swimming pool and a paddling pool, and some have child-minding services. For older children and teens there are many kinds of sports and recreational programmes.

In the Algarve boat tours and trips through the grottoes are offered on the western coast; there are also trips up the Rio Arade from Portimão to Silves or on the Guadiana along the Spanish border. Ferries offer a pleasant ride to the offshore lagoon islands in the east Algarve. Or try a lagoon trip through the Ria Formosa near Faro. Several large aquaparks (▶Holiday Activities) cater for kids and adults. Zoomarine Park hosts dolphin shows and swimming with dolphins. It is easy to spend the whole day here. Zoo Lagos (▶Lagos) is also worth a visit. Trips to the southwestern tip of Europe near Sagres or the nature reserve on the ▶Costa Vicentina, or a visit to the *câmara obscura* in ▶ Tavira are also interesting.

Excursions

Algarve waves – paradise for real water-lovers

Electricity

The mains supply is 220 volts AC. An adapter is required for devices with British or non-European plugs.

Emergency

● EMERGENCY NUMBERS

EMERGENCY NUMBERS

▶ **General emergency**
Tel. 112 (toll-free)
Police, fire department, ambulances, medical attention etc.

▶ **Hospitals**
   ▶ Health

▶ **Police**
P.S.P. · Polícia de Segurança Pública
Tel. 289 899 899

▶ **Breakdown service**
Tel. 808 201 301 (Euroscut, Via do Infante); also ▶Arrival

INTERNATIONAL AIR AMBULANCE SERVICES

▶ **Cega Air Ambulance (world-wide service)**
Tel. +44(0)1243 621097
Fax +44(0)1243 773169
www.cega-aviation.co.uk

▶ **US Air Ambulance**
Tel. 800/948-1214 (US; toll-free)
Tel. 001-941-926-2490 (international; collect)
www.usairambulance.net

Etiquette and Customs

Friendliness
The politeness and friendliness of the Portuguese is well known. Yet in regions where tourists invade the country in droves this aspect of the national character is severely put to the test. A hearty welcome in tourist information centres or in restaurants highly frequented by tourists cannot therefore be counted on; in contrast, the reception in more remote villages, unfrequented parts of town or old general stores is a different story.

Welcome
When meeting the Portuguese personally, visitors should not be surprised to be included in the traditional welcome with two pecks on the cheek, even as a stranger – hands are shaken only during formal

meetings. The same goes for farewells: after a pleasant evening there will be two pecks for goodbye.

Many Portuguese are very patient and expect the same from foreigners. There are frequently situations where the wait lasts longer than expected and the reason for the delay and what is actually being done about it is not clear. Flying into a rage or insisting on an explanation seldom meets with success. It is far better to accept the matter and exercise some patience. Even the most confusing situation will be resolved in time and the lengthiest of waits will come to an end eventually.

Patience

Service is included in the bills of **hotels and restaurants**. An additional tip of about 10% of the amount on the bill is nevertheless customary – even for that quick cup of coffee. Simply leave a small amount on the table or on the saucer after paying the bill. The chambermaids in the hotels also appreciate an extra tip; the amount depends on the length of the stay. An adequate tip should also be given to **taxi drivers, baggage porters and tour guides**.

Tipping

Fado

Fado is typical Portuguese music; the word is derived from Latin »fatum« (fate). Fado originated in Lisbon. In addition, a special kind of fado can be heard in Coimbra. With a little luck, good fado can be heard in the Algarve at special festivals. Otherwise fado is organized in southern Portugal mostly only for the tourists. While these events are not especially authentic, they at least give some impression of what fado is like. The singing of the ***fadista***, a man or a woman, is normally accompanied not only by a normal guitar or a twelve-stringed fado guitar, but also by posture and gestures. The songs are about lost or impossible love, homesickness, wanderlust or a general yearning.

Songs of fate

Some bars in the Algarve or larger hotels offer *noites de fado* (fado nights). There is no admission charge, but guests are expected to eat a meal. Reservations (from 7.30 or 8pm) are recommended. The fado begins after dinner.

Fado bars

Festivals, Holidays and Events

As in the rest of Portugal, celebrations in the Algarve are extravagant – the country is known especially for its many saints' days. Every town and almost every village has its own patron saint, for whom a

Saints' days

festival is held sometime in the year. The saints' festivals are not just religious occasions but are celebrated as folk festivals. They usually begin with an extensive mass in honour of the saint, and the churches are filled to the last seat. These are often followed by a *romaria*, a pilgrimage or procession, in which an image of the saint is carried through the town followed by a long train of people. Then comes a fair-like celebration with lots of music and folklore dancing. Some seasonal events, like the almond blossom, are also celebrated.

Folklore Hotels and restaurants regularly offer typically Portuguese folklore performances with music, dance and local groups wearing traditional costume for the tourists. Concert series, folklore events, film and dance festivals are organized in the summer of every year.

Calendar of events Information is available at the local tourist information centres. The local press or special event calendars (*agenda cultural*) often on display in tourist information offices or hotels are also worth a glance.

 CALENDAR OF EVENTS

EVENT INFORMATION

▸ **www.allgarve.pt**
Website with comprehensive information for all of the Algarve

NATIONAL HOLIDAYS

1 January: New Year
February: Shrove Tuesday
March/April: Good Friday
25 April: Freedom Day (national holiday: anniversary of the Carnation Revolution on 25 April 1974)
1 May: Labour Day
May/June: Corpus Christi
10 June: national holiday (day of the death of the national poet Luís de Camões on 10 June 1580)
13 June: holiday in Lisbon (Santo António day)
24 June: holiday in Porto (São João day)
15 August: Assumption Day
5 October: national holiday (proclamation of the republic on 5 October 1910)
1 November: All Saints' Day
1 December: national holiday (restoration of Portugal's independence from Spain on 1 December 1640)
8 December: Immaculate Conception
25 December: Christmas
In addition to national holidays all cities in the Algarve also celebrate another local holiday (Dia do Município).

JANUARY

▸ **Janeiras at the beginning of the year**
Musicians walk through the villages and sing »janeiras«, songs for

the beginning of the year of secular and religious origin.

▶ Medieval festival
In Paderne the year begins with a trip back to the Middle Ages: costumes and medieval market

▶ Festa das Chouriças
The sausage festival in Querença in the Algarve mountains involves a procession and samples to taste.

FEBRUARY/MARCH

▶ Carnival
Carnival is celebrated everywhere in the country, but especially in these Algarve towns: Loulé, Moncarapacho and Portimão. Loulé is known in all of Portugal for its carnival parade (three days with parades: Saturday, Sunday, Tuesday). The parade consists of 20 floats decorated all over with paper almond blossoms.

MARCH/APRIL

▶ Easter
Some towns have processions on Good Friday and Easter Sunday.

▶ Anniversary of the Carnation Revolution
This national holiday commemorates the Carnation Revolution on 25 April 1974 and the end of the decades-long dictatorship. It is celebrated in many places with speeches, folk festivals and music events.

APRIL/MAY

▶ Festa da Mãe Soberana
On the second Sunday after Easter a famous *romaria*, pilgrimage, to the chapel Nossa Senhora da Piedade, is held in Loulé. The Madonna is carried up a difficult path to the mountain chapel. Afterwards there is a lively folk festival in the village.

▶ Festa da Espiga
In the mountain village Salir on Ascension Day, 40 days after Easter, the grain festival is celebrated – one of the oldest festivals in the Algarve and very typical for the hinterland.

APRIL – OCTOBER

▶ Fiesa
Big sand sculpture festival between Pêra and Algoz

MAY

▶ May Day
Like 25 April, the first day in May is celebrated in many places with speeches, music and markets.

▶ Festa da Grande Fonte
In Alte the beginning of May is celebrated at the romantic springs on the edge of town with a big picnic. There are also parades, music and dancing.

JUNE

▶ Festival Med
Five days of concerts with world music in Loulé, also arts and crafts, street theatre, dancing from various countries.

▶ Festas dos Santos Populares
In all Portugal the patron saints are commemorated in June. The festival of Santo António, the patron saint of the absentminded and of lovers, and at the same time of the city of Faro, is held on 13 June with a procession and a folk festival.

JULY – SEPTEMBER

▶ Allgarve Festival

Summer festival with top class concerts (classical, jazz, rock, pop), theatre, opera and dance as well as sporting events everywhere in the Algarve. www.allgarve.pt/en

AUGUST

▶ Seafood Festival

The Festival dos Mariscos in Olhão is one of the Algarve's biggest folk festivals and something for the taste buds of seafood lovers. Also good live music.

▶ Sardine Festival

On the riverbank in Portimão sardines are the focal point for eight days. There are concerts every evening with famous Portuguese rock-pop musicians.

SEPTEMBER

▶ Cataplana Experiencia

At the marina in Vilamoura the best Portuguese cooks prepare the best cataplana recipes.

▶ Festas de Alcoutim

Large fête in beautiful Alcoutim on the Guadiana: music, sports, games

OCTOBER

▶ Feira de Santa Iria

This fair is known far beyond the borders of the town where it takes place: Faro.

DECEMBER

▶ Christmas

There are always concerts in the time before Christmas, the most important family holiday in Portugal. New Year's Eve is not celebrated as noisily as in other parts of Europe.

Food and Drink

Going out to eat occupies quite an important place in Portuguese life. For lunch (*almoço*) many Portuguese go to a favourite place close to their work, and for supper (*jantar*) they like to meet friends or acquaintances in a restaurant. Family festivities and birthdays are also often celebrated outside the home. Groups of people celebrating anniversaries are a common sight in local bars.

Eating out

On the Algarve coast there are many quite touristy restaurants, which has the advantage that the menu is often in English. But these restaurants rarely serve authentic Portuguese cuisine. Good local cooking is best eaten in very **simple restaurants**. Here the food is generally freshly cooked and agreeable. The simple *tascas* also serve tasty, simple meals. Portuguese fare is generally plain and light, though not particularly varied. Fish and seafood lovers can have a good time

Local cuisine

← *A long procession: Easter in Loulé*

Is the roof sturdy? Portuguese ham is aromatic and appetizing.

in Portugal. Those who enjoy vegetables and salad are often out of luck – salads should be ordered on the side. Sauces are virtually absent from Portuguese cuisine; fish is occasionally served with potatoes and melted butter.

Mealtimes Lunch is generally served between 12.30pm and 2pm, supper between 8pm and 10pm. There are also restaurants that are open from noon to 11pm and serve meals the whole time. Others are only open in the evening; these are usually more expensive. Reserve a table in this kind of restaurant.

Breakfast Breakfast (*pequeno almoço*) is **by no means the most important meal** in everyday Portugal. Many Portuguese people breakfast in simple bars on the way to work. Hotels and guesthouses normally offer a breakfast that matches continental European standards. The larger hotels put on a breakfast buffet, and guesthouses provide coffee or tea with rolls and jam or cheese and cold meat. Breakfast in a bar usually means sandwiches or rolls (*sanduíche*) with cheese (*com queijo*) or ham (*com fiambre*), buttered toast (*torrada*) or a ham and cheese toasted sandwich (*tosta mista*).

! *Baedeker* TIP

Taste cataplana!

Cataplana originally referred to the copper pot used to cook real delicacies: mussels, fish or meat, paprika, onions and potatoes. Classical cataplana is often on the menu in the Algarve, so there are plenty of chances to try it.

Don't miss this: the delicious homemade dessert arroz doce – rice pudding – is served with cinnamon.

Both lunch and the evening meal normally consist of an appetizer, a main course and a dessert. The appetizer (*entrada*) is often one of the superb Portuguese soups. The main course consists of a fish or meat dish with chips, potatoes or rice and perhaps some vegetables and salad. The meal is topped off by a final course (*sobremesa*) consisting of a delicious and often homemade dessert (*doces*), ice cream or fruit. Bread and butter are usually served beforehand, sometimes with cheese or olives.

At times, small quantities of seafood are placed on the table in advance of the main meal. Though unrequested, bear in mind that such trifles must be paid for, and in the case of seafood that can increase the bill considerably.

Beverages

International drinks such as cola and tonic water (*água tónica*) are available as well as mineral water (*água mineral*), either carbonated (*com gás*) or still (*sem gás*). There are also good fruit juices (*sumo*) though they are rarely freshly squeezed.

Beer (*cerveja*) is a very popular drink in Portugal. The most common is Sagres, brewed near Lisbon; Sagres Boémia is a brown ale. Superbock is somewhat sweeter. If you order *cerveja* you will get a bottled beer. An *imperial* is a small draught beer, a *caneca* a large one.

Wine   A table wine (*vinho da mesa*) or house wine (*vinho da casa*) usually accompanies a meal. *Vinho tinto* is red wine and *vinho branco* white wine. Preferred wines are Dão wines, **wines from the Douro**, and those from the Ribatejo and from the Colares region north-west of Lisbon. Recently **Alentejo wines** have become more popular. *Vinho verde* is a light sparkling, young wine that comes from northern Portugal; about 20% of Portuguese wine production is produced like this. The refreshing »green wine« gets its name from the production method. The grapes are picked early and only fermented a short time.

Algarve wines were regarded as being among Portugal's best wines for a long time, and were mostly drunk as table wines. Recently the quality of Algarve wines has improved significantly thanks to smaller wineries that have completely revamped their production. The official map of Portugal's wine regions shows that the Algarve has four regions. About half of the Algarve vines grow in »Lagoa«, with *c* 2000ha/5000 acres. »Tavira« is the southeastern wine-growing region in Portugal and stretches to the Spanish border with *c*1500ha/3700 acres. The smallest regions in the Algarve are »Lagos«, the most southwestern region in Europe, and »Portimão«, the region around the central fishing port city. Algarve grape varieties are mainly Negra Mole and Periquita or Trincadeira for red, and Crato Branco for white wines.

Cataplana is on the menu of many restaurants in the Algarve.

Portugal's most famous wine is port. The name comes from the nor- *Portport*
thern Portuguese city Porto, where the largest producers are located.
The wine-growing region itself is located significantly farther east on
the slopes of the Douro. The slatey soil on which the grapes grow
imparts a distinctive taste to the wine.
After picking the grapes, a mixture of partially fermented red wine
and brandy is stored in wooden casks or bottles for several years.
Sweet port is used as a dessert wine, while the drier varieties serve as
aperitifs.

The high-alcohol spirit *medronho* is very widespread in the Algarve. *Medronho*
It is made from the fruit of the arbutus, which grows primarily in
southern Portugal.
Bagaço, and *aguardente velha*, old brandy, are also popular spirits.
Unlike at home, glasses are usually filled to the brim. **Ginjinha**, a
cherry liqueur that can be ordered with (*com*) or without (*sem*) cher-
ries, is fairly sweet.

Coffee is served as *café* or *bica*, a small strong coffee, or as *galão*, in a *Coffee*
glass with milk. If you order *café com leite* you will normally get coffee with warm milk in a cup. *Meia de leite* is served with a little less
milk – also in a cup. The freshly brewed *meia de leite à máquina* (also
served with milk) is often more aromatic.

Health

Medical Assistance

Telephone numbers of hospitals (*hospital*, pl.: *hospitais*) and health *Hospitals*
centres (*centro de saúde*) can be found in the first pages of the telephone book or under »*hospitais*«. Most hospitals have a 24-hour
emergency service. In urgent cases, go directly to the casualty department (*urgência*) of the nearest hospital. Staff at the hotel reception
desk will also assist in case of illness. English is spoken in most hospitals. There are health centres in many smaller locations, which are
open during the day. Many English-speaking doctors and dentists
practise in Portugal, particularly on the Algarve or other resorts; the
embassies and consulates will be able to furnish particulars (▶ Information).

Treatment on location normally has to be paid by the patient, so *Health insurance*
comprehensive health insurance is advised. A detailed invoice will be
required by the insurer before reimbursing any costs. Generally it is
advisable to take out additional insurance to cover costs should
transport home be necessary.

▶ MEDICAL ASSISTANCE

▶ **Emergency**
Tel. 112
Emergency doctor, ambulance

▶ **Red Cross**
Faro: Tel. 289 899 903 Portimão:
Tel. 282 485 640

▶ **Emergency services**
Albufeira: Tel. 289 597 000
Faro: Tel. 289 891 100
Lagos: Tel. 282 770 100
Portimão: Tel. 282 450 300,
Tel. 707 282 828
Tavira: Tel. 808 24 24 24

For UK residents, the European Health Insurance Card (EHIC) entitles the holder to state-provided medical treatment free or at a reduced cost while visiting any country in the European Economic Area (EEA). The EHIC is available from post offices.

Pharmacies

Pharmacies (*farmácias*) supply foreign preparations alongside the **medication** produced in Portugal, and they are sometimes cheaper than in their country of manufacture. Regular **opening hours** of pharmacies are Mon–Fri 9am–1pm and 3pm–7pm, Sat 9am–1pm. The addresses of pharmacies offering a **night-time and Sunday service** are listed on signs outside the shops. Information on pharmacies on duty after hours (*farmácias de serviço*) can also be obtained in the daily papers and under tel. 118.

Holiday Activities

Language Schools

Travel agencies also offer special language-learning holidays. Various institutes in the Algarve offer Portuguese language courses. They generally last from two to four weeks.

Excursions

There are many ways of exploring the Algarve on short or longer excursions. The large hotels normally offer tours to various Algarve sights. In the tourist centres, bus tours and **boat tours** along the coast can be booked in many places. Boat trips on the Guadiana are offered in the eastern Algarve.
Excursions in your own car, by local bus or train are also possible. Trains only stop in the larger towns and in smaller towns along the

⏵ USEFUL ADDRESSES

LANGUAGE SCHOOLS

▶ **Faro**
CIAL
Rua Almeida Garrett 44
Tel. 289 807 611
Fax 289 803 154

▶ **Lagos**
Centro de Línguas de Lagos
Rua Dr. Joaquim Tello 32-1 Esq.
Tel./Fax 282 761 070

▶ **Portimão**
CLCC – Centro de Língua,
Cultura e Comunicação
Rua D. Maria Luísa 122
Tel. 282 430 250

EXCURSIONS

▶ **GuadianaTour**
Pesca e Turismo Lda.
Altura ? Barrocal
8950-418 Castro Marim

Tel. 281 956 634
mob. 968 831 553, 965 648 189
www.guadianatour.com
Boat tours from Vila Real de Santo
António on the Guadiana to
Alcoutim and from Vila Real de
Santo Antonio to Tavira

▶ **Formosamar**
Centro Náutico, Marina de Faro
Tel. 289 817 466
www.formosamar.pt
Tours through the Ria Formosa
and drives to the Ilha Deserta.

▶ **Santa Bernarda**
Rua Júdice Fialho 4
8500-702 Portimão
Tel./Fax 282 422 791
mob. 967 023 840
www.santa-bernarda.com
Tours with a beautiful two-masted
boat along the cliff coast

Mountain biking along the west coast

Slide & Splash: a blue labyrinth of tubes makes for fun sliding.

SPAS

▶ **Sociedade das Termas de Monchique, Ldª**
Caldas de Monchique 8550-232
Monchique
Tel. 282 910 910, fax 282 910 991
www.monchiquetermas.com

! **Baedeker TIP**

Health and beauty in the Algarve
Of some 30 Portuguese spas, Caldas de
Monchique (see Serra de Monchique) is
located in the Algarve. Respiratory, liver,
gastro-intestinal and rheumatic ailments are
treated here.

▶ **Associação das Termas de Portugal**
Avenida Miguel Bombarda 110, 2°
1050-167 Lisboa
Tel. 217 940 574/05, 217 940 602
www.termasdeportugal.pt

THEME AND ANIMAL PARKS

▶ **Krazy World**
Theme park with an imaginative mini-golf course, small zoo, restaurant, swimming pool and much more ▶Albufeira

▶ **Zoomarine**
Zoo with aquarium, dolphin shows and swimming with dolphins ▶Albufeira

▶ **Go carts – Kartódromo de Almancil**
On the road N 125 in Almancil

▶ **Zoo Lagos**
Small zoo near ▶Lagos

▶ **Slide & Splash**
East of Portimão near ▶Lagos on the N 125

▶ **Aqualand Algarve**
North of ▶Armação de Pêra near Porches right on the N 125

▶ **Aquashow Family Park**
Near Quarteira on the N 396
www.aquashowpark.com

▶ **Parque da Mina**
Near Caldas de Monchique in the ▶ Serra de Monchique

▶ **Family Golf Park**
In ▶Vilamoura

ALGARVE FROM THE AIR

▶ **Floating in a hot air balloon**
Avenida da Falésia, Vilamoura
Tel. 289 316 576

▶ **Aero Algarve**
Aé000dromo Municipal de
Portimão
Near Alvor – Penina

Tel. 282 495 828
www.aeroalgarve.com

▶ **Air Nimbus**
Herdade dos Salgados
Vila das Lagoas Lote 8 E
1º D – Vale Rebelho
Albufeira
Tel. 961 705 028
www.airnimbus.pt

coast. Buses go to some of the villages in the interior, but do not run very often to remote areas (▶ Transport). An excursion taking in more than one place is difficult without a car (▶Tours). Another option is a **bicycle tour** into the interior, which is however mountainous (▶Sports & Fun). Mountain bikes are suitable for shorter tours along the coast or on unpaved roads or tracks in the hinterland.
Anyone staying in the eastern Algarve can drive to Seville – it takes a couple of hours on four-lane roads and the motorway. From the eastern Algarve a trip to Mértola in south-east Alentejo is also possible.

Information

 USEFUL ADDRESSES

IN AUSTRALIA

▶ **ICEP/Portuguese Trade and Tourism Office**
Suite 507/147 A King Street
Sydney, NSW 2000
Tel. 2 9221 9866, fax 2 9221 0966
info@visitportugal.com

IN CANADA

▶ **ICEP**
60 Bloor Street W, Suite 1005
Toronto
Ontario M4W 3B8
Tel. 416 921 7376
Fax 416 921 1353

icep.toronto@iceptor.ca
info@visitportugal.com

IN THE UK

▶ **ICEP/Portuguese Trade and Tourism Office**
Portuguese Embassy
11 Belgrave Square
London SW1X 8PP
Tel. 0845 35512112
(brochure request and information service; local call rate)
Fax 020 7201 6633
www.visitportugal.com
www.imagesofportugal.com

IN THE USA

▶ **ICEP**
590 Fifth Avenue, 4th Floor
New York, NY 10036
Tel. 212 723 0200 99
Fax 212 764 6137
tourism@portugal.org
info@visitportugal.com

IN THE ALGARVE

▶ **Associação Turismo do Algarve**
Avenida 5 de Outubro 18
8000-076 Faro
Tel. 289 800 403, fax 289 800 466
www.visitalgarve.pt

▶ **»turismo«**
There are tourist information
centres (*turismos*) in all larger cities
and some of the smaller towns that
will provide information on the
town and the surrounding region
and at times assist with the search
for accommodation. The turismos
opening hours vary from office to
office; normal opening times are
Mon–Fri 10am–1pm and
3pm–5pm. The offices in some
towns are planned to move but the
new addresses were not yet released
when this book went to press.

EMBASSIES AND CONSULATES IN PORTUGAL

▶ **Australian Embassy**
Avenida da Liberdade, 200
2nd floor
P-1250-147 Lisbon
Tel. 21 310 1500, fax 21 310 1555
www.portugal.embassy.gov.au

▶ **Canadian Embassy**
Avenida da Liberdade 198-200
3rd floor
P-1269-121 Lisbon
Tel. 21 316 4600
Fax 21 316 4692
http://geo.international.gc.ca/
canada-europa/portugal/

▶ **Irish Embassy**
Rua da Imprensa a Estrela 1-4
P-1200-684 Lisbon
Tel. 21 392 9440
Fax 21 397 7363

▶ **British Embassy**
33 Rua de So Bernardo
P-1249-082 Lisbon
Tel. 21 392 4000, fax 21 392 4185
ppalisbon@fco.gov.uk
www.uk-embassy.pt

▶ **Embassy of the United States of America**
Avenida das Foras Armadas
Sete Ríos
P-1600-081 Lisbon
Tel. 21 727 3300
Fax 21 726 9109 or 217 271 500
(consular section)
www.american-embassy.pt

INTERNET

▶ **www.visitalgarve.pt**
Official website of the Associação
Turismo do Algarve

▶ **www.allgarve.pt**
All events in the Algarve in one
website

Language

Foreign
languages
The foreign languages that are most widely understood and spoken
in Portugal, besides Spanish, are English or French. Visitors will not

usually encounter any communication problems in hotels and larger restaurants. It is advisable however – even if only as a gesture to your hosts – to pick up a few words or simple phrases in Portuguese.

Portuguese is of Romance origin and has also retained some of the earlier influences of the Celtic period and those of later Germanic and Arabic invaders. Written Portuguese can be quickly identified as a Romance language and those with knowledge of Latin and other Romance languages may partly understand.

Portuguese

Spoken Portuguese, however, generally poses difficulties: it sounds almost like a Slavonic language. The

> **? DID YOU KNOW ...?**
>
> ■ Among the most-spoken languages in the world Portuguese is in seventh place. Outside Portugal it is spoken in Brazil as well as in the former Portuguese colonies in Africa.

soft pronunciation, the stringing together of individual syllables, the many sibilants and the number of differently pronounced vowels are striking. Another feature is the strong stress on certain syllables, which frequently results in the swallowing of unstressed syllables.

The majority of Portuguese words are stressed on the penultimate syllable. Generally: if a word ends with the letter m, or s, or with the vowel a, e, or o, then the stress will be on the penultimate syllable. If a word ends with l, r, z or with an ã, i or u, then the last syllable will be stressed. Deviating stresses are marked with accents.

Pronunciation

Accents (´ and ` as well as ˆ) also determine the pronunciation of vowels. Vowels with a tilde (~) are nasalized.

PORTUGUESE PHRASE BOOK

Pronunciation

a	unstressed like a whispered e
á	long a (ah)
c	before a, o and u like k; before e and i like s
ç	like s
ch	like sh
e	unstressed like a whispered i, virtually swallowed at the start of a word before s (»escudo« is pronounced »shkúhdu«; »Estoril«: »shturíu«)
ê	like a closed e (eh)
é	like an open e
g	before a, o and u like g; before e and i like the French j in »journal«

gu	like g
h	is silent
i	after u nasalized (»muito« is pronounced »muínto«)
j	like the French j in »journal«
l	like the English double -l in »hall«, like a so▶ u at the end of a word
lh	like ly
m	nasalizes the preceding vowel at the end of a word
n	nasalizes the preceding vowel at the end of a▶ word
nh	like ny
o	unstressed and like u at the end of a word
ô	like a closed o (oh)
ó	like the open o in »ostrich«
qu	like k
r	r on the tip of the tongue, strongly rolled r a the beginning of a word
rr	strongly rolled r
s	voiceless like s before vowels; between vowel▶ vocalized like the s in »rose«; before hard consonants and at the end of a word like a voiceless sh; before soft consonants like j in the French »journal«
v	like v
x	like sh
z	like the vocalized s in »rose«; at the end of a word like sh

At a glance

Yes/No	Sim/Não
Mrs./Mr.	Senhora/Senhor
Maybe	Talvez
Please	Se faz favor
Thank you	Obrigado/Obrigada
You're welcome/My pleasure	De nada/Não tem de quê
I beg your pardon!/Excuse me!	Desculpe!/Desculpa!
All right/Okay!	Está bem/De acordo!
When?	Quando?
Where?	Onde?
What?	Que?
Who?	Quem?
I beg your pardon?	Como?
How much?	Quanto?
Where to?	Aonde? Para onde?

A good start in the disco: Olá – como vai?

Where from?	Donde?
What time is it?	Que horas são?
I do not understand.	Não compreendo.
Do you speak English?	Fala Inglês?
Can you help me please?	Pode ajudar-me, se faz favor?
I would like …	Queria …
I (do not) like that.	(Não) Gosto disto.
Do you have …?	Tem …?
How much is it?	Quanto custa?

Getting aquainted

Good morning/day!	Bom dia!/Boa tarde!
Good evening!	Boa tarde!/Boa noite!
Hallo!	Olá!
How are you?	Como está?
Thank you. And you?	Bem, obrigado/obrigada.
	E o senhor/a senhora/você/tu?
Goodbye!/Cheerio!/See you!	Adeus!/Até logo!
See you next time!	Até à próxima!

On the road

left	ã esquerda
right	ã direita
top	em cima
bottom	em baixo

straight ahead	em frente
nearby	pert o
far	longe
How do I get to … please?	Se faz favor, onde está …?
How far is that?	Quantos quilómetros são?

Breakdown

My car has broken down.	Tenho uma avaria.
Could you tow me to the next repair shop?	Pode rebocar-me até à oficina mais próxima?
Is there a repair shop close by?	Há alguma oficina aqui perto?

Petrol station

Where is the next petrol station please?	Se faz favor, onde ésta a bomba de gasolina mais próxima?
I would like … litres …	Se faz favor … litros de …
…regular petrol	…gasolina normal
…super	…súper
…diesel	…gasóleo
…unleaded	…sem chumbo
…leaded	…com chumbo
…with …octane	…com …octanas
Fill her up, please.	Cheio, se faz favor.

Accident

Help!	Socorro!
Careful!	Atenção!!
Caution!	Cuidado!
Please call … quickly	Chame depressa …
…an ambulance.	…uma ambulãncia.
…the police.	…a polícia..
…the fire brigade.	…os bombeiros.
It was my/your fault.	A culpa foi minha/sua.
Please give me your name and address.	Pode dizer-me o seu nome e o seu endereço, se faz favor?

Dining out

| Where can I find… | Pode dizer-me, se faz favor, onde há aqui … |
| …a good restaurant? | …um bom restaurante? |

All that's missing is a serviette (guardanapo) and toothpicks (palitos) …

…a restaurant that is not too expensive?	…um restaurante não muito caro?
…a typical restaurant?	…um restaurante típico?
Is there a bar/a café nearby?	Há aqui um bar/um café?
I would like to reserve a table for four for this evening.	Pode reservar-nos para hoje à noite uma mesa para quatro pessoas, se faz favor?
Can you please give me...?	Pode-me dar..., se faz favor?
knife	faca
fork	garfo
spoon	colher
glass	copo
plate	prato
napkin	guardanapo
toothpick	palitos
salt	sal
pepper	pimenta
Here's to you! Cheers!	À sua saúde!
The bill, please.	A conta, se faz favor.
Did you enjoy your meal?	Estava bom?
The food was excellent.	A comida estava êcelente.

Accommodation

Can you recommend … please?	Se faz favor, pode recomendar-me
…a good hotel	…um bom hotel?
…a guesthouse	…uma pensão?
Do you have any vacancies?	Ainda tem quartos livres?
a single room	um quarto individual
a double room	um quarto de casal
a room with two beds	um quarto con duas camas

with a bath	com Casa de banho
... for one night.	…para uma noite.
... for one week.	…para uma semana.

Doctor

Can you recommend a doctor?	Pode indicar-me um médico?
I have pain here.	Dói-me aqui.

Bank

Where is the nearest …	Onde há aqui …
…bank?	…um banco?

Post office

stamp	selo
How much is …	Quanto custa …
…a letter …	…uma carta …
…a postcard …	…um postal …
to England?	para a Inglaterra?
Can I send a fax to... from here?	Posso mandar aqui um fax para...?

Numbers

0	zero
1	um, uma
2	dois, duas
3	três
4	quatro
5	cinco
6	seis
7	sete
8	oito
9	nove
10	dez
11	onze
12	doze
13	treze
14	catorze
15	quinze
16	dezasseis
17	dezassete

18	dezoito
19	dezanove
20	vinte
21	vinte e um
22	vinte e dois
30	trinta
40	quarenta
50	cinquenta
60	sessenta
70	setenta
80	oitenta
90	noventa
100	cem
101	cento e um
200	duzentos
1000	mil
2000	dois mil
10,000	dez mil
1/2	um meio
1/3	um terço
1/4	um quarto

Ementa/menu – Sopas/soups

Açorda	bread and garlic soup
Caldo verde	Portuguese cabbage soup
Sopa de legumes	vegetable soup
Sopa de peíe	fish soup
Sopa alentejana	garlic soup with egg

Entradas/appetizers

Amêijoas	cockles
Azeitonas	olives
Caracóis	snails
Espargos frios	cold asparagus
Melão com presunto	melon with smoked ham
Pão com manteiga	bread and butter
Salada de atum	tuna salad
Salada à portuguesa	mixed salad
Sardinhas em azeite	sardines in olive oil

Peíe e mariscos/fish and seafood

Amêijoas ao natural	cockles, boiled

Atum	tuna
Bacalhau com todos	dried cod with garnish
Bacalhau à Bráz	dried cod, chips, scrambled eggs
Caldeirada	fish stew
Camarão grelhado	grilled prawns
Cataplana	scallops, fish or meat, bell peppers, onions, potatoes
Dourada	gilthead bream
Ensopado de enguias	eel stew
Espadarte	swordfish
Filetes de cherne	silver perch fillets
Gambas na grelha	grilled prawns
Lagosta cozida	boiled crayfish
Linguado	sole
Lulas à sevilhana	baked squid
Mêilhões de cebolada	mussels with onions
Pargo	sea bream
Peixe espada	silver scabbard fish
Perca	perch
Pescada à portuguesa	Portuguese-style haddock
Salmão	salmon
Sardinhas assadas	fried sardines

Carne e aves/meat and poultry

Bife à portuguesa	Portuguese beef steak
Bife de cebolada	steak with onions
Bife de peru	turkey steak
Cabrito	kid
Carne de porco à Alentejana	pork with cockles
Carne na grelha/Churrasco	meat from the (charcoal) grill
Coelho	rabbit
Costelata de cordeiro	lamb cutlet
Costeleta de porco	pork chop
Escalope de vitela	veal cutlet
Espetadas de carne	skewered meat
Fígado de vitela	calf's liver
Frango assado	fried chicken
Frango na pucara	chicken in a clay pot
Iscas	braised liver
Lebre	hare
Leitão assado	suckling pig roast
Lombo de carneiro	saddle of mutton
Pato	duck
Perdiz	partridge
Peru	turkey
Pimentões recheados	filled bell peppers

Porco assado . . . . pork roast
Rins . . . . kidneys
Tripas . . . . tripe

Legumes/vegetables

Batatas . . . . potatoes
Beringelas fritas . . . . fried eggplant
Bróculos . . . . broccoli
Cogumelos . . . . mushrooms
Ervilhas . . . . peas
Espargos . . . . asparagus
Espinafres . . . . spinach
Feijão verde . . . . green beans
Pepinos . . . . cucumbers

Sobremesa/dessert

Arroz doce . . . . rice pudding
Compota de maçã . . . . stewed apples
Gelado misto . . . . mixed ice cream
Leite creme . . . . butterscotch pudding
Maçã assada . . . . baked apple
Pêra Helena . . . . pear belle-hélène
Pudim flan . . . . pudding with caramel sauce
Sorvete . . . . sorbet
Tarte de amêndoa . . . . almond tart

Lista de bebidas – list of beverages

Aguardente . . . . schnapps
Aguardente de figos . . . . fig brandy
Aguardente velho . . . . aged brandy
Bagaço . . . . pomace brandy
Ginjinha . . . . cherry liqueur
Madeira . . . . Madeira wine
Medronho . . . . brandy made with the fruit from
                                                          the strawberry tree
Porto . . . . port wine

Cerveja e vinho/beer and wine

Cerveja/Imperial . . . . draught beer
Caneca . . . . large draught beer

Vinho branco/tinto	white/red wine
Vinho verde	light wine with natural acidity

Bebidas não alcoólicas/alcohol-free beverages

Água mineral	mineral water
Bica	espresso
Café (com leite)	coffee (with milk)
Chá com leite/limão	tea with milk/lemon
Galão	coffee with milk in a glass
Meia de leite	coffee with lots of milk
Garoto	espresso with milk
Laranjada	orangeade
Sumo de laranja	orange juice

Days of the week

Segunda-feira	Monday
Terça-feira	Tuesday
Quarta-feira	Wednesday
Quinta-feira	Thursday
Sexta-feira	Friday
Sábado	Saturday
Domingo	Sunday
Feriado	holiday

Literature

Rioletta Sabo, Jorge Nuno Falcato: *Portuguese Decorative Tiles: Azulejos*, Abbeville Press, USA 1998 – Beautiful coffee-table book about Portugal's tile art – an »Azulejo trip« through the whole country

Julie Stratham, June Parker: *Walking in the Algarve: 40 Coastal and Mountain Walks*, Cicerone 2009. Walking guide by a resident Englishwoman that goes beyond the well-worn trails.

Novels   **António Lobo Antunes**: *The Inquisitor's Manual*, Grove Press 2003. Focuses on the situation in Portugal before and after the revolution using the example of one family and its employees. The patriarchal lord of the manor, once a minister under Salazar, is still lord and master in his own house.

José Saramago: *The Year of the Death of Ricardo Reis*, The Harvill Press 1998. Mixing fact, fantasy and folklore in characteristic style, Saramago depicts Portuguese society during the 1930s as fascism and socialism sweep through a Europe still unsettled by the First World War.

Godfrey Spence: *The Port Companion: A Connoisseur's Guide*, Hungry Minds Inc., US 1997. Information on more than 300 ports with an excellent review section. For those who wish to become port connoisseurs.

Port guide

David Birmingham: *A Concise History of Portugal*, Cambridge University Press, 2003. This book is just what it says – an overview that's not too long, and readable too.

History

José Saramago: *Journey to Portugal*, The Harvill Press 2002. Portugal's Nobel Prize-winner describes a journey across his country, starting in the north-east. Copious descriptions of the sights, somewhat less about actual life in Portugal; first published in 1994.

Portugal general

Marion Kaplan: *The Portuguese: The Land and Its People*, Carcanet Press, 2006. A lively all-round survey, covering the life of the Portuguese as well as their literature and history.

Media

English **daily newspapers and glossy magazines** are generally available in the Algarve in larger cities and holiday centres one or two days after publication. There are several Portuguese publications printed in English, such as the *Anglo-Portuguese News* and *The Portugal News* newspapers, and the magazine *Essential Algarve*. The **daily newspapers of Portugal** are *Público* and *Diário de Notícias*, which along with the day's news stories contain what's-on listings and useful addresses as well as telephone numbers of doctors, hospitals and pharmacies. The largest weekly papers are *Expresso* and *Visão*.

International and national press

Money

Portugal's official currency is the euro. Any bank will exchange foreign currency.

Euro

Money can be drawn from cash dispensers which are found in all the larger towns. The machines are equipped with multilingual ope-

Cash dispensers

● CONTACT DETAILS FOR CREDIT CARDS

In the event of lost bank or credit cards you can contact the following numbers in UK and USA (phone numbers when dialling from abroad):

▶ **Eurocard/MasterCard**
Tel. 001 / 636 7227 111

▶ **Visa**
Tel. 0800 / 811 84 40

▶ **American Express UK**
Tel. 0044 / 1273 696 933

▶ **American Express USA**
Tel. 001 / 800 528 4800

▶ **Diners Club UK**
Tel. 0044 / 1252 513 500

▶ **Diners Club USA**
Tel. 001 / 702 797 5532

Have the bank sort code, account number and card number as well as the expiry date ready.

The following numbers of UK banks can be used to report and cancel lost or stolen bank and credit cards issued by those banks:

▶ **HSBC**
Tel. 0044 / 1442 422 929

▶ **Barclaycard**
Tel. 0044 / 1604 230 230

▶ **NatWest**
Tel. 0044 / 142 370 0545

▶ **Lloyds TSB**
Tel. 0044 / 1702 278 270

rating instructions. Money can be withdrawn from dispensers using all common credit cards.

Banks, major hotels, higher class restaurants, car rental companies as well as some retail shops will accept most international **credit cards**. Visa and Eurocard are widely used, American Express and Diners Club are used somewhat less frequently.

Nightlife

Discos, bars
Nightlife on the Algarve coast often takes place in the discos and bars of the large hotels. In the tourist centres of the central Algarve there are also several large clubs, whose popularity rises and falls from one year to the next. **Albufeira** is definitely a night-owl venue: right in the centre there are whole streets of bars, like Rua Cândido dos Reis or Largo Engenheiro Duarte Pacheco, and in the Montechoro neighbourhood bars line the street on the famous »strip«. Between Albu-

Foam party in the legendary Kadoc disco, one of the most popular in the Algarve, between Albufeira and Vilamoura.

feira and Vilamoura there is what is probably the most popular club in the Algarve, »Kadoc«. **Lagos** also has nightspots, and most of the bars and discos are in the old quarter here; there is also always something going on at the marina. In **Praia da Rocha** the coastal road is closed to traffic at night when all the bars are open. People from nearby Portimão go to Praia da Rocha in the evenings, too. **Monte Gordo** is the nightlife centre of the eastern Algarve, and also has enough pubs, bars and discos. In Faro as well the nights are lively on weekends. The bars, mostly found in three or four streets of the old quarter, are frequented by students. In Tavira and in Olhão the cafés in the covered markets stay open until late, and the atmosphere is quieter.

In the casinos – in Praia da Rocha, Vilamoura and Monte Gordo – French and American roulette, blackjack and baccarat are generally played; there are also slot machines. There is usually a restaurant attached, and these have begun to present international shows. The casinos are normally open daily from 3pm to 3am. **Casinos**

Opening Hours

In places that have adjusted to tourists the chances are good that there will be a kind of low-season atmosphere in the winter months. Many shops – especially souvenir shops – restaurants, smaller hotels and bed & breakfasts could be closed then or have shorter opening times. This of course does not apply to shops and restaurants that are frequented by local people. In the hinterland the opening times usually do not depend on the season. **Tourist centres**

Churches   Most churches in the Algarve are closed during the week and only opened for mass. In order to visit the most important churches it is necessary to pay **admission** – in Lagos it is only possible to enter the Igreja de Santo António by going through the museum; in Faro a ticket to climb the tower is also admission to the church etc.

Water and theme parks   Many of the amusement parks are closed in the winter even though they post official opening times. The only solution is to ask at the closest tourist information or to go and see.

Post · Telecommunications

Telephone   Telephone calls within Portugal and abroad can be made from public call boxes, post offices and private telephone companies. In the **post office** and with **private telephone companies**, register the call at the counter first and pay afterwards. Either coins or a telephone card (*cartão para telefonar*) can be used in **public call boxes**; the card can be purchased at post offices or from telephone companies. To use a **mobile phone** that is not registered in Portugal, dial the country code of Portugal (+351 or 00 35 1) before entering the number of a participant in Portugal. Reception for mobiles is fine throughout the country.

Post   Letters and postcards from southern Portugal to the UK generally take three to four days by regular mail. Letters sent by the considerably more expensive express service *correio azul* will usually get to the UK within two days. **Stamps** (*selos*) can be purchased at the post

 INFORMATION AND DIALLING CODES

DIRECTORY ENQUIRIES
▶ **Tel. 118**
www.118.pt

DIALLING CODES
▶ **Dialling code to Portugal**
from the UK and Republic of Ireland:
tel. 00 35 1
from the USA, Canada and Australia:
tel. 00 11 35 1
The countrywide nine-digit telephone number follows the country code.

▶ **Dialling code from Portugal**
to the UK: tel. 00 44
to the Republic of Ireland:
tel. 00 353
to the USA and Canada: tel. 00 1
to Australia: tel. 00 61
The 0 that precedes the subsequent local area code is omitted.

▶ **Phoning within Portugal (mobile)**
For telephone calls to numbers in Portugal, use the country code:
tel. 00 35 1

office (*correios*) or in shops with the »CTT Selos« sign. **Postage** for letters up to 20g/0.7oz (*cartas*) and cards (*postais*) is € 0.57 within Europe; for *correio azul* it is € 1.75. **Letter boxes** for regular mail are red free-standing columns or red boxes on the walls of houses. The letter boxes for *correio azul* are blue. **Post offices** are generally open Mon–Fri 9am–12.30pm and 2.30pm–6pm.

Prices · Discounts

The days of exceptionally low-priced trips to Portugal are over. In many parts of the country it is still possible to find moderately priced accommodation and restaurants, but in the tourist hotspots the prices are comparable to those in the UK. However there are still ways to plan for a moderately priced holiday. Reasonable guesthouses are available that are neat and clean but do not offer any extras. It is a good idea to be on the lookout for inexpensive restaurants – many simple bars provide good food at low prices. Public transportation is not very expensive, nor is taking the taxi.

 WHAT DOES IT COST?

Double room
from €45.00

Simple meal
€7.00

Train ticket Faro – Tavira
from €2.20

Draught beer
about €1.50

Petrol
about €1.50 per litre

A »bica«
about €0.60

Shopping

In general gold and silver items as well as shoes and leather items can be bought at reasonable prices in Portugal, but the prices in the Algarve's tourist centres are usually higher than in the rest of the country. Shopping is good in Lagos, Portimão and Faro. With some luck simple clothing of good quality at low prices can be found on the **weekly markets** or gypsy markets that take place in some places regularly on a certain weekday. Crafts especially are popular gifts.

365 days of low prices – that doesn't always apply in the Algarve.

Azulejos, **hand painted tiles**, make a pretty, typically Portuguese souvenir. New azulejos can be found everywhere in souvenir shops or in markets. Finding azulejos that are copies of authentic designs is more difficult. They are easiest to find in antique shops.

In Portugal many folk art **products are used in everyday life** – especially ceramics in various shapes and styles, depending on the region. A special ceramics souvenir from the Algarve are the miniature chimneys, which are imitations of the famous Algarve chimneys. The gaily coloured **Barcelos rooster**, which actually comes from northern Portugal, is also well known and can be found in the Algarve in many souvenir shops in various functions – from bottle cork to keychain.

Lace tablecloths, hand-woven fabrics, baskets, wood and cork carvings are available in specialty shops in larger towns or in markets. In Monchique **curule chairs** are produced: beautiful folding chairs with high armrests.

A popular gift from Portugal is **port** from the Douro region in northern Portugal. It is available in all price categories and from various years. The lightly sparkling vinho verde or a bottle of ginjinha, a cherry schnapps, also make good alcoholic souvenirs. An Algarve souvenir is **medronho**, a strong spirit made from the fruits of the local strawberry trees. A music souvenir could be a **fado recording** on CD or DVD. They are sold on the markets at reasonable prices. Good fado can be acquired e.g. at FNAC in AlgarveShopping (▶Albufeira). Recordings by the most famous Portuguese *fadista* Amália Rodrigues or fados by Alfredo Marceneiro or by Carlos Ramos are recommended. Newer fado interpretations are by Dulce Pontes, Mísia, Mariza, Cristina Branco or Camané. The group Madredeus, which interprets Portuguese folk music, is world-famous.

▶ SELECTION OF RURAL MARKETS

▶ Paderne
First Saturday of the month
Fresh fruit and vegetables, house-hold items, clothing, souvenirs

▶ Estói
Second Sunday of the month
Rural market where pretty much everything can be bought: house-hold goods, clothing, ceramics and even animals

▶ Odiáxere
Fourth Monday of the month
A large market is set up on the Largo do Moinho.

▶ Alte
Third Thursday of the month
People from Alte and the sur-rounding villages meet on the Largo José Cavaco Vieira to shop and chat once a month on market day.

Market in Olhão: the stands are set up every Saturday right by the seaside.

! *Baedeker* TIP

Forum Algarve

A large shopping centre with every imaginable kind of shop. There are countless restaurants for relaxing after a marathon shopping trip. All of this is found in attractively designed architecture: Forum Algarve, Faro, on the road to the airport.

▶ **Loulé**
Saturdays
Large country market on the road towards Bouliqueime. Stalls are set up opposite the Convento de Santo António to sell fruit, vegetables, ceramics, baskets, wood and leather work.

▶ **Moncarapacho**
First Sunday of the month
People flock to this market from the whole area and stock up on household items, plastic and ceramic bowls, shoelaces, boots and clothing. Some even buy seed or a sheep or donkey here.

▶ **Olhão**
Saturdays
In the covered market and outside musical cassettes, baskets, clothing and household items are sold. Of course fruit, vegetables, fish and meat are also available.

▶ **Monchique**
Second Friday of the month
On the Largo do Mercado in the centre of Monchique there is a bustle when the markets stalls are put up. Food and household goods are available.

▶ **São Brás de Alportel**
Saturdays
Household items and simple clothing as well as pottery and wood carvings can be bought here reasonably.

Popular souvenirs: colourfully decorated ceramics

Sports & Fun

Hiking in Portugal is getting more and more popular. The entire in- Hiking
terior region is suitable, especially Serra de Monchique. Some travel
agents offer hiking holidays in the Algarve where it is really possible
to explore the beautiful regions of the Algarve. Signs and markers are
often missing on the trails, but recently more trails have been made,
e.g. the Via Algarviana, which runs through the Algarve east to west.
In the eastern Algarve the organization Odiana has developed 19 circular hiking trails that run through the regions Alcoutim, Castro
Marim and Vila Real de Santo António, each with its own theme,
and offer information on flora, fauna, irrigation systems, traditional
architecture and so on. Information brochures on the individual
routes are available at the Odiana office in Castro Marim.

Only the smaller roads in the Algarve interior are suitable for bike Biking
tours. Tours through beautiful landscape are possible here but it is
important to remember that it gets mountainous away from the
coast. The bigger roads along the coast have too much traffic and
there are generally no bicycle paths, only the occasional right lane
for slow-moving vehicles. In Faro, Albufeira, Armação de Pêra, Carvoeiro, Lagos, Praia da Rocha, Tavira, Vilamoura, Quarteira and
Monte Gordo bicycles can be rented – and motor scooters for less
challenging tours.

A kite buggy on the deserted Praia da Bordeira near Carrapateira

Angling   Freshwater angling and sea angling are a popular recreation activity for the Algarvios. Sea angling – insofar as it's not done commercially – requires no licence or fees. In Sagres, Vilamoura, Portimão and Lagos boats can be chartered for angling on the high seas. It is also possible to fish from the coast using long fishing rods. Angling in rivers and lakes requires a permit (the tourist information centres will furnish particulars).

Horseback riding   Anyone wanting a riding holiday or even just to take a few lessons has various options in the Algarve. There are about 20 stables, which also give riding lessons.

Sailing   The best-equipped **marina** in the Algarve is **Vilamoura**. Albufeira and Portimão also have large, modern yacht harbours. Sailing clubs in many towns in the Algarve have boats for charter and offer courses for beginners and advanced sailors. There are sailing facilities in the Algarve in Albufeira, Armação de Pêra, Alvor, Lagos, Monte Gordo, Portimão, Praia da Oura, Praia da Rocha, Quinta do Lago, Olhão, Tavira, Vale do Lobo, Vilamoura and on the Praia da Falésia.

Surfing   The beaches of the Costa Vicentina in the western Algarve are best suited for surfing since the surf is strongest here. There is a surfing school on the Praia do Amado near Carrapateira.

Windsurfing ▶   Windsurfing or kitesurfing courses and equipment rental are available at numerous beaches in the Algarve. There are good conditions for windsurfing on the central and western Algarve coast between Quinta do Lago and Sagres.

Diving   The rocky south-west of the Algarve coast is suitable for diving. There are excellent and in places untouched diving areas at depths of 5–30 m (15–100ft). There are many diving centres that run courses and hire out equipment.

Tennis   Almost all of the larger hotels have their own tennis courts. There are also many public tennis courts, of which the ones belonging to the tennis academy in Vale do Lobo are the best.

Waterskiing   Waterskiing lessons and equipment are available in the larger tourist centres of the Algarve.

Golf   Golfing on the Algarve began in the early 1930s when British residents built a basic course in Praia da Rocha. Penina, the first larger golf course, was created in the 1960s – and designed by the British golfing legend Sir Henry Cotton.

Spectator sports   Important for motorsports fans: in 2008 in the hinterland of Portimão the Autódromo Internacional do Algarve with a 4.7km/2.9mi-long racecourse was opened.

ADDRESSES FOR SPORTS HOLIDAYS

DIVING

▶ **Scubado Dive Centre**
Porto da Baleeira
8650 Sagres
Tel./fax 282 624 821

▶ **Blue Ocean Divers**
Lagos, Estrada de Porto de Mos
Motel Ancora, Apartado 789
Tel. 964 665 667
www.blue-ocean-divers.de

▶ **Divers Cape**
Porto da Baleeira
8650 Sagres
Tel. 965 559 073
www.diverscape.com

HIKING

▶ **Via Algarviana**
www.viaalgarviana.org
Tel. 289 412 959

▶ **Hiking in the Serra de Monchique and on the coast**
▶ **Hiking in the eastern Algarve**
Odiana; information on established routes: Castro Marim, Rua 25 de Abril 1 Tel. 281 531 171
www.odiana.pt

GOLF
Albufeira Region

▶ **Balaia Golf Village**
Albufeira

Practising on the beach: surfing school on Praia do Amado

Golf on the cliffs right above the sea – the Algarve is a golfer's mecca!

Tel. 289 570 200
www.balaiagolfvillage.com

▶ **Pine Cliffs Resort**
Albufeira
Tel. 289 500 113
www.pinecliffs.com

▶ **CS Salgados Grande Hotel**
Albufeira
Tel. 289 244 200
www.cshotelsandresorts.com

Almancil Region

▶ **Barringtons Golf Academy**
Almancil
Tel. 289 351 940
www.barringtons-pt.com

▶ **Pinheiros Altos**
Almancil
Tel. 289 359 900
www.pinheirosaltos.com

▶ **Quinta do Lago Norte**
Almancil
Tel. 289 390 700
www.quintadolagogolf.com

▶ **Quinta do Lago Sul**
Almancil
Tel. 289 390 700
www.quintadolagogolf.com

▶ **San Lorenzo Golf Club**
Almancil
Tel. 289 396 522
www.sanlorenzogolfcourse.com

Castro Marim Region

▶ **Castro Marim Golfe & Country Club**
Castro Marim
Tel. 281 510 330
www.castromarimresort.com/golf

▶ **Quinta do Vale**
Castro Marim
Tel. 281 351 615
www.quintadovale.com

Lagoa Region

▶ **Silves Golf**
Carvoeiro, Lagoa
Tel. 282 340 900, 282 440 130
www.pestanagolf.com

▶ **Gramacho Golf Course**
Lagoa
Tel. 282 340 900
www.pestanagolf.com

▶ **Vale da Pinta Golf Course**
Lagoa, Carvoeiro
Tel. 282 340 900
www.pestanagolf.com

▶ **Vale de Milho Golf**
Lagoa
Tel. 282 358 502
www.valedemilhogolf.com

Lagos Region

▶ **Boavista Golf – Quinta da Boavista**
Lagos
Tel. 282 000 111
www.boavistagolf.com

▶ **Palmares Golf**
Lagos
Tel. 282 790 500
www.palmarcsgolf.com

Loulé Region

▶ **Ocean Golf Course**
Loulé
Tel. 289 353 465
www.valedolobo.com

▶ **Royal Golf Course**
Loulé
Tel. 289 353 465
www.valedolobo.com

Olhão Region

▶ **Colina Verde Golf Course**
Moncarapacho, tel. 289 790 110
www.golfcolinaverde.com

Portimão Region

▶ **Alto Golf and Country Club**
Alvor
Tel. 282 410 820
www.altoclub.com

▶ **Golfe do Morgado**
Portimão
Tel. 282 402 150
www.cs-hoteis.com

▶ **Le Méridien Penina Golf & Resort**
Portimão, tel. 282 420 200
www.lemeridien.com/peninagolf

▶ **Resort Golf Course**
Portimão
Tel. 282 420 223
www.lemeridien.com/peninagolf

Tavira Region

▶ **Benamor Golf**
Tavira
Tel. 281 320 880
www.benamorgolf.com

▶ **Quinta da Ria**
Tavira
Tel. 281 950 580
www.quintadariagolf.com

▶ **Quinta de Cima**
Tavira
Tel. 281 950 580
www.quintadariagolf.com

Vila do Bispo Region

▶ **Parque da Floresta**
Vila do Bispo
Tel. 282 690 013
www.parquedafloresta.com

Vilamoura Region

▶ **Supergolf Vilamoura – Academy Golf Course**
Vilamoura
Tel. 289 300 680
www.supergolf-vilamoura.com

▶ **Oceânico Laguna Golf Course**
Vilamoura
Tel. 289 310 333
www.oceanicogolf.com

▶ **Oceânico Millennium
Golf Course**
Vilamoura
Tel. 289 310 333
www.oceanicogolf.com

▶ **Oceânico Pinhal
Golf Course**
Vilamoura
Tel. 289 310 333
www.oceanicogolf.com

▶ **Oceânico Old Course**
Vilamoura
Tel. 289 310 333
www.oceanicogolf.com

▶ **Oceânico Victoria
Golf Course**
Vilamoura
Tel. 289 310 333
www.oceanicogolf.com

▶ **Vila Sol Golf**
Vilamoura
Tel. 289 300 505
www.vilasol.pt

HORSE RIDING

▶ **Region Albufeira**
Centro Hípico Vale Navio
Estrada da Branqueira
Tel. 289 542 870

▶ **Region Portimão**
Centro Hípico de Vale de Ferro
Sítio Vale de Ferro –
Apartado 104
8501-903 Mexilhoeira Grande
Tel. 282 968 444
www.valedeferro.com

▶ **Region Lagos**
Centro Hípico Tiffany's
Vale Grifo
Almádena
Tel. 282 697 395
www.valegrifo.com

SAILING

▶ **Quima Yachting**
Castelo da Nave
8550-244 Monchique
Tel. 282 912 993
www.quima-yachting.com

SURFING / WINDSURFING / KITESURFING

▶ **Centro de Desportos
Aquáticos**
Quinta do Lago
8135-024 Quinta do Lago
Tel. 289 394 929
lagowatersports@sapo.pt
www.levante.pt

▶ **Centro Náutico da
Praia de Faro**
Avenida Nascente – Praia de Faro
Tel. 289 819 348
Fax 289 819 348
centronautico@hotmail.com

▶ **Escola Windsurf**
Estrada da Meia Praia Bairro
1.º de Maio 4
8600-315 Lagos
Tel. 282 792 315
www.windsurfpoint.com

▶ **EOLIS – Escola de Kitesurf e
Windsurf**
Av. Ria Formosa 38 (Centro
Comercial, loja nº 33)
8800-591 Cabanas de Tavira
Tel. 962 337 285
www.kitesurfeolis.com

▶ **Algarve Watersport**
Rua Ilha da Madeira 20
8600-692 Lagos
Tel. 960 460 800

Time

Western European Time applies in Portugal, which is the same as Greenwich Mean Time. From the end of March to the end of October, Western European Summer Time applies, the same as British Summer Time.

Transport

By Car

The best way to explore much of the Algarve is definitely by car. The hinterland is difficult to access by public transportation. The roads are generally good, but some older roads away from the main traffic routes might be in poor condition. In remote areas the roads might be unsurfaced, but they are also easily passable.

The **driving style** of many motorists presents greater difficulties. They drive fast in the Algarve, especially on the N 125, and on smaller roads the pace is no slower. On mountain roads be prepared for approaching drivers taking tight curves. In the dark be prepared for oncoming cars with dimmed or no lights – even on four-lane roads.

The **N 125** runs along the southern coast and is heavily frequented, especially between Lagos and Faro. The **motorway** IP 1/E 01 or A 22 (Via do Infante de Sagres) runs further inland and is generally used for through traffic because of its distance from towns. It is still free, but there is a possibility that it will become a toll road in the foreseeable future.

The traffic regulations do not differ much from those in other parts of continental Europe. The Portuguese drive on the right and traffic signs comply with international standards. As a rule, drivers who have been in possession of their licence for less than a year are not allowed to drive faster than 55mph/90kmh on roads outside towns and cities; they must affix the corresponding sticker of the Portuguese Automobile Club (ACP) to their car. The international green insurance card must be presented in the event of damage. If the driver of the car is not also the owner, then he or she may need a notarized

Traffic regulations

 Good to know

- **Mobile phones** may only be used with a hands-free kit while driving.
- The **drink-drive limit** is 0.5mg/ml. Drivers who get caught with higher levels can expect stiff penalties.
- There is a general **requirement to wear a seat belt**.
- A **warning vest** must be in the car, which is to be worn when leaving the vehicle in the case of a breakdown.

power of attorney from the owner of the vehicle. A warning vest must be in the car. Vehicle inspections and speed checks are generally fairly frequent in Portugal. The **speed limit** for passenger cars and motorcycles is 30mph/50kmh within built-up areas and 55mph/90kmh outside towns. The speed limit on four-lane roads is 63mph/100kmh, on motorways 75mph/120kmh. For vehicles with trailers the speed limit is 45mph/70kmh outside towns, and 50mph/80kmh on motorways. The minimum speed on motorways is 25mph/40kmh. Traffic on the right has **right of way** on smaller roads which are not specially marked. Main roads with priority are marked by a yellow diamond. Smaller priority roads are for the most part not signposted as such, but the roads merging in will have a stop sign. Motorized road users always have the right of way over non-motorized users.

Car Rental

Persons under 21 years of age are not permitted to rent a car in Portugal. To rent a car you must have had a driving licence for at least one year. A rental car of the lowest category will cost at least € 150 per week; at times, Portuguese car rental firms undercut the price of the international companies considerably.

By Taxi

Taxi costs in Portugal are fairly reasonable. Most taxis are ivory-coloured but the old black taxis with a green roof are still sometimes in service. The vehicles are equipped with a taximeter, and outside towns there are fixed tariffs that passengers can enquire about beforehand. Up to 50% higher fees often apply for journeys at night or for carrying baggage. There will frequently be an extra charge for an empty run in the case of longer drives overland. Passengers should negotiate a special tariff beforehand for pleasure trips. It is customary to give a tip of 10%.

By Bus

For public transport EVA-Transportes and Frota Azul are the agents of choice. There are good bus connections between larger Algarve towns; there are several buses a day – often *expressos*, express buses. Along the coast between Lagos and Ayamonte (Spain) the Linha Litoral stops in all major towns. Smaller towns and villages in the hinterland can also be reached by bus, but not especially frequently. The bus stations (*estação rodoviária*) are as a rule centrally located. In the central Algarve certain bus lines service the coast and the hinterland. Holders of a **tourist pass** (*passe turístico*) can ride as often as they like. The tourist pass is valid for three days. Tourist information or the bus stations have more information. When going to Lisbon or the rest of Portugal it pays to take the express buses from the larger towns.

⟩ USEFUL ADDRESSES

CAR RENTAL

▶ **Avis**
Reservations in the UK:
Tel. 0844 581 0147
www.avis.com

▶ **Europcar**
Reservations in the UK
Tel. 0845 758 5375
Reservations in Portugal
Tel. 21 940 77 90
www.europcar.com

▶ **Hertz**
Reservations in the UK
Tel. 08708 44 88 44
www.hertz.com

▶ **Auto Jardim**
Faro Airport
Tel. 289 800 881
Albufeira:
Av da Liberdade, Edifício »Brisa«
Tel. 289 580 500
Fax 289 587 780
www.auto-jardim.com

AUTOMOBILE CLUB

▶ **ACP**
Avenida 5 de Outubro 42
8000-076 Faro, tel. 289 898 950

▶ **ACP breakdown service**
Tel. 707 509 510

▶ **Additional emergency
telephone numbers:**
▶Emergency services

BY BUS OR COACH

▶ **EVA-Transportes**
www.eva-bus.com

▶ **Frota Azul**
www.frotazul-algarve.pt

BUS TERMINALS

▶ **Albufeira**
Alto dos Caliços
Tel. 289 580 611/614

▶ **Faro**
Av. da República
Tel. 289 899 760

▶ **Lagos**
Rossio S. João
Tel. 282 762 944

▶ **Loulé**
Rua Nossa Senhora de Fátima
Tel. 289 416 655

▶ **Olhão**
Av. General Humberto Delgado
Tel. 289 702 157

▶ **Portimão**
Largo do Dique
Tel. 282 418 120

▶ **Tavira**
Rua dos Pelames
Tel. 281 322 546

▶ **Vila Real de Santo António**
Av. da República
Tel. 281 511 807

BY RAIL

▶ **Caminhos de Ferro
Portugueses**
Tel. 808 208 208, www.cp.pt

BY AIR

▶ **Faro Airport**
Tel. 289 800 801, www.ana.pt

▶ **TAP Air Portugal**
Tel. 707 205 700
(call centre for all of Portugal)
www.flytap.com

By Train

In the southern Algarve a railway line runs between Vila Real de Santo António and Lagos almost parallel to the coast, stopping in almost all small and large towns, but the trip is worthwhile because it goes through very beautiful landscape. The railway stations of some smaller towns are located far outside town. There are good and fast intercity connections to Lisbon and further north.

By Ship

There are connections across the Guadiana between Vila Real de Santo António in Portugal and Ayamonte in Spain (runs daily between 8am and 7.30pm). Since the building of the motorway bridge across the Guadiana this ferry has become less important. There are also boats that travel regularly to the offshore lagoon islands near Faro.

By Air

The Algarve's international airport is **Aeroporto de Faro**. It is located 7km/4mi outside town. European holiday flights arrive and depart from here. There are also regular flights by TAP (Air Portugal) and Portugália to Lisbon and Porto.
A bus runs to the centre of Faro, stopping at the railway station and the bus terminal, but not very regularly. A taxi from the airport to Albufeira, for example, costs about € 40.

Travellers with Disabilities

Travelling in Portugal is not always easy for tourists with physical disabilities. Airports, larger train stations, modern hotels and the most important museums and sights are for the most part equipped to allow the disabled visitor access in relative comfort. ICEP offices (►Information) or local tourism offices provide general information.

 INFORMATION FOR THE DISABLED

UNITED KINGDOM
► **Tourism for All**
c/o Vitalise, Shap Road Industrial Estate, Shap Road, Kendal
Cumbria LA9 6NZ
Tel. 08 45 124 99 71
www.tourismforall.org.uk

USA
► **SATH (Society for Accessible Travel and Hospitality)**
347 5th Ave., no. 605
New York, NY 10016:
Tel. (212) 4 47 72 84
www.sath.org

When to Go

In the summer count on lots of tourists, booked up hotels and crowded beaches. From June until September the temperatures are not intolerable but can get quite high, so the spring and autumn months are ideal for a holiday in the Algarve. Between mid-March and early June, and from early September until early November the temperatures are comfortable and the weather is relatively stable on the whole. It is still possible to swim at this time, too. In spring the Algarve greens and blossoms as well. Even in winter the temperatures only briefly go below 10°C/50°F; with luck there will be some warm or at least mild days between December and March, but it can also be very rainy at this time.

All year round

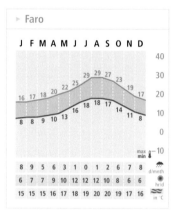

The Atlantic is generally colder than the Mediterranean Sea's; in the summer it rarely goes above 20°C/70°F and in the winter it drops to 15°C/60°F. In the eastern Algarve the water temperature is about 2°C/4°F higher than in the west.

Tours

FARO 51

LISBOA 265

THREE TOURS THROUGH
THE BEAUTIFUL INTERIOR OF THE ALGARVE:
EXPERIENCE RURAL TRANQUILLITY FAR FROM THE
BUSTLE ALONG THE COAST. THEN THERE IS
A TOUR OF THE SPECTACULAR WEST COAST OF
THE ALGARVE WITH ITS IMPRESSIVE SCENERY.

TOURS THROUGH THE ALGARVE

Anyone who takes all the tours described here will have a complete impression of the Algarve interior, its variety of landscape and some very remote villages. The coastal region is for the most part left out of the tours – these towns should be explored individually and with more time. All of the tours are round trips that take one long day.

TOUR 1 **Central Algarve Hinterland**
Only a few miles from the coast: gently rolling hills with lush blossoms in spring, charming and sleepy villages with whitewashed houses, a bustling rural town with a market hall that is busy in the morning and a proud provincial town that was once the much-praised capital of the Moorish province of Al-Gharb ▶ **page 132**

TOUR 2 **Quiet eastern Algarve: mountains and river landscape**
Roman ruins, old mountain villages remote in space and time, endlessly winding roads, the border river Guadiana where hardly anyone goes, and, to finish, sundown in a beautiful coastal town of the Sandy Algarve ▶ **page 134**

TOUR 3 **Rugged and deserted – the western Algarve**
First a traditional spa resort whose hot springs were visited by the Romans and later by Portuguese kings, then to the highest peak of the Algarve, to the wild western coast with its jagged cliffs, empty beaches and massive Atlantic waves, and finally to the westernmost point in Europe and back to tourist territory ▶ **page 137**

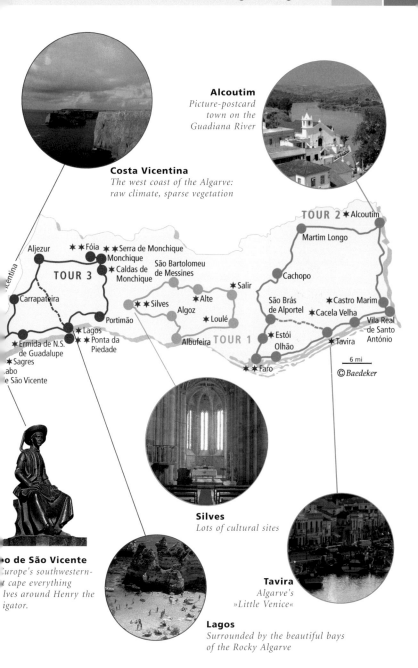

Alcoutim
*Picture-postcard
town on the
Guadiana River*

Costa Vicentina
*The west coast of the Algarve:
raw climate, sparse vegetation*

TOUR 2 ✱Alcoutim

Martim Longo

Aljezur

✱✱ Fóia   ✱ ✱ Serra de Monchique
Monchique

Cachopo

TOUR 3   ✱ Caldas de   São Bartolomeu
Monchique   de Messines

✱ Salir

Carrapateira   ✱ ✱ Silves   ✱ Alte   São Brás   ✱ Castro Marim
de Alportel   ✱ Cacela Velha

Algoz   Vila Real
Portimão   ✱ Loulé   de Santo
António

✱ Lagos   Albufeira   TOUR 1   ✱ Estói
✱ Ermida de N.S.   ✱ ✱ Ponta da   Olhão   ✱ Tavira
de Guadalupe   Piedade
✱ Sagres   ✱ ✱ Faro

6 mi

© Baedeker

Silves
Lots of cultural sites

o de São Vicente
urope's southwestern-
cape everything
lves around Henry the
igator.

Tavira
*Algarve's
»Little Venice«*

Lagos
*Surrounded by the beautiful bays
of the Rocky Algarve*

Holiday in the Algarve

Sun tanning, swimming, relaxing

People come to the Algarve coast to relax, soak up the sun and swim – and south-western Europe has much to offer in this area. The high season lasts almost all year. But beware: in some years there is still heavy rainfall in May or June and from October there is hardly ever uninterrupted sunshine. The summer months guarantee beautiful weather, so sunscreen with a high protection factor as well as other sun protection are definitely a must.

Beaches

Along the south and the west coast of the Algarve there are masses of beautiful beaches – in the Rocky Algarve (Windward Coast) to the west there are some sandy coves in enchanting landscape between high cliffs, and in the so-called Sandy Algarve (Leeward Coast) in the east there are miles-long sandy beaches almost like Mediterranean beaches, because the Atlantic influence is reduced here. The western coast is rougher, the waves are higher and the water is always colder. There are wonderful beaches here that get few visitors. With a little luck you will find a beach bar, and otherwise nature can be enjoyed from its wildest side from morning until evening. The central Algarve coast gets very full in the high season, but for that the tourist infrastructure is fully developed: large and good hotel complexes, restaurants, cafés, bars, lots of nightlife.

East, west or centre?

When booking a beach holiday, check which location has good beaches nearby. Flat sandy beaches are in the east, and the atmosphere there is quite relaxed. In the region between Faro and Tavira the beaches are on the lagoon islands off the coast, which are mostly accessible by boat. This is important for daily planning: a short siesta in the hotel is not as convenient here as in the east, where the beaches are right on the coast. On the west coast there is less accommodation. The beaches are farther away and require a bit more improvisation, but the natural setting is the best here. The centre of the Algarve coast, between Quarteira and Lagos, is ideal for people who want a little variety, like shopping in a pedestrian zone or relaxing in ice cream bars or cafés.

> ! **Baedeker TIP**
>
> **Train trip through the eastern Algarve**
> A train ride from Faro to Vila Real de Santo António is very enjoyable. It takes about an hour and part of the trip runs right along the lagoon. Starting in Lagos is also possible, but there is usually a long stop in Faro. Departure times can be found in the railway stations or under www.cp.pt.

Children in the Algarve

The most important consideration for an Algarve holiday with small children is the type of beach or accommodation that is geared for children and possibly has activities for them or child-minding services. Hotels like this can be found in the tourist-oriented central Al-

Splashes of colour: poppy field in the Algarve hinterland

garve, and increasingly in the east too. The beach conditions are also good here – there are long beaches in the east, though swimming here can be dangerous, or shallow coves where the water is quieter. Further to the west places like Salema or Luz are suitable for holidays with children.

It is generally not well known that the hinterland of the Algarve has lots of small gems and beautiful landscape. There is no point in planning a cultural holiday in southern Portugal, but small towns and villages that are not on the coast make for pretty excursions and give an idea of normal Portuguese everyday life, which is for the most part lacking on the coast. Apart from that the Algarve also has sites of cultural interest: from Roman times and the age of discovery, though unfortunately little of the Moorish past remains.

The »other Algarve«

The simplest way to get about is by car. Remote beaches can hardly be reached in other ways. It is also enjoyable to take buses or trains for longer distances. Biking along the coast is no fun: drivers don't really watch out for cyclists, there are no bike paths and it is really quite dangerous. Further inland, biking is fun but the inclines make it a sport, not recreation.

How to drive through the Algarve?

Tour 1 Central Algarve Hinterland

Length of tour: *c* 100km/60mi   **Duration:** 1 day

Most of this tour goes through gentle garden landscape, passing through pretty villages and small rural towns, and ending with a visit to Silves, the old Arab capital.

From ❶**Albufeira** drive on the N 125 and the N 270 or the motorway to ❷ ✷ **Loulé**. Via the N 270 stop to the south of the village at the pilgrimage chapel Nossa Senhora da Piedade above the road and enjoy the view. In Loulé there is a market every morning and bustling activity around the market hall. Apart from that the small old part of Loulé is definitely worth a visit. From Loulé continue to ❸ ✷ **Salir**. Take either the small road northwards to Salir or take a detour through Querença, another village located in beautiful landscape. Salir is one of the prettiest villages in the Algarve. It is spread out over two hills with beautiful views from here of the patchwork fields and gardens around it. The village church lies on one of the two hills, the remains of the Moorish castle walls on the other. From here drive west on the N 124 – past the ✷ **Rocha da Pena** hills, which go up to 479m/1572ft – to ❹ ✷ **Alte**. Alte is one of the postcard villages of the Algarve hinterland and it can get crowded here. The village itself with its pretty white houses is worth exploring, as are the church and the springs on the eastern end.

The next stop is ❺ **São Bartolomeu de Messines**. A stroll through the centre of this small rural town is nice, but there are no real tourist sights. Anyone who wants a little more time for the cultural attractions of Silves should drive through without stopping. The road is hardly ever used and goes through a very remote region.

❻ ✷✷ **Silves** can be seen from far off. Right at the entrance to the town, a Manueline roadside cross on the right is sheltered under a roof. A visit to the cathedral is worthwhile; it has a number of Gothic features, which are rare in the Algarve. The impressive castle, built of red sandstone, dominates the town. Finally the archaeological museum is very interesting; a 12th/13th-century cistern was integrated into the exhibition rooms.

DON'T MISS

- Visit the Loulé market hall during the morning hours.
- Salir: stroll to the castle hill with the remains of a Moorish castle
- Picnic in Alte on the square by the springs
- Silves: the castle above the town, which goes back to Moorish times

Take the N 269 back. This quiet country road leads through a peaceful area. **❼Algoz**, a typical Algarve village that gives no hint of the activity a few miles away on the coast, lies on the route to Albufeira, 11km/6mi away.

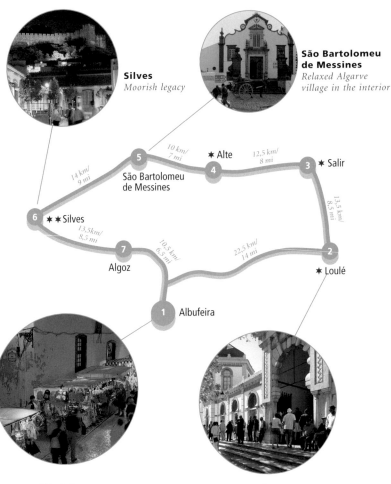

Silves
Moorish legacy

São Bartolomeu de Messines
Relaxed Algarve village in the interior

10 km/7 mi

★ Alte

12,5 km/8 mi

5

São Bartolomeu de Messines

4

3 ★ Salir

14 km/9 mi

13,5 km/8,5 mi

6 ★★ Silves

13,5km/8,5 mi

7

Algoz

10,5 km/6,5 mi

22,5 km/14 mi

2

★ Loulé

1 Albufeira

Albufeira
Busy streets and lanes even in the late evening

Loulé
Recommended: a morning visit to the beautiful market hall

Tour 2 The Quiet Eastern Algarve: Mountains and River Landscape

Length of tour: just under 200km/ 120mi

Duration: 1 day

This route through the eastern Algarve will take a long day to complete; it goes through very remote mountain regions. The first part of the route, via Martim Longo to Alcoutim, is especially curvy and time-consuming. The drive along the banks of the Guadiana in the east is delightful. Depending on when the coast is reached, there is still time for visiting one or two coastal towns, but this tour does not allow for a good look round Tavira or Olhão; both towns are worth seeing and should be visited on separate days.

From ❶ ✳✳ **Faro** follow the N 2 via Estói to São Brás de Alportel. The traffic becomes lighter away from Faro. Anyone who gets an early start and wants to take a short tour right away can stop in ❷ ✳ **Estói** at the Roman ruins of Milreu, and also see if the palace gardens are open. After Estói the road leads through gentle garden scenery as far as ❸ **São Brás de Alportel**. A short stop in this pretty rural town is worthwhile to absorb the atmosphere. Anyone interested in regional rural life, clothing and customs should stop at the excellent Museu do Trajo. Continue on the N 2, which leads north towards Lisbon via Almodôvar. A drive with many curves leads finally to the remote village of Barranco Velho. Shortly afterwards turn right onto N 124, which passes through ✳ **Serra do Caldeirão** to Cachopo. Here and south of Barranco Velho the landscape is very charming. The winding road runs through a lonely mountainous area with few villages. The village of ❹ **Cachopo** is a good place for a short break – it gives an impression of how remote and lonely the villages of the Algarve can be. Then follow the road eastwards toward Martim Longo via Vaqueiros. Shortly after Vaqueiros a 3km/2mi track runs towards Parque Mineiro Cova dos Mouros above Ribeiro da Foupana and affords pretty views of the river valley. It ends at ❺ **Martim Longo**, the largest village in this, the poorest region of the Algarve. From Martim Longo follow the N 124 again eastwards, an easy drive of 30km/ 18mi to ❻ ✳ **Alcoutim**. A visit to the castle in this town on the Gua-

 DON'T MISS

■ Estói: the ruins of the water sanctuary with the fish mosaics
■ A visit to Museu do Trajo in São Brás de Alportel
■ Alcoutim, a pretty village right on the Guadiana
■ Castle in Castro Marim
■ Cacela Velha: small hamlet right above the lagoon

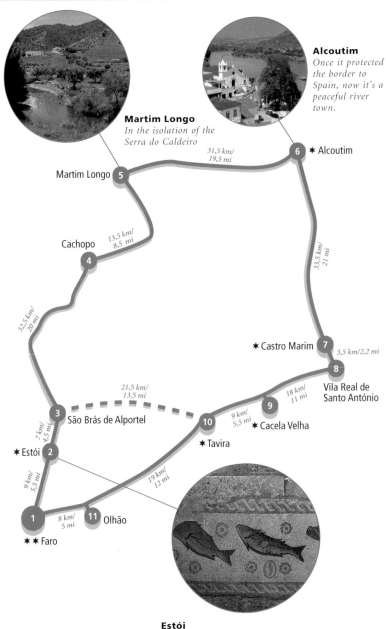

Alcoutim
Once it protected the border to Spain, now it's a peaceful river town.

Martim Longo
In the isolation of the Serra do Caldeiro

31,5 km/ 19,5 mi

Martim Longo **5**

6 ★ Alcoutim

13,5 km/ 8,5 mi

Cachopo
4

33,5 km/ 21 mi

32,5 km/ 20 mi

★ Castro Marim **7**

3,5 km/2,2 mi

8

21,5 km/ 13,5 mi

3
São Brás de Alportel

Vila Real de Santo António

18 km/ 11 mi

10

9

9 km/ 5,5 mi
★ Cacela Velha

7 km/ 4,5 mi

★ Estói **2**

★ Tavira

9 km/ 5,5 mi

19 km/ 12 mi

1

8 km/ 5 mi

11 Olhão

★ ★ Faro

Estói
Ruins of a Roman water sanctuary

! *Baedeker* TIP

Above the riverbanks

In Alcoutim there is a nice place to relax with a view of the Rio Guadiana: on a small terrace above the river there are a few tables and chairs where a kiosk sells drinks and snacks. There is a view across the river to Spain; occasionally a boat crosses over.

diana is worthwhile. Take a break in a café along the river-bank and enjoy the view across to Sanlúcar de Guadiana on the Spanish side.

From Alcoutim a narrow road leads southwards along the beautiful Guadiana. The river-bank on both the Spanish and the Portuguese sides is slightly hilly; the road runs a little above and sometimes right next to the river. The village of Guerreiros do Rio (»river warrior«) is especially lovely and has a small museum on the history, flora and fauna of the Guadiana.

South of Odeleite turn onto the N 122/IC 27, which quickly leads to ❼ ✳ **Castro Marim**, a town with two fortified castles. ❽**Vila Real de Santo António**, a little further to the south just before the Guadiana flows into the Atlantic Ocean, is worth a short visit. The town was planned in a chequerboard pattern, and a stroll on the promenade along the banks of the Guadiana is nice. The drive on the N 125 pa-rallel to the coast back to Faro provides an opportunity to stop in the hamlet of ❾ ✳ **Cacela Velha**, time allowing; or let the day wind down in pretty ❿ ✳ **Tavira** or in ⓫ **Olhão**.

Cacela Velha: Hamlet on the edge of the lagoon

As an alternative to the motorway or the busy coastal road, after Tavira return to Faro through the countryside on the N 270, which leads through pretty scenery. In São Brás de Alportel turn off towards Faro.

Alternative routes

Holidaymakers who are staying on the eastern coast between Tavira and Vila Real de Santo António can take the N 397 directly from Tavira to Cachopo and thus shorten the tour a bit. But allow for enough time for this route: the road through the beautiful scenery of the Serra de Alcaria do Cume has many curves.

Tour 3 Rugged and Deserted – the Western Algarve

Length of tour *c* 185km/115mi   **Duration:** 1 day

This tour leads through a great variety of scenery. The foothills gradually give way to the Serra de Monchique, with the highest peak in the Algarve. Then comes the west, whose ruggedness is markedly different from the other regions of the Algarve. Cabo de São Vicente is the southwestern tip of Europe. There is only enough time for a thorough tour of Lagos if you start the tour early enough. Anyone who wants to linger along the route can leave out Cabo de São Vicente. In that case the tour is only 100km/60mi long.

Start in ❶**Portimão** going towards Monchique on the N 266. Shortly after Portimão this road leads through thinly settled regions. The road climbs and opens attractive vistas repeatedly. A few miles before Monchique there is a special place: ❷✳ **Caldas de Monchique**, a traditional spa resort that is quite a bit smaller than Monchique itself but has more atmosphere. There are cafés here for a relaxing break.

❸ **Monchique**, the main town of the ✳✳ **Serra de Monchique**, marches up a slope; meander through the steep streets to get good views of the valley. Almost all of the small streets in the north-western

DON'T MISS

- Coffee break under tall trees in the charming spa village Caldas de Monchique
- Fóia: view from the Algarve's highest peak
- Costa Vicentina: there are beautiful beaches near Carrapateira
- Cabo de São Vicente – Europe's south-westernmost point

part of the village lead into beautiful mountain landscape: to get a little exercise, take a short walk here.

After the visit to Monchique by all means take a small detour to the highest peak of the Algarve, ❹✳✳ **Fóia** (902m/2960ft above sea le-

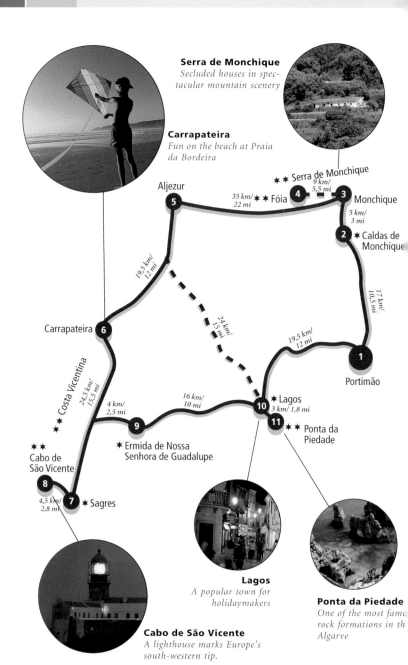

Serra de Monchique
Secluded houses in spectacular mountain scenery

Carrapateira
Fun on the beach at Praia da Bordeira

Aljezur **5**

★★ Serra de Monchique

35 km/ ★★ Fóia **4** 9 km/ **3** Monchique
22 mi 5,5 mi

5 km/
3 mi

2 ★ Caldas de
Monchique

19,5 km/
12 mi

17 km/
10,5 mi

Carrapateira **6**

24 km/
15 mi

19,5 km/
12 mi

1

Portimão

Costa Vicentina

24,5 km/
15,5 mi

4 km/
2,5 mi

16 km/
10 mi

★ Lagos
3 km/ 1,8 mi

10

11 ★★ Ponta da
Piedade

★★

Cabo de
São Vicente

9

★ Ermida de Nossa
Senhora de Guadalupe

8

4,5 km/
2,8 mi

7 ★ Sagres

Lagos
A popular town for holidaymakers

Cabo de São Vicente
A lighthouse marks Europe's south-western tip.

Ponta da Piedade
One of the most fam(o)us rock formations in th(e) Algarve

vel). The road to the peak starts right in Monchique (there and back 16km/10mi). Despite a forest of radio antennas and transmitters at the top, there is also a grand view of almost the whole coastline and a beautiful view northwards into the interior towards the Alentejo.

Return to Monchique on the same road and leave the town southwards; after only 2km/1.2mi turn off onto the N 267 to the west. This winding road leads through superb mountain scenery, which becomes increasingly rugged and barren as the influence of the Atlantic on the vegetation makes itself felt. In ❺**Aljezur** stop briefly and walk through the historic town centre up to the fortifications. If you have time, visit one of the small museums in the old part of town.

Then continue the tour on the N 120 and drive southwest on the N 268. Near ❻ **Carrapateira** it's possible to drive right by the water. This area shows clearly to what extent the ✳ ✳ **Costa Vicentina**, the western coats of the Algarve, differs from the touristy southern coast. Drive as far as ❼ ✳ **Sagres**. Do not miss visiting the Fortaleza de Sagres south of the town and ❽ ✳ ✳ **Cabo de São Vicente**, the most southwestern promontory of the European continent. There is no better place to imagine how Portuguese mariners felt in the 15th century when they set sail towards the horizon. From Cabo de São Vicente take the same road back via Sagres, drive to Vila do Bispo and turn off here onto the N 125, which is relatively quiet in this region. Beyond the town of Raposeira there is a little-noticed treasure to the left of the road: ❾ ✳ **Ermida de Nossa Senhora de Guadalupe**, the oldest church in the Algarve.

Then finally comes ❿ ✳ **Lagos**. The town centre is small but its narrow streets and many pavement restaurants are an invitation to stroll and spend some time there. To end the tour with a work of nature, take a small detour 2km/1.2mi south to ⓫ ✳ ✳ **Ponta da Piedade**, certainly the most bizarre rock formation on the Algarve coast – in the evening light the rocky towers and arches shimmer beautifully. From Lagos it is just about 20km/13mi to the starting point at Portimão.

Alternatively, follow this route in the opposite direction, which has the advantage of touring Lagos earlier in the day when you are still fresh and ending the day in the atmospheric little spa of Caldas de Monchique. However, it could be a disadvantage to have to decide early in the day whether to visit Cabo de São Vicente or to shorten the tour.

Alternative route

To visit Sagres and Cabo de São Vicente in a separate tour, turn off 6km/3.5mi south of Aljezur on the N 120. This way the distance to Lagos is only 24km/14mi.

Shortening the tour

Sights from A to Z

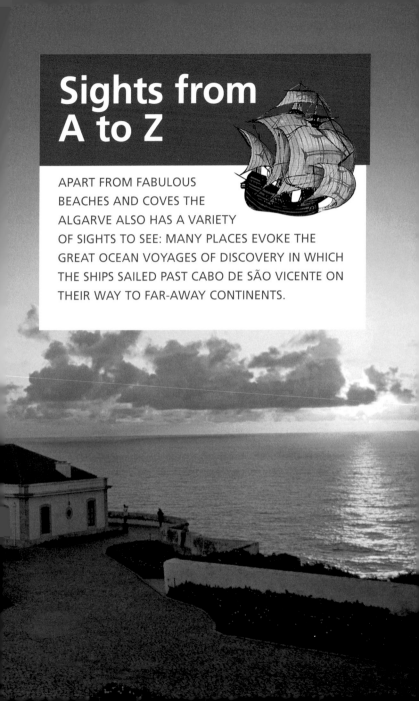

APART FROM FABULOUS BEACHES AND COVES THE ALGARVE ALSO HAS A VARIETY OF SIGHTS TO SEE: MANY PLACES EVOKE THE GREAT OCEAN VOYAGES OF DISCOVERY IN WHICH THE SHIPS SAILED PAST CABO DE SÃO VICENTE ON THEIR WAY TO FAR-AWAY CONTINENTS.

★ Albufeira

F 5

Conselho: Albufeira (capital)   **Population:** 17,000

Until the middle of the 20th century Albufeira was a little fishing village in a beautiful location. Then it became a well-kept secret, and in the 1960s and 1970s the dream destination of sun worshippers from various European countries who cultivated a bohemian lifestyle and turned night into day here.

Albufeira on the southern coast of the Algarve about 35km/20mi west of Faro is the first sizeable town in the eastern part of the Barlavento, the section of coast that is marked by rocky cliffs and small picturesque coves. Albufeira started out in one of these sandy coves bordered by cliffs.

The dream ended in the 1970s when Albufeira, like other places in the Algarve, became the focus of interest of big travel companies and before long was one of the **foremost holiday centres** in the Algarve. With the influx of visitors a distinctly tourist infrastructure developed in Albufeira and on the surrounding beaches. Every imaginable kind of water sport is available here, as are tennis and golf; horse riding is possible in the whole area. A large marina was built west of Albufeira.

History

Albufeira looks back on a long and turbulent history. The Romans settled here in the first half of the 2nd century BC, but because of Albufeira's ideal location it can be assumed that they already found settlements here when they came. They built a fortress on the cliffs and named it Baltum, together with the settlement; in the sea they constructed a basin for extracting salt, which they needed to conserve fish. The Visigoths came into the region in the 5th century AD and were taken over in AD 716by the Arabs, who called the city Al-Buhara or Al-Buhera, the origin of the present name Albufeira, meaning **lagoon**. Albufeira became an important port by trading with North Africa. Its conquest by Christian troops in 1189 only lasted 2 years; it was only in the mid-13th century that it was conquered by knights of the Order of Santiago and fell conclusively to Portugal. Trade with North Africa stopped completely and the city lost its status.

In the 16th century the residents of Albufeira successfully warded off Arab, English and French pirates. The **earthquake** of 1755 caused great devastation: a tidal wave washed away many houses close to the shore. Albufeira's next catastrophe took place during the civil wars in the 19th century. The guerrilla troops of the infamous »Remexido« (►Famous People), a follower of the absolutist king Miguel I, laid siege to the town and finally set it on fire.

← *Lighthouse at Cabo de São Vicente*

Industrial development in Albufeira began in the 19th century with the fish processing on a large scale. In the early 20th century Albufeira mainly lived from exporting fish and dried fruits. There were several shipyards and five factories, where mainly women worked. The economic situation declined rapidly in and around Albufeira in the 1950s. Shipyards and factories had to close, and the population declined. Albufeira began to flourish again with the onset of tourism, but had to accept the fact that the appearance and character of the city and surroundings changed completely.

The town centre is an extensive pedestrian zone. The typical Portuguese mosaics that pave the streets are very pretty. Small, whitewashed houses give the centre an appealing look. There are souvenir shops, jewellery shops and boutiques everywhere. Albufeira is an **Eldorado for night owls** when it gets dark – it is the perfect place for pub crawls, and there is a vast selection. The same applies for restau-

Albufeira's centre

There is activity in the streets of Albufeira's old centre until late evening.

! *Baedeker* TIP

A vista of white houses

Above Praia dos Pescadores to the east, steep steps lead up to a small lookout. From here the town's im-pressive location can be best seen: a spectacular view of the houses of Albufeira, the municipal beach and the coast.

rants and cafés: some streets look like one large eatery, especially Rua Cândido dos Reis.

Albufeira's location, **like an amphitheatre** that climbs up the steep slopes of the cove, is still an attraction, but the density of the houses in town and above the bay cannot be overlooked. Not much remains of the fishing village and the well-kept secret; tourism dominates the scene completely in the summer months. Sunbathers crowd the broad municipal beach; only a few fishermen still keep boats here and actually go fishing.

What to See in Albufeira

Rua 5 de Outubro
The centre of Albufeira's pretty pedestrian zone is Rua 5 de Outubro, which is always very busy during the tourist season. Southwards it extends to a tunnel that was carved out of the rock in the 1930s, the connection to the municipal beach, Praia do Peneco.

Museu Municipal de Arqueologia ⏱
Steps lead from the southern end of Rua 5 de Outubro up to Praça da República. The old town hall is located on the east side of the square and now houses the Museu Municipal de Arqueologia with its archaeological collection; opening times in the summer: Tue – Sun 2pm – 8pm, in the winter: 10.30am – 4.30pm.

Igreja da Misericórdia
Diagonally opposite, the little Igreja da Misericórdia is integrated inconspicuously into the row of houses. Only the Manueline-style portal of red sandstone stands out a bit.

Largo Cais Herculano
Follow Rua da Bateria eastwards to Largo Cais Herculano, a street with many fish restaurants and bars. In the past the new catch was sold immediately in the **open fish market** – today it is sold in the modern market hall north of the bypass.

Praia dos Pescadores
In front of Largo Cais Herculano lies Praia dos Pescadores with its colourful fishing boats, a municipal beach that used to be only used by fishermen; today only a few can be seen plying their trade. On Praia dos Pescadores a **pier** stretches into the sea, providing a small promenade and a place for anglers to while away the hours.

Largo Engenheiro Duarte Pacheco
Rua Cândido dos Reis – in the summer months it is one large roadside eatery – is the connection to Largo Engenheiro Duarte Pacheco. **Albufeira's main square** is named after the engineer Duarte Pacheco, who was minister of building under Salazar and in charge of building the tunnel between Rua 5 de Outubro and the municipal beach.

Albufeira *Map*

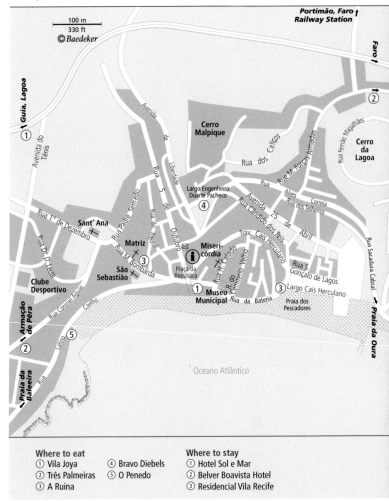

Where to eat
① Vila Joya
② Três Palmeiras
③ A Ruina
④ Bravo Diebels
⑤ O Penedo

Where to stay
① Hotel Sol e Mar
② Belver Boavista Hotel
③ Residencial Vila Recife

The square, which has recently been remodelled and renovated, is the city's lively centre, where locals and especially tourists meet. Cafés, restaurants and snack bars line the sides, interspersed with postcard stands and fashion jewellery sellers. The town's churches are depicted on the fountain in the square.

Two churches west of Rua 5 de Outubro are worth a visit. The Renaissance-style Igreja de São Sebastião still has the **Manueline side en-**

Igreja de São Sebastião

▶ VISITING ALBUFEIRA

INFORMATION
Rua 5 de Outubro
Tel. 289 585 279

SHOPPING
Albufeira's town centre is one big shopping zone, with souvenir shops and boutiques especially on Rua 5 de Outubro. AlgarveShopping, with more than 130 shops, on the N 125 just before Guia (coming from the east) is the largest shopping centre in the Algarve.

GOING OUT
Probably the most famous nightclub in the Algarve is »Kadoc« on the road between Albufeira and Vilamoura.

Those looking for something less spectacular or who don't want to be so far from bed after a long night will find plenty of bars and discos in Albufeira – most of them on Rua Cândido dos Reis and Largo Engenheiro Duarte Pacheco. The »strip« east of the town centre between Praia da Oura and Montechoro is also known for its nightlife.

WHERE TO EAT
▶ **Expensive**
① *Vila Joya*
Road to Praia da Galé
Tel. 289 591 795
This restaurant is considered to be one of the best in Portugal.

Pub on Largo Engenheiro Duarte Pucheco

▶ Moderate

② *Três Palmeiras*
Areias de São João
Tel. 289 515 423
A well-known restaurant approx.
2.5km/1.5mi east of the centre, pop-
ular with both locals and tourists.

▶ Moderate/Inexpensive

③ *A Ruina*
Cais Herculano
Tel. 289 512 094
Freshly caught seafood and a splendid
view of the »beach of the fishermen«.
It is especially pleasant on the roof
terrace.

④ *Bravo Diebels*
Largo Eng. Duarte Pacheco 50
Tel. 289 589 240
As almost everywhere in the centre of
Albufeira, the menu here is very
tourist-oriented; in addition there is
good German beer. The service is
exceedingly friendly and fast.

⑤ *O Penedo*
Rua Latino Coelho 15
Tel. 289 586 110
Situated directly above the cliffs with
a beautiful view across the city and
the water. The fish dishes are good.

WHERE TO STAY

▶ Luxury

Sheraton Algarve e Pine
Cliffs Resort
Praia da Falésia
Tel. 289 500 100
www.sheraton-algarve.com
East of Albufeira in the direction of
Quarteira, this is considered to be one

Sheraton Algarve: buffet on the cliffs above the beach

of the most beautiful hotels on the Algarve: 215 rooms and suites in a spacious two-storey building.

▶ Mid-range

① Hotel Sol e Mar
Rua José Bernardino de Sousa
Tel. 289 580 080
Fax 289 587 036
www.grupofbareta.com
This 74-room hotel, located between the cliffs on the main beach, heralded the beginnings of the tourist industry in Albufeira in the early 1960s.

② Belver Boavista Hotel
Rua Samora Barros 20
Tel. 289 589 175; fax 289 589 180
www.hotelboavista.pt/belver
Beautiful hotel with a view of the ocean, though the water is not right on the doorstep. Charming and elegant interior decoration, no organized recreational programmes.

Hotel Alfa Mar
Praia da Falésia
Tel. 289 501 351; fax 289 501 069
www.alfamar.pt
Large hotel (264 rooms), beautifully situated between Albufeira and Quarteira above Falésia beach. Wide range of sports offered.

▶ Mid-range/Budget

Auramar Beach Resort
Praia dos Aveiros
Tel. 289 599 100
www.grupofbareta.com
Located east of Albufeira on the coast; friendly atmosphere, all the necessities without many extras.

③ Residencial Vila Recife
Rua Miguel Bombarda 6
Tel. 289 583 740
www.grupofbareta.com
Centrally located, though somewhat removed from the hustle and bustle, in a beautiful house. 92 modern, simply furnished rooms.

trance of a previous church on the site. The Museu de Arte Sacra with a small collection of sacred articles is also housed in the church. Hours: Tue – Sun 10.30am – 12.30pm and 2.30pm – 4pm.

Igreja Sant'Ana   The architecture of Igreja Sant'Ana on Largo Jacinto d'Ayete at the corner of Rua 1° de Dezembro is worth looking at. The typical whitewashed 18th-century Algarve church seems quite rural in the urban setting. The dome and the Baroque gables that frame it on all four sides are striking.

Around Albufeira

Beaches   West of Albufeira there are several small beaches in picturesque coves as well as the long **Praia da Galé**, which stretches to Armação de Pêra. Everywhere there are small or large places to eat as well as good facilities for water sports: diving, surfing, water skiing. Praia da Galé is preferred by surfers; diving and snorkelling is best between Albufeira and **Praia do Castelo** on the popular Praia de São Rafael and on **Praia da Baleeira**.

Breathtaking: the cliffs above Praia da Falésia

Pretty little beaches east of Albufeira are **Praia da Oura**, **Praia da Balaia** and **Praia de Maria-Luisa**, which belong to the tourist suburbs Montechoro and Areias de São João. There are good water sports conditions and places to eat on all of the beaches.

Olhos de Água lies 7km/4mi east of Albufeira on the coast. The name comes from the freshwater springs that can be seen on the beach at low tide and which the residents called »**water eyes**«. The in part rocky beach is quite pretty but mostly very full during the tourist season.

Olhos de Água

Praia da Falésia is a well-kept broad beach about 12km/7mi east of Albufeira. Praia da Falésia is distinguished by the high cliffs that glow brightly in the right light and stretch along the coast for miles. They are most impressive in the evening at sunset.
The beach is roomy even though one of the Algarve's largest holiday resorts with apartments, bungalows and hotels is located on top of the cliffs.

✱
Praia da Falésia

Paderne is located 10km/6mi north-east of Albufeira in the middle of pretty, slightly hilly countryside. This picturesque village radiates a

Paderne

pleasant restfulness although it is not too far from the tourist activity on the coast. Known to the Arabs as Badirna, the village was conquered in 1248 by the Portuguese under Dom Paio Peres Correia. The parish church was built in the 16th century, and still has some Manueline elements from that period.

About 2km/1.2mi to the south there is a **fortress** whose origins go back to a Moorish fort. The castle can be reached via a small road (signposted »Castelo«) that turns off the main road near the cemetery at the western edge of town and heads south. It leads under the motorway, and the ruins can be seen from far off.

Boliqueime Boliqueime is a village 10km/6mi north-east of Albufeira that has begun to sprawl. **Cavaco Silva**, who was the Portuguese prime minister for many years and is now president, comes from here. Lídia Jorge (▶Famous People), one of Portugal's most famous authors, also grew up here. Her novel *The Day of the Prodigies* describes everyday life in sleepy Boliqueime during the Salazar era and the hope that grew after the Carnation Revolution.

Guia In Guia, 6km/4mi north-west of Albufeira, Igreja de Nossa Senhora da Guia, which was built in the 18th century, is decorated with pretty tiles inside.

<table>
<tr><td>

! **Baedeker** TIP

Hot stuff: piri-piri

Guia is known for a culinary specialty in Portugal – frango piri-piri or frango da Guia is at the top of every menu in town. Young chickens are prepared with a delicious sauce, and hot piri-piri is added to the dish. If the thought makes you break out in a sweat, order it without piri-piri.

</td></tr>
</table>

On the N 125 near Guia is the popular **Zoomarine Park**, which draws about 400,000 visitors annually. Various animals are kept on the grounds between ponds, gardens and restaurants: on the one hand parrots that perform for the visitors, but mainly – as the name suggests – various kinds of aquatic life. **Sharks** can be seen and **sea lions**, **dolphins** and **seals** have their own show. There is also a large swimming pool so that visitors can swim too. Swimming with the dolphins is a special attraction. Not last there are carousels, a giant wheel and a cinema.

It takes at least four hours just to see the main attractions and animal shows. Hours: from March until November daily 10am – 6pm, July, August until 7.30pm.

Algoz Algoz is a typical Algarve rural town about 10km/6mi north-west of Albufeira and a good 15km/9mi east of Silves. It lies in the middle of beautiful landscape, parts of which still look untouched. Ermida de Nossa Senhora do Pilar on a hill at the southern edge of town is worth a short detour. It offers a beautiful view of Algoz and the surroundings.

About 3km/2mi north of Algoz via the road to São Bartolomeu de Messines lies Krazy World, an amusement park with a unique mini-golf course, a petting zoo, snake pond, crocodiles and many more attractions. There are also a swimming pool and a restaurant on site. Opening times from May until Sept daily 10am – 6pm, irregular opening times in other months (www.krazyworld.com)

Krazy World

⊕

✳ Alcoutim

L 3

Conselho: Alcoutim   **Population:** 4500

Alcoutim is a remote border town in the north-eastern Algarve on the banks of the Guadiana River, which forms the border to Andalusia here. The seclusion is what gives the place its charm; very few tourists come here on weekdays.

About 40km/24mi to the south – near ►Vila Real de Santo António – the Guadiana empties into the Atlantic Ocean. In Alcoutim itself the Ribeira de Cadavais flows into the Guadiana. There are only modest tourist facilities. Alcoutim and the areas to the west and the south are among the most secluded parts of the Algarve. The population density is low and there is much poverty because jobs are few and far between. On the Spanish side of the river lies **Sanlúcar de Guadiana** – a tranquil scene that gives no hint of the animosity that existed between these two towns for centuries.

Alcoutim was already a river port in Phoenician times, and it is presumed that the Celtiberians settled here too. In the 2nd century BC the town became Roman and was called Alcoutinium. In AD 415 the Alans conquered Alcoutim, followed shortly afterwards by the Visigoths; the Arabs took over in the 8th century. In 1240 the Portuguese

History

 VISITING ALCOUTIM

INFORMATION
Rua 1° de Maio
Tel. 281 546 179

WHERE TO EAT
► **Moderate/Inexpensive**
Estalagem do Guadiana
Tel. 281 540 120
The Portuguese flock to this hotel restaurant on weekends. Regional specialties.

WHERE TO STAY
► **Budget**
Estalagem do Guadiana
8970 Alcoutim
Tel. 281 540 120
Fax 281 546 647
Tidy little hotel in a lovely setting right above the river. The rooms are adequately furnished and there is a swimming pool for relaxation.

! **Báedeker TIP**

Restful river ride

The Uadi Ana, a small excursion boat, sails on the Guadiana from Vila Real de Santo António to Alcoutim in about 2.5 hours. It leaves in the morning and there is enough time in Alcoutim to explore the town and have lunch before returning to Vila Real de Santo António – www.guadiana.tour.

under Sancho II conquered Alcoutim. In the early 14th century Alcoutim was given to the knights of the Order of Santiago; in 1371 Portugal and Castile concluded the so-called **Peace of Alcoutim** here. Fernando I and Henrique II of Castile signed the peace treaty after a formal **meeting at the river**, which ended armed conflicts between the two countries temporarily. In the 17th century Alcoutim was again the site of battles between Spain and Portugal after Portuguese noblemen revolted in 1640 and initiated the restoration of Portugal's independence from Spain. In 1668 Spain recognized Portugal's independence conclusively. Alcoutim experienced the last political conflicts at the time of the Liberal Wars in the 1830s, when liberals and absolutist Miguelists fought each other on the Guadiana.

Full up on the weekend

The brilliant white houses below the castle stretch down to the river. A stroll through the narrow streets of the unspoiled little town is worthwhile. There are some pretty spots on the river and in the town itself, and a small promenade along the river. Several churches and the fortifications bear witness to the eventful history of Alcoutim.

It's better not to come on weekends because – at least in the summer months – peace and tranquillity are not to be found. Flocks of visitors storm the place on Saturdays and Sundays, as this pretty town on the Guadiana has become a popular destination for day-trippers. A table in one of the few restaurants is hard to find on Sunday afternoons, and the otherwise deserted castle is mobbed.

What to See in Alcoutim

✱
Castelo

Because of its location Alcoutim had an important strategic function from early on. The present castle goes back to an Arab fortification from the 11th century, but there were probably larger fortified walls earlier. It is known that Dom Dinis I ordered the town to renovate the walls and the castle in 1304.

The fort has not been used for military purposes since 1878. It had various functions afterwards, serving for a while as a slaughterhouse. In 1973 extensive archaeological excavations and restorations according to original plans were begun. Today the visitor will find an **exhibition of archaeological finds** at the castle; old foundations that were exposed during the excavations can be seen. Opening hours: daily 9.30am – 5.30pm, in the summer until 7pm.

Ermida de N. S. da Conceição

The Ermida de Nossa Senhora da Conceição is located west and above the fort. Steps lead in a semi-circle up to the unpretentious chapel, which dates from the 16th century; the Manueline doorways are the only part still remaining. In the early 18th century the building was thoroughly restored and its appearance changed considerably. Inside, the Baroque altar from this time is noteworthy.

The location of the parish church on the banks of the Guadiana is striking. In place of a simple church without aisles, a new building with nave and side aisles was constructed in early Renaissance style between 1538 and 1554, financed by the Order of Santiago. Only the attractive Renaissance doors have remained. Notice the capitals inside as well as the baptistery with a 16th-century low relief.

Igreja Matriz

The little Igreja da Misericórdia on the Praça da República was built in the early 16th century, but restored and remodelled several times afterwards. In the course of the centuries repeated **severe floods** caused problems for the town. A mark on the outer wall of the church showed the highest flood level in December 1876.

Igreja da Misericórdia

Alcoutim on the Guadiana, the river on the border to Spain

Take the ferry to Spain From the harbour it is possible to cross over to Spain. A little ferry runs across to Sanlúcar de Guadiana. There is also a place for yachts that came up the Guadiana to tie up on the riverbanks.

Around Alcoutim

Guerreiros do Rio From Alcoutim a road runs along the banks of the Guadiana southwards through beautiful scenery. In the sleepy village of Guerreiros do Rio, about 12km/7mi south of Alcoutim in an idyllic location on the banks of the Guadiana, fishermen offer boat tours on the river. The former elementary school houses the **Museu do Rio**, with displays on history, flora and fauna, and on the life of the people along ☉ the river. Opening times: Tue – Fri 9am – 1pm and 2pm – 5pm.

★ Aljezur

C 4

Conselho: Aljezur   **Population:** 4000

Far from the international bustle of the tourist centres along the southern coast, Aljezur is suitable for individual travellers who are less interested in luxury and good tourist facilities than in experiencing nature.

The small town is in the western Algarve about 40km/25mi north of Sagres. The N 120, which runs through Aljezur from Lagos, continues northwards through the Alentejo region and then on to Lisbon. The climate is a bit rougher than in the eastern Algarve and the vegetation differs greatly from that of the south-eastern Algarve. The landscape is much more barren, with no lovely gardens, and is characterized by low shrubs and macchia. This region owes its peace and quiet not least to the fact that the whole coastline south and north of Aljezur is under nature protection (▶Costa Vicentina).

History It is assumed that Aljezur was established by the Arabs. In 1246 the town was conquered by the Portuguese Order of Santiago under Dom Paio Peres Correia, but due to its remote location never became an important town.

A river separates the old and new town Aljezur shows its best side to those who enter from the north. Cross the little river, Ribeira de Aljezur, and drive directly towards the **old quarter**, which stretches up to the castle. This quarter has been smartened up a bit and several small museums are worth a visit. The new town opposite, which is called **Igreja Nova**, is a completely normal, relatively unspectacular small Algarve town with typical day-to-day life.

⏵ VISITING ALJEZUR

INFORMATION
Largo do Mercado
Tel. 282 998 229

WHERE TO EAT
▶ Inexpensive
Restaurante Primavera
Rua 25 de Abril
Tel. 282 998 249
A small restaurant which serves good basic regional dishes.

WHERE TO STAY
▶ Budget
Hostel Amazigh
8670-065 Aljezur
Tel. 917 998 182, 282 997 502
www.amazighostel.com
Simple and nice modern hostel; there are double rooms and dorms as well as family rooms. The common kitchen and lounge are also basic but tasteful.

What to See in Aljezur

The municipal museum is located in the 19th-century former town hall. Mainly archaeological finds from the region are on display. Opening times: Mon – Fri 9am – 1pm and 2.30pm – 6.30pm ⏰
Museu Municipal

Religious art of all kinds is shown in the annex to the simple Igreja Misericórdia. Opening times: Tue – Sat 9.30am – 1pm and 2.30pm – 6pm
Museu de Arte Sacra ⏰

The Museu Antoniano in the 17th-century Capela de Santo António with numerous exhibits is dedicated to St Anthony, the patron saint of Lisbon. Opening times: Tue – Sat 9am – 1pm and 2.30pm – 6.30pm
Museu Antoniano ⏰

This small museum shows works by the painter José Cercas, who came from Aljezur, as well as works by other Portuguese artists. Opening times: Tue – Sat 9.30am – 1pm and 2.30pm – 6.30pm
Casa Museu José Cercas ⏰

Steep streets lead up to the castle, which goes back to the Arab period; now it is nothing but a ruin. The outer walls and a cistern remain. There is a good view of the surroundings from the top, including the valley of the Ribeira de Aljezur, which runs into the Atlantic Ocean north of the town.
Castelo

Around Aljezur

There are excellent beaches near Aljezur, but some are difficult to reach and in all rougher than the beaches on the southern Algarve coast as far as wind and water are concerned. Strong currents change
Beaches

View of the town centre of Aljezur from the castle

the conditions from year to year. The most beautiful beaches are described at ►Costa Vicentina.

✳ Almancil

Conselho: Loulé   **Population:** 8800

Almancil is known for two reasons: the Igreja de São Lourenço is one of the most interesting churches in the Algarve for its art. The cultural centre right next to the church has gained a reputation among art and music lovers.

Almancil (or Almansil) is widely dispersed and located about 13km/8mi north-west of Faro. The busy N 125 runs right through the centre of the town and is the main reason for Almancil's lack of urban character. But with its many shops and banks, Almancil is the shopping centre for the nearby luxury resorts of Vale do Lobo and Quinta do Lago.

What to See in Almancil

✳
Igreja de São
Lourenço

The Igreja de São Lourenço is located outside town on the road to Faro: it can be seen from far off. The building probably dates back to the 15th century. A small chapel was built first. The present-day Baroque church is unpretentious on the outside – only the brilliant white dome catches the eye.

The church is famous for its unusual tile decoration in the relatively small interior. Both the walls and the vaulted ceiling, even the dome, are covered with blue and white azulejos. The high altar made of talha dourada with the figure of **St Lawrence** make for a warm contrast. The six tile pictures on the side walls show scenes from the saint's life. On the right-hand wall at the back a scene depicts

 ## VISITING ALMANCIL

INFORMATION
Rua de Vale Formoso
Almancil
Tel. 289 392 659

WHERE TO EAT
► Expensive
Casa Velha
Quinta do Lago
Tel. 289 394 983
First-class atmosphere in an old country house, French cooking.

Henrique Leis
Vale Formoso
Almancil
Tel. 289 393 438
Henrique Leis from Brazil cooks up international gourmet cuisine with a French accent. Excellent fish and seafood dishes.

Florian
Rua Van Zanten
Quinta do Lago
Tel. 289 396 674
Top-class restaurant. Extensive wine list, large selection of Portuguese wines.

► Moderate
São Gabriel
On the road between Vale do Lobo and Quinta do Lago
Tel. 289 807 611
Refined restaurant with a terrace.

Casa do Lago
Quinta do Lago
Tel. 289 394 911
Basic, pleasantly furnished restaurant. Its plus is the location in the lagoon landscape of Ria Formosa. Large selection of fish dishes.

► Budget
Pastelaria Venezuela
Rua do Vale Formoso
For afternoon tea: simple pastelaria with first-class cakes.

WHERE TO STAY
► Luxury
Hotel Quinta do Lago
Tel. 289 350 350
www.hotelquintadolago.com
The best address on the Algarve coast, a luxury resort with 150 rooms, very attractive surroundings and lots of green areas. A quiet holiday is possible here, but there is a variety of sports activities for anyone who wants them.

Hotel Dona Filipa
Tel. 289 357 223
Fax 289 357 201
www.donafilipa.com
Luxury hotel with 136 rooms – a spacious resort with lots of greenery, excellent infrastructure and various sports opportunities.

Even the dome of Igreja de São Lourenço is decorated with azulejos.

St Lawrence talking to Pope Sixtus and lamenting that he cannot die a martyr's death. Then he learns that he will be martyred within the next three days. The following five panels show the saint's martyrdom: the authorities had him burned at the stake because he had distributed church funds, which the emperor wanted to collect from him, to the poor.

The pictures have been dated at 1730. At that time the production of large tile pictures was very popular in Portugal. Political events, cityscapes, allegories and religious scenes such as these were depicted on tiled walls. The azulejos in São Lourenço were painted by the Baroque artist **António Oliveira Bernardes**. It is not known in which factory the tiles themselves were produced. They were possibly imported from Italy or Holland. Opening times: Mon – Fri 10am – 1.30pm and 12.30pm – 5.30pm, Sat 10am – 1.30pm, Sun 2.30pm – 5.30pm

Centro Cultural São Lourenço A short distance below the church the Centro Cultural São Lourenço was established in the 1980s. The restoration of the beautiful rooms was modelled on traditional Algarve architecture. They are now used for rotating **exhibits**. Concerts and series of concerts, ranging from **classical to jazz music**, are also held in the cultural centre. Occasionally avant-garde music is on the programme. There is also a sculpture garden and a patio for outdoor events. Opening times: Tue–Sun 10am–7pm ☉

Around Almancil

Quinta do Lago, the »estate on the lake«, is a very **exclusive holiday resort** 6km/3.5mi south of Almancil. The expansive grounds are occupied by well-spaced villas and bungalows, some of which are privately owned and some of which can be rented. There are broad lawns between the houses with small artificial ponds; decorative umbrella pines grow everywhere and spread a pleasant aroma. For **golfers** – including beginners – Quinta do Lago is a paradise. Various courses can be combined, and if that's not enough there are always the courses in neighbouring Vale do Lobo.

★
Quinta do Lago

Everything is bit finer in Quinta do Lago than in the rest of the Algarve. This can be seen already in »Quinta Shopping« at the entrance to the resort. If it's expensive and luxurious, it's on sale here. Street cafés and stylish restaurants round off the shopping experience. Numerous roundabouts have to be negotiated to reach the parking lot of the Praia do Quinta do Lago. A 300m/1000ft-long bridge spans the lagoon and offers access to the endlessly long sandy beach without getting wet feet – it is not surprising that renting loungers costs the earth here. To the west Praia do Quinta do Lago merges with Praia do Anção, where beach bars are the place to meet. Apropos restaurants: the selection in and around Quinta do Lago is wide and almost always top-class.

> ! **Baedeker TIP**
>
> **Hike around the lagoon**
>
> At the wooden bridge that leads to Praia da Quinta do Lago two beautiful hiking trails begin: the 3.3km/2mi São Lourenço Trail and the 2.3km/1.4mi da Quinta do Lago Trail. A short hike on the trails along the lagoon, which is part of the Ria Formosa Nature Park (see p.219), is an experience. Watch local fishermen or shell collectors; birds can be seen close – with a little luck there might even be a swarm of flamingos!

The »wolf's valley« a few miles west of Quinta do Lago is just as luxurious. Here too pretty villas with small gardens and swimming pools, expansive lawns and many pines characterize the landscape. There are also golf courses and tennis courts, and in all a wide selection of recreational activities. Despite all the opportunities to be active, Vale do Lobo offers plenty of peace and quiet. The small centre of Vale do Lobo is also pretty. The cafés and restaurants – some with a sea view – are good places to relax.

★
Vale do Lobo

★ Alte

F 4

Conselho: Loulé   **Population:** 800

Alte is on the excursion programme of almost every travel agent. As soon as the last bus has left, it reverts to a quiet and idyllic village: whitewashed Algarve houses, unevenly cobbled lanes, flower gardens and flower pots at doorways, and hibiscus, geraniums and oleander in flower everywhere.

Alte is a pretty showpiece of a village in the Algarve hinterland, a good 20km/13mi from the coast – north of Albufeira at the foot of the Serra do Caldeirão. It is best to take the quiet country road that runs from São Bartolomeu de Messines eastwards into the foothills. Alte is located in relatively untouched hilly landscape. The gentle Algarve garden landscape stretches this far; to the north of Alte the landscape becomes a little more barren. In the fertile surroundings olives, figs, oranges, lemons and especially almonds thrive.

What to See in Alte

Igreja Matriz   The Igreja Matriz rises in the village centre; it was built in the early 16th century. The original **unadorned Manueline main door** has been preserved. This pretty village church is usually open; enter on the right side through the sacristy. In the interior with its beautiful wood ceiling a Manueline arch stands out; it separates the choir with the high altar from the nave. In the choir ceiling there are **three capstones**: the front one symbolizes the Portuguese voyages of discovery; the middle, moon-shaped one the discoveries in the orient; and the blue one at the back the sea route to India that the Portuguese opened up. The pulpit with steps decorated with azulejos is also worth a look. The Baroque side chapels contain images of popular saints. In the Capela de Nossa Senhora de Lurdes in the left aisle, a black saint is portrayed. This side chapel is decorated with tiles from Seville.

> ! **Baedeker TIP**
>
> **May 1 in Alte**
> Alte is known for its festival on May 1 when the streets and alleys are decorated with flowers. There are flower processions, and a big dance festival that attracts dancing groups and spectators from miles around. May 1 is traditionally a picnic day in and around Alte, also at the Fonte Grande.

Fonte das Bicas   The Fonte das Bicas is an idyllic little place on the eastern edge of the village. At the *bicas*, the water taps, the villagers fill their plastic jugs with fresh **spring water** – people even come from far off, since the water is thought to have healing properties and is supposed to be

⏵ VISITING ALTE

INFORMATION

Alte
Estrada da Ponte 17
Tel. 289 478 666

Salir
Rua José Viegas Guerreiro
Tel. 289 489 733

SHOPPING

The souvenir shops in Alte and in the Casa Memória sell regional items and have information on acquiring cheese, honey or medronho directly from the producers around Alte.

WHERE TO EAT

► Inexpensive
O Folclore
Av. 25 de Abril
Typical regional home cooking is served here, mostly consisting of simply prepared meat dishes.

WHERE TO STAY

► Mid-range
Hotel Alte
Estrada de Santa Margarida, Montinho
Tel. 289 478 523
www.altehotel.com
The only hotel in town, a well-kept place with 25 rooms, swimming pool and tennis courts; located a short distance out in the countryside – experience the peace and quiet of the hilly hinterland here.

► Budget
Casa d'Alvada
Quinta do Freixo – Benafim
Tel. 289 472 185
wwww.quintadofreixo.org
On a farm between Alte and Salir north of the Rocha da Pena. 10 quiet, basic rooms are rented as an »agro-turismo« initiative.

---

responsible for the high life expectancy of the people from Alte. An azulejo picture shows St Anthony; there are also verses from a poem by the poet Cândido Guerreiro (1871 – 1953) who came from Alte. A restaurant and a kiosk make it possible to linger a while.

Follow the stream for 300m/1000ft to the Fonte Grande, the »big spring«. Tables and benches are set up for **picnicking**; there is also a restaurant and a kiosk.   **Fonte Grande**

Around Alte

The village of Salir is just as pretty as Alte but much quieter; it is located 15km/9mi to the east and extends over two hills. On the western hill there are scanty remains of a Moorish castle. These walls are important because this is one of the few places at all in the Algarve where **authentic Arab remains** can still be seen. The small Castelo neighbourhood with tiny white houses and many flowers is especially picturesque. The larger part of the village is located on the other hill; it is dominated by a water tower and a plain village church. The   ★ **Salir** church square offers a beautiful view of the mountainous surroundings. Small-scale farming on red earth characterizes the countryside.

✳ **Rocha da Pena**

Between Alte and Salir a signposted lane leads north from the N 124 to Rocha da Pena, a small mountain chain that rises to 479m/1572ft. Rocha da Pena was declared a **nature reserve** because of its unusual flora and fauna. There are good lookout points and a cave where Arabs are supposed to have hidden in the 13th century from attacks by Christian forces. At a roundabout with an old carob tree in the middle a 4.7km/2.9mi-long hiking path begins; it is not in very good shape and is signposted poorly, sometimes not at all.

✳ Alvor

D 5

Conselho: Portimão   **Population:** 7000

Alvor's tourist attraction is the Praia de Alvor, a miles-long, broad sandy beach that extends on both sides of town. To the east it joins Praia dos Três Irmãos, which is bordered by steep cliffs.

Alvor is a fishing village with a tourist atmosphere between Lagos and Portimão on the wide Baía de Lagos, Lagos Bay, about 1km/0.5mi inland. West of Alvor the estuaries of four rivers from a lagoon. Many of the villagers work as fishermen in the lagoon.

History

It is assumed that Alvor goes back to a settlement in the 5th century BC. In the Arab period – it was called Albur then – it was the site of a castle, which was conquered by the Portuguese in 1250 under the reign of Afonso III. Alvor entered Portuguese history because **King João II** died here in 1495. He was buried in the cathedral of Silves and his remains were later taken to Batalha. Alvor was almost completely destroyed in the earthquake of 1755 and the accompanying floods.

✳ **Tourism and yet almost a village**

Alvor is a pleasant place between the two holiday centres Portimão and Lagos; while it has been influenced by tourism it has still managed to keep its pretty appearance as a village. The centre of the village is a maze of narrow alleys with low white fishermen's houses. A few restaurants, cafés and souvenir shops line the streets. Down at the edge of the lagoon a broad promenade was added, and the old fish auction hall from past times still stands. East of Alvor near Torralta and on the Praia dos Três Irmãos there are larger hotel blocks.

✳ **Igreja Matriz**

The village has a charming sight in the Igreja Matriz. With its origins in the 16th century it is a typical Algarve village church in which some elements of the old architecture have been preserved. Its Man-

The Manueline interior of the pretty village church in Alvor has been preserved.

ueline main doors are remarkable. Inside there are also **Manueline features**: the arch over the altar area is decorated with a spiral stone band; the decorative capitals of the six columns consist of stone fishermen's ropes and plant ornamentation. The altar painting is framed with modest talha dourada.

Around Alvor

Mexilhoeira Grande – about 4km/2.5mi north-west of Alvor – has also been able to keep its village character. At the top of the village the Igreja Matriz, with its Renaissance doors and Manueline side doors, is worth seeing. The door of the bell tower also has Manueline decorations. Trees have been planted on the pretty church plaza. There is an excellent view here towards Alvor and the sea. **Mexilhoeira Grande**

In order to reach the **necropolis of Alcalar** leave the N 125 near the Alvor exit and follow a narrow road north to Alcalar and Casais. After 5km/3mi on this road a sign points to the right to the excavation site. Archaeologists exposed several megalith gravesites, which were probably made between 2000 and 1600 BC. Some of the grave offerings found here are on display in the Archaeological Museum of Silves and in the Museu Municipal of Lagos. The reception and exhi- **★ Alcalar**

▶ VISITING ALVOR

INFORMATION
Rua Dr Afonso Costa 51
Tel. 282 457 540

WHERE TO EAT
▶ Moderate
O Luís
Praia dos Três Irmãos
Tel. 282 459 688
Come here to enjoy a wonderful view
of the water and good cooking:
excellent fish, tasty seafood and meat
dishes.

WHERE TO STAY
▶ Luxury
Hotel Pestana Alvor Praia
Praia dos Três Irmãos
Tel. 282 400 900, fax 282 400 975
www.pestana.com
Large hotel on the beautiful beach
between Alvor and Portimão: a six-
storey luxury hotel that does not look
very luxurious from outside. There is a
variety of activities and entertainment,
and the almost 220 rooms are beautifully furnished.

▶ Mid-range
*Apartamentos Turísticos Prainha
Clube*
Praia dos Três Irmãos
Tel. 282 480 000, fax 282 458 950
www.prainha.net
What is special about this apartment
and villa complex with 60 living units
is its ultimate location right above the
cliffs. Walk to beautiful swimming
coves or along an equally beautiful and
endless sandy beach. There are several
restaurants in this high-class resort,
which provides good accommodation
for families.

Holiday accommodation for families: Apartamentos Turísticos Prainha

bition building also has more information on the history of Alcalar. Opening times: Tue – Sat 10.30am – 1pm and 2pm – 6.30pm, in the cooler half of the year 9.30am – 1pm and 2pm – 5pm

Remains from Roman times can be found near Abicada (Vila roma-na). Near Figueira a signposted road turns off from the N 125 (»Ruinas romanas«) towards the south. Follow it 1.5km/1mi towards the coast. The way runs parallel to the railway tracks first, then it passes an abandoned farm and ends by a group of houses. Directly below is the excavation site of Abicada. The area is fenced in but can be viewed from all sides. The villa was probably occupied between the first and fourth centuries AD and at that time was probably right on the seaside; various mosaic floors are well preserved.

Abicada

Armação de Pêra

E 5

Conselho: Silves   **Population:** 6000

Apartment blocks, hotel complexes, half-finished high-rise skele-tons and tall construction cranes combine to give Armação de Pêra a dejected appearance. The miles-long, wide beach east of town might make up for these disadvantages.

Armação de Pêra is located between Portimão and Albufeira about 45km/28mi west of Faro. Astonishingly, only a few miles to the north lies an attractive but not exactly uninhabited landscape. Therefore travellers coming to Armação de Pêra from the N 125, that is from the north, suspect nothing at first – until the view of the bizarre sky-line appears from behind a hill. Coming closer the colourful little fishing boats at the edge of town appear unusually picturesque. The seaside promenade is also passable, and even a little of the former village can still be seen: the remains of the 17th-century fortress with the little Capela de Santo António. Armação de Pêra shows its most pleasant side east of the coastal road.

Around Armação de Pêra

Hotels and resorts are lined up to the west. Some of these are even very attractively designed holiday villages situated on cliffs above the sand beaches. There are deep coves that the Atlantic carved out of the cliffs over thousands of years between large rock promontories. Popular sandy bays are Praia dos Irmãos, Praia dos Beijinhos, Praia de Salomão, Praia da Cova Redonda, Praia Maré Grande.

Holiday accommodation and beaches

On a high promontory about 1km/0.5mi west of Armação de Pêra is a true gem – especially since there are few feasts for the eyes in this

★

Nola Ermida de Nossa Senhora da Rocha

▶ VISITING ARMAÇÃO DE PÊRA

INFORMATION
Avenida Marginal
Tel. 282 312 145

WHERE TO EAT

▶ **Moderate**

Clipper
Avenida Marginal
Tel. 282 314 108
The Clipper is aimed exclusively at

tourists; the food is not elaborate but
good.

O Serol
Rua Portas do Mar 2
Tel. 282 312 146
Considered one of the best fish
restaurants in the Algarve; free tables
are rare.

Beautiful luxury: restaurant in the Vila Vita Parc holiday resort

WHERE TO STAY

▶ Luxury

Holiday Park Vila Vita Parc
Alporchinhos
Tel. 282 310 100
Fax 282 320 333
www.vilavitahotels.com
Just about 200 rooms outside Armação de Pêra in a luxurious holiday resort. The range of amenities in the resort is large, first class, expensive and best suited for people looking for relaxation – the Vila Vita grounds are somewhat secluded and ideal for having a proper holiday.

▶ Mid-range

Holiday Inn Algarve
Avenida Beira Mar
Tel. 282 320 260
Fax 282 315 087
www.hialgarve.com
Popular hotel with a pool and direct access to the beach. It is located on the busy road coming into town. It has 150 rooms in all – the ones with a sea view are very quiet and recommended in all cases. There are good water sports facilities right in front of the hotel.

▶ Mid-range/Budget

Casa Bela Moura
Estrada de Porches
Alporchinhos - Apartado 323
Tel. 282 313 422
Mobile 918 031 800
www.casabelamoura.com
A small »turismo rural« house with 8 rooms in all.

Casa do Catavento
Alcantarilha
Escorrega do Malhão
Tel. 282 449 084
Fax 282 449 638
www.casadocatavento.com
This »turismo rural« accommodation is located inland 8km/5mi north of Armação de Pêra and 8km/5mi east of Silves. It is only open from 1 February until 31 October; 4 rooms.

area. Ermida de Nossa Senhora da Rocha was built above the sea on a 35m/120ft-high cliff. The chapel contrasts in brilliant white with the blue water. In front of it a miradouro, a lookout point, runs out into the Atlantic in a point. The adjacent promontories can be seen clearly from there.

The chapel has early Gothic features. Two columns mark a small porch. One **column capital** is still quite well preserved; the other has weathered in the course of centuries. There are always a few candles lit in the foyer – many Portuguese come here to honour the Senhora da Rocha. The unusual **six-sided pointed roof** over the altar can be seen from far off. Next to the church there is a cistern.

Pêra

About 2km/1.2mi from Armação de Pêra inland there is a quiet pretty village that gives no hint of the lively activity along the nearby coast. Pêra does not get many visitors. The surrounding landscape with its many gardens, small farms and citrus orchards is also pretty. In front of one of the two churches there is a square with a view of the sea.

Ermida de Nossa Senhora da Rocha – an absolute gem high above the sea

Alcantarilha   Alcantarilha, 3km/2mi north of Armação de Pêra, goes back to an Arab settlement. Alcantarilha means »small bridge« in Arabic. The heavily used N 125 cuts the village in two, but there are still some pretty places. The parish church with Manueline elements inside is pretty. Adjacent to the church there is a capela dos ossos (bone chapel).

! *Baedeker* TIP

Olaria Pequena pottery

Colourfully painted plates and bowls, vessels made of brown and black clay, copies of traditional Algarve chimneys … The shops in Porches have a huge selection. Olaria pottery at the eastern edge of Porches is recommended especially – on the right-hand side coming from Porches on N 125. Watch pottery being decorated here.

Along with Tavira, Moncarapacho and Loulé, **Porches** is a centre for the production of pottery. The village is located 4km/2.5mi north-west of Armação de Pêra on the N 125. The street is lined with numerous shopping centres which sell every possible kind of typically Portuguese **pottery**.

Aqualand   Between Porches and Alcantarilha is the fun park **Aqualand** with a big water chute. Opening times: early June until mid-September daily 10am – 6pm.

View of Carvoeiro: the beach isn't always this quiet.

Carvoeiro

Conselho: Lagoa   **Population:** 6000

For a long time Carvoeiro was still a pretty fishing village, but then this peaceful spot developed into a complete tourist centre. At first many Portuguese had their summer homes in Carvoeiro; in the early 1980s an international building boom began.

Yet the town has been able to maintain some of its flair. The centre above the small cove still consists of charming little streets and alleys that lead up the slope. The houses are carefully whitewashed; new villas and small apartment buildings were added between the old fishermen's houses. Care was given to make the new buildings around the former village attractive and many of the holiday villages are built in **Moorish style**. Carvoeiro got its good reputation from this thought-out planning, but construction has spread, so that the whole coastline around Carvoeiro is built up. There is more than adequate infrastructure, with countless cafés and restaurants. In the high season there is background music around the clock – not to mention the usual nightlife. On the beach fishermen offer boat rides

▶ VISITING CARVOEIRO

INFORMATION
Praia do Carvoeiro
Tel. 282 357 728

WHERE TO EAT
▶ **Moderate**
Tia Ilda
Rua do Paraíso 18
Tel. 282 357 830
Popular restaurant above the edge of
town serving good Portuguese and
international food

WHERE TO STAY
▶ **Mid-range**
Apartamentos Rocha Brava
Alfanzina
Tel. 282 350 370

Fax 282 350 371
www.rochabrava.com
Very expansive and attractive holiday
village with 375 rooms above the cliffs.
The furnishings of the apartments and
the facilities are very good. Because of
the location it is best to have a car.

Hotel Tivoli Carvoeiro
Tel. 282 351 100
Fax 282 351 345
www.tivolihotels.com
Almost all of the 300 rooms in this
comfortable hotel have a view of the
sea. The amenities include several
restaurants and bars as well as a
swimming pool, sauna, two tennis
courts and other sports facilities.

along the coast. There are fantastic views of the cliffs from the sea.
The Atlantic Ocean has been working on the bizarre formations of
soft limestone for thousands of years.

Around Carvoeiro

★ ★
Algar Seco
Grand rock formations can be admired near Algar Seco, especially
2km/1.2mi east of Carvoeiro. A unique landscape has been created
here by wind and weather over the years. It is best explored on foot.
Walk through a **natural maze of plateaus, rock columns, narrow
openings and natural arches**, even past a small pond that is connected to the sea and rises and falls with the tides. The sea churns
below in caves and grottoes. Depending on the lighting the limestone
takes on different colours, and is especially beautiful at sunset. There
is a **small café** – protected by the rocks but with a view of the sea –
in the middle of the limestone world. Relax here with a drink and
soak up the atmosphere of the bizarre surroundings.

**Praia da
Marinha**
East of Algar Seco there are several fabulous sandy coves; among the
most beautiful is undoubtedly Praia da Marinha with steps leading
down from the cliffs. A path leads eastwards from here along the picturesque rocky coast to Ermida de Nossa Senhora da Rocha (►Ar-

*In the midst of bizarre rock formations: Praia da Marinha →
is one of the most beautiful bays for swimming near Carvoeiro.*

mação de Pêra). Good shoes are required as well as care, since the path is not secured and leads right along the cliff. The views of the coast are sensational. The walk to the chapel of Nossa Senhora da Rocha takes about 2 hours.

✳ Castro Marim

L 4

Conselho: Castro Marim   **Population:** 7000

The town, located 5km/3mi from the coast, has an interesting history. The marshy plains of the Guadiana surround Castro Marim. This swamp region with its varied plant and animal world has been protected as Reserva Natural do Sapal de Castro Marim.

History

The name Castro Marim – »**castle by the sea**« – indicates that the settlement in the extreme south-east of the Algarve was once right on the coast. Archaeological evidence indicates pre-Roman settlement of Castro Marim. The Phoenicians probably built a trading port here. The name of the town also suggests that the Celtiberians were present; fortified settlements of the Celtiberians were called *castros*. Both in Roman times – at that time the town was called

Castro Marim: for centuries it was an important fortification and secured the Portuguese-Spanish border.

Castrum Marinum – and under Arab rule Castro Marim was important because of its site on a major communication route. In 1319
Dom Dinis I declared the city to be the **headquarters of the Knights
of Christ**, the order that later played a major role in the Portuguese
voyages of discovery and conquest.
Although the order moved its seat
to Tomar in 1356, Castro Marim
remained a strategically vital **fortified town** for centuries to secure
the border to Spain. In the 14th
and 17th centuries the fortifications were expanded considerably.
In the time of the Inquisition Castro Marim was a feared prison
camp. Because of the destruction
caused by the earthquake in 1755
and the rebuilding of nearby Vila
Real de Santo António in 1774,
Castro Marim lost its significance
within a short time.

CASTRO MARIM

INFORMATION

Turismo
Rua José Alves Moreira 2
Tel. 281 531 232

*Reserva Natural do Sapal
de Castro Marim*
Tel. 281 510 680
Fax 281 531 257

The centre of Castro Marim is located between several hills that are
surmounted by fortifications. The centre around the elongated Praça
1° de Maio, with its trees and benches, and the Igreja de Nossa
Senhora dos Mártires is very attractive.

What to See in Castro Marim

From the Praça 1° de Maio steps lead up to the Igreja de Nossa Senhora dos Mártires. The church was built in the 18th century by the
Knights of Christ. The balustrade on the side, which consists of typical crosses of the Knights of Christ, testifies to this. Note also the
harmonious form of the dome.

**Igreja de Nossa
Senhora dos
Mártires**

Above the little town centre is the extensive fort, which can be
reached on foot from the Praça 1° de Maio. Between 1319 and 1356
the **Knights of Christ** (▶Baedeker Special, p. ???) occupied it. The fort
was restored and enhanced in the 16th and 17th century in order to
withstand artillery. Inside the massive walls are the **Igreja da Misericórdia** with an impressive Renaissance doorway and a square residence with four round corner towers. Inside it is a small museum on
the history of the fort. The excellent view from the fortress walls over
the town and the newer fort opposite as well as across the Guadiana
to Spain are the most impressive part of the visit. Opening times:
daily 10am – 5pm

**✱
Castelo**

🕐

Castelo Novo or Castelo de São Sebastião rises above the town centre
on the south. The fortress was built in the 17th century in the course
of the wars of restoration between Spain and Portugal.

Castelo Novo

A SHORT BUT DELIBERATE VISIT

At first sight Castro Marim appears to be the birthplace of the Knights of Christ. The order, which played a key role in the 15th and 16th century Portuguese expansion history, was founded in 1319 and had its headquarters on a hill near the city. The members of the order stayed on the right banks of the Guadiana until 1356, then they moved away to a former castle of the Knights Templar in Tomar.

But the short visit hides a clever and strategic move. For the Knights of Christ were nothing more than former **Knights Templar**, who were banned in 1312. The Order of the Knights Templar was founded in 1119 to protect pilgrims in the Holy Land and played a major role in the crusades of the Middle Ages. It was awarded various privileges by the pope. The Templars' prestige and power grew quickly and they soon owned huge estates. In Portugal they settled on the Rio Nabão and built the famnous castle of **Tomar** there. The Templars also had lots of influence

and huge estates in France – much to the grief of Philip the Fair. In the early 14th century Philip searched carefully for a way to acquire these lands. He went so far as to accuse the order of apostasy and to claim that they had connections to Islam. The pope, who was dependant of France, declared that the accusations were justified. So the Knights Templar were banned in all Christian countries.

New only in appearance

But in Portugal the order was only dissolved in appearance. Some time after the dissolution of the Templars

the »Ordem de Cristo«, the Order of the Knights of Christ, was founded. But the members of the order were the same ones; they only changed their name and the cross on their white robes. While it was a red cross with eight points before, now a small white cross was set inside the red one.

The **properties** of the Templers devolved to the Knights of Christ – and in principle everything stayed the same. The headquarters were moved to the Algarve for awhile. When everything had quieted down there was nothing to keep them from moving (back) to Tomar.

Out into the world

Defending the Christian faith, fighting Islam and **enlarging the Portuguese sphere of power** were the aims of the order. They changed the world when they put these to practice. In the following centuries the Knights of Christ had significant influence on the **Portuguese history of discovery and conquest** and thus on the whole history of the world. Major seafarers of the 15th and 16th century were members of the order: Bartolomeu Dias, Vasco da Gama, Pedro Álvares Cabral. Henry the Navigator became grand master of the order in 1418. Several kings were also members of the Knights of Christ, especially **Manuel I**.

The Knights of Christ invested money in seafaring and the **cross of the Knights of Christ** became more or less the sign of the times, marking the **sails of the caravels** and the sailors' clothing – in this way it was spread into the whole world from Portugal. Reorganizing into a monastic order in 1523 began its decline; in 1789 the Knight of Christ were secularized and in 1910 when the republic was declared it was dissolved altogether.

Igreja Santo António The Igreja de Santo António stands on the third hill to the east outside the town centre. The depictions of the saint inside are worth seeing.

Around Castro Marim

Reserva Natural do Sapal de Castro Marim Around Castro Marim there is a marshy region, which was made a **nature reserve** in 1975: the Reserva Natural do Sapal de Castro Marim. The 2089ha/5162 acres of swamps and marshes are a breeding ground for oystercatchers, herons, storks and ospreys. 153 different species of birds live here. The fauna includes 440 varieties including numerous grasses and swamp plants. Tourism has hardly reached this area, but **bird watching** is possible thanks to various (not signposted) unpaved trails into the salty swamps. There are also numerous salt works.

> ! **Baedeker TIP**
>
> **Bird watching**
> A good place for it is about 2km/1.2mi west of Castro Marim. Leave town on Rua de São Sebastião towards Faro and Tavira. On the roundabout follow the exit to the N 125. Cross the small bridge after a short distance and after a few metres turn onto a track on the left. Park the car here and follow the track into the nature reserve.

✶ ✶ Costa Vicentina

Wide, almost deserted sandy beaches that stretch over several miles, interspersed with bizarre rock formations against which the Atlantic throws itself with full force, broad plateaus with sparse vegetation, an occasional farm and rarely a village – the Costa Vicentina is a wild natural paradise, a fabulously beautiful coastal landscape.

This section of coastline, which stretches from the Cabo de São Vicente in the extreme south-west via Odeceixe in the north-west Algarve into the Alentejo, is part of the **Parque Natural do Sud-oeste Alentejano e da Costa Vicentina**, an area of 75,000ha/185,000 acres that has been a nature reserve since 1988. It is an important habitat for flora and fauna that exist in only few places on earth. 200 various types of birds have been counted. This is also an excellent breeding ground for many rare migratory birds. Moreover about 60% of Portugal's reptiles and 65% of its amphibians live in the Costa Vicentina region. The sea flora includes more than half of all registered algae in Portugal, and about 110 various kinds of fish inhabit its waters.

Hardly any tourists There is hardly any tourism in the Costa Vicentina so far, and no mass tourism at all. This is not only because the coast is a protected natural zone, but especially because of the raw climate. A strong

The Atlantic crashes full force onto the Costa Vicentina.

wind usually blows across the barren high plateaus, and on some days takes the fun out of a day at the beach. The water temperature is generally three to four degrees lower than further east in the Algarve. Anyone not bothered by strong winds and cool water will enjoy the Costa Vicentina's **splendid natural landscape** without having to share it with masses of people. Accommodation is limited. Sagres and its surroundings are the best places to stay. The fishing village Carrapateira is the place for free spirits looking for peace and quiet. Further to the north Odeceixe used to be an insider's tip among green tourists – but anyone who wants to go there in the summer now has to start looking for accommodation early.

Sights and Beaches on the Costa Vicentina

The southwestern outpost of the Costa Vicentina is Cabo de São Vicente (►Sagres).

Cabo de São Vicente

West of ►Vila do Bispo lies the highest point of the south-western Algarve coast, the Torre de Aspa at 156m/512ft. An obelisk on the barren high plateau marks the point. Further to the west the cliff drops to the Atlantic from a height of a good 150m/500ft There is a grand view at the coast there, and waves break at full force on the rocks below.

Torre de Aspa

▶ VISITING COSTA VICENTINA

INFORMATION

Turismo Sagres
Rua Comandante Matoso
Tel. 282 624 873

Turismo Aljezur
Largo do Mercado
Tel. 282 998 229

HIKING

A trail leads from Sagres for miles along the coast.
It is possible to hike through the entire stretch of the Costa Vicentina that belongs to the Algarve.

WHERE TO STAY

▶ **Mid-range**
Memmo Baleeira Hotel
▶Sagres

▶ **Budget**
Pensão das Dunas
Carrapateira
Rua da Padaria 9
Tel. 282 973 118
www.pensao-das-dunas.pt
Nice bed & breakfast at the edge of town; make reservations in the summer.

Praia do Castelejo
The beaches north of Torre de Aspa are beautiful, and some are very secluded. Access to Praia do Castelejo (turn off from the road leading to Torre de Aspa) is relatively easy. On weekdays the bay, which is interspersed with sharp slate rocks, is often deserted. On weekends locals come on days when the weather is good. A beach bar serves drinks and food. Praia do Castelejo changes again and again due to currents.

Praia da Cordama, Praia da Barriga
From the small road leading to Praia do Castelejo, tracks turn off to Praia da Cordama and to Praia da Barriga further north – the latter can also be reached from a road that turns off N 268. Both bays are also very beautiful and have flat sandy beaches framed by high cliffs. But none of these natural beaches have protection from the wind, which mostly comes from the west.

! **Baedeker TIP**

Surfing
There are surfing schools here in the summer as well as a self-service bar – all with a wonderful view of the coast!

About 9km/5.5mi north of Vila do Bispo a small road turns off the N

268 to Praia do Amado – the way to the beach is signposted. Parking is available right above the beach, with an easy walk down to a wide cove with fine sand framed by a fabulous setting of small rocky points.

Praia do Amado ★

Praia da Bordeira is another wonderful beach a few miles further north beyond Cabo Pontal. There is a small lagoon between the beach and the mainland, which makes it a good place for children.

Praia da Bordeira

Anyone looking for a holiday site beyond the tourist masses is in the right place in **Carrapateira**. There is little accommodation in this village 13km/8mi north of Vila do Bispo, which means that the beaches around Carrapateira are not especially full.

Baedeker TIP

A grand view

Just west of Carrapateira there is a path that offers an excellent view of the fabulous coastal scenery. It runs past Praia do Amado, Cabo Pontal and Praia da Bordeira.

From ►Aljezur a road leads south to Praia da Arrifana. The promontory (114m/374ft) of the same name rises above the cove, which has ideal conditions for surfing. There are also a few fish restaurants.

Praia da Arrifana

The semicircular Praia de Monte Clérigo with its light-coloured sand and rugged rocks also makes a beautiful scene. There are rooms for rent in the small fishing hamlet above the cove, and several beach restaurants.

Praia de Monte Clérigo ★

The drive from Aljezur to Odeceixe in the extreme north-west of the Algarve is about 14km/8mi on the N 120. About 1000 people live in the village with narrow alleys and authentic architecture. In the winter hardly any visitors come; in the summer mainly individual tourists stay here.

Odeceixe

From Odeceixe small roads lead on both sides of the Ribeira de Seixe to Praia de Odeceixe, a beautiful wide sandy bay 3km/2mi away. The beach restaurants are only open in the high season.

Praia de Odeceixe ★

★ Estói

Conselho: Faro   **Population:** 800

Estói is typical of the eastern Algarve hinterland. Some pretty houses are grouped around the church. The village is known because of the palace and Roman excavations.

Igreja Matriz The parish church, which was originally built in the 17th century, almost seems too big. It is dedicated to São Martinho and was heavily damaged in the 1755 earthquake. The bishop of the Algarve at that time, Francisco Gomes do Avelar, had it rebuilt in the early 19th century to plans by Francisco Xavier Fabri. He brought the Italian architect to southern Portugal after the earthquake as an expert consultant for the rebuilding of Algarve cultural treasures. The church's interior renovation was carried out mainly in the 1840s by local craftsmen. The most valuable possession of the church is the 55cm/22in gilded silver monstrance. The figure of St Vincent with a crow on the right side altar was found in the ruins of the destroyed church; it dates from the 17th century.

ESTÓI

WHERE TO SLEEP · EAT

▶ **Mid-range/Luxury**

Estalagem Monte do Casal
Cerro do Lobo
Tel. 289 990 140, 289 991 503
www.montedocasal.pt
Refined country house between Estói and Moncarapacho with beautiful rooms and suites. The restaurant has a good reputation.

Palácio de Estói / Pousada The palace of Estói was built in the late 18th century in the Rococo style for the Visconde de Carvalhal. Later it was owned by another nobleman, and in 1989 devolved to the city of Faro. After the palace had stood empty for many years, a pousada was opened in it and in a modern annex in 2009.

The **palace gardens** continue to be open to the public. The park was constructed in the 18th and 19th century on several levels. On the middle level there is a terrace with a pavilion and water pool with an Italian group of figures in the middle. The place is decorated with several tile pictures of allegorical and mythological scenes. Among them are Leda and the swan. Busts of Portuguese politicians and literary figures, including the Marquês de Pombal, Luís de Camões and Almeida Garrett, crown the walls. Steps lead to an avenue with old trees and to the former entrance. Here too a wall has been decorated with pretty **blue and white azulejo pictures**. The Casa da Cascata, in which lush green plants thrive, is decorated with mosaic stones from nearby Milreu. A statue of the **Three Graces** also catches the eye. It was inspired by a sculptural group by the Italian Antonio Canova. The palace of Estói lies in beautiful landscape with extensive orange orchards. North-west of the palace walls there is still an old *nora*, a typical Algarve well, which no longer functions.

Milreu On the western edge of Estói along the road to Santa Bárbara de Nexe are the ruins of Milreu. Archaeological excavations have been carried out here for more then 120 years. They were begun by the historian and archaeologist Estácio da Veiga in 1877.

In Roman times Milreu was the »summer residence« of wealthy families from Faro, the former Ossonoba. The Roman name Ossonoba

Steps decorated with azulejo tiles in the park of Palácio de Estói

was also used for Milreu. In excavations the foundations of a **Roman villa** and remains of thermal baths were found. They were built in the 2nd and 3rd centuries AD on the remains of an older villa. In the 4th century AD the villa was decorated with mosaics depicting fish and other maritime designs. A **cult building**, which also dates from the 4th century AD, stood south of the villa. In the course of the 6th century AD it was converted to a Christian church. The complex was continuously occupied into the early 10th century. When the dome of the church caved in, the residents moved away. The next permanent occupants probably only arrived in the early 16th century. A farmhouse in the north-eastern part of the complex testifies to this.

After passing a reception building with a small exhibition on the history of Milreu, visitors reach the excavation site. The Via Romana divides it into a northern and southern half. North of the paved Roman street is the excavation site of the patrician house, which was

Milreu Plan

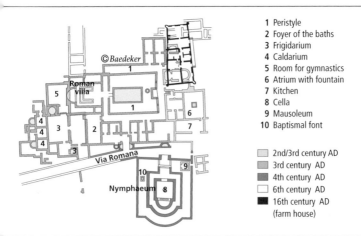

©Baedeker

1 Peristyle
2 Foyer of the baths
3 Frigidarium
4 Caldarium
5 Room for gymnastics
6 Atrium with fountain
7 Kitchen
8 Cella
9 Mausoleum
10 Baptismal font

☐ 2nd/3rd century AD
☐ 3rd century AD
☐ 4th century AD
☐ 6th century AD
■ 16th century AD
(farm house)

probably built by a wealthy Roman citizen. It has the typical floor plan of a Roman villa with a columned courtyard (peristyle), around which living, eating and reception rooms are grouped. Some floor mosaics can still be seen. The most important excavated finds from the villa, a bust of Hadrian and a bust of the empress Agrippina Minor, are exhibited in Faro.

West of the villa are the Roman baths with a changing room (apodyterium), warm bath (caldarium) and cold bath (frigidarium). The remains of a floor heating system and the attached furnace can also be examined. A basin decorated with fish mosaics is well preserved.

South of the Via Romana there is a semicircular walled ruin: a 4th-century nymphaeum. This Roman cult site is unique on the Iberian peninsula in that it is a temple surrounded by a colonnade. Inside the temple is the elevated podium with the cella, which has a water basin in the middle – an indication that this is a **water sanctuary**. The mosaic images of fish and sea creatures also indicate a water cult. An early Christian baptismal font and a burial site testify that the Roman sanctuary was converted to a church in the 6th century AD. Opening times: Tue – Sun 9.30am – 12.30pm and 2pm – 5pm

Around Estói

Santa Bárbara de Nexe

The hamlet Santa Bárbara de Nexe is located about 6km/4mi west of Estói, nestled in countryside full of orchards. From here there is a view of the nearby mountains.

The parish church is one of the few smaller Algarve churches that are opened daily. It has a charming location above the village street, and a beautifully cobbled church square. The church was built in the 15th century. The altar is separated from the nave by a Manueline pointed arch decorated with carved stone ropes and coral, while the Manueline ceiling of the choir is spanned by carved ropes and a Gothic net vault. Several side chapels – the middle one in the left aisle has a pretty statue of Santo Amaro – are decorated with talha dourada.

★ Faro

H 5

Conselho: Faro   **Population:** 35,000

The international airport is only a few miles west of Faro – for most tourists the gateway to the Algarve. But few of them ever venture into the city itself. The pretty historic centre has elegant lanes, interesting museums, street cafés, restaurants and excellent shopping.

As the district and regional capital, Faro is the administrative and economic centre of the Algarve. It is a port and something of an industrial city, and has a university. Faro is not a downright holiday resort like Lagos or Albufeira, because an extensive system of lagoons separates it from the coast, and the beaches are thus a bit farther away. But as a **shopping city** and for a **cultural tour** Faro is definitely worth a visit. It is assumed that the present name »Faro« comes from the time of the Arabs: in the 11th century Ben Said Ben Hárum established a principality here and in the course of time the name »Faro« probably developed from his name. On the other hand there is an obvious connection to the Portuguese word *farol*, meaning lighthouse.

Capital of the Algarve

 DON'T MISS

- Centro Histórico: idyllic old city quarter
- Climb the cathedral tower: view of the lagoon landscape
- Get the shivers: bone chapel next to the Igreja do Carmo
- Sea and fishing: Museu Maritimo
- Shopping in the little town centre

Faro was presumably founded by the Phoenicians. Under Roman rule – the city was called **Ossonoba** then – it developed into an important administrative city, and the harbour also played a major role. In AD 418 the Visigoths conquered the city and Faro became an episcopal see. The Visigoths began building a Christian church, which they dedicated to the Virgin Mary. Because of the veneration of Mary, which played a major role at that time, the city was called Santa Maria de Ossonoba under the Visigoths.

History

Between 714 and 1249 Faro was Arab, but the capital of the province of Al-Gharb (Algarve) was Xelb, today's Silves. The Portuguese king

Afonso III conquered Faro in 1249. That year the end of Arab rule in southern Portugal was sealed, and in 1250 the Algarve cities were annexed to the kingdom of Portugal. In 1577 the episcopal see was moved from Silves to Faro. Afterwards the city was completely destroyed twice: in 1596 in an attack by the Earl of Essex and in 1755 by the great earthquake which also destroyed Lisbon completely. Faro has been the capital of the province of Algarve since 1756. In the early 19th century the city had to submit to occupying forces once more for a short time – in 1808 Napoleonic troops attacked. Faro has had a university since 1982, which also gives the city a student atmosphere.

Pretty and busy city centre

What gives the Algarve metropolis its charm is that Portuguese everyday life takes place here. Tourists are attracted to the city by its extensive pedestrian and shopping zone. Most of the houses date from the 18th and 19th centuries. There are small or large squares everywhere with pretty trees, parks and street cafés. The **historic city centre** – surrounded by a city wall – is gathered around the cathedral a little apart from the pedestrian streets; it has a special atmosphere.

What to See in Faro

★★
Centro Histórico / Vila Adentro

★
◄ Arco da Vila

The historic centre of Faro, which is in part surrounded by a 13th-century city wall, is extremely pretty. One of the entrances is right by the tourist information office on the way to Jardim Manuel Bivar: the Arco da Vila, built in the 18th century by the Italian architect Francisco Xavier Fabri as a city gate with a bell tower on top and a figure of Thomas Aquinas. In the passage a horseshoe arch from Moorish times can be seen. In the narrow streets of the Centro Histórico there are a few galleries and antique shops, cafés and restaurants. In the spring there are **storks' nests** on the numerous towers and wall spurs. The parent storks circle above Faro's old city centre, and only the beaks of the young can be seen over the edge of the nests.

Largo da Sé, Paço Episcopal

In spring the Largo da Sé too looks its best. The spacious square is bordered by orange trees that blossom in March and April and spread a pleasant scent. The Largo da Sé is bordered on the north and west side by the Paço Episcopal, the bishop's palace. The long west wing was added to the original building in the late 18th century by Fabri when it was decided to open a priest's seminary here. After 1974 the building was used temporarily as a reception centre for **retornados**, returnees from former Portuguese colonies. In 1986 it again became a priest's seminary. On the square in front of the building a monument commemorating Bishop Francisco Gomes do Avelar was erected in 1940; he had promoted the idea of a seminary

← *Arco da Vila – one of the city gates in the historic centre of Faro* in the late 18th century and worked for the rebuilding of the many churches that had been destroyed by the earthquake. On the northeast corner of Largo da Sé is the Faro city hall (*câmara municipal*).

The most conspicuous building on the Largo da Sé is the cathedral. Part of its history is visible on the outside already: large parts of the originally Gothic church were destroyed by the **earthquake** in the 18th century and rebuilt. Of the previous church only the tower and a window on the south side survived. The Visigoths already built a first church in honour of Santa Maria, probably on this site. Later there was a mosque here, and the Portuguese then built a church over its remains, as was so often the case after the Arabs were driven out.

In all Gothic, Renaissance and Baroque elements can be made out in the church. The tower rises clearly above the building. The Gothic origins of the structure can be seen primarily in its doorways. The

▶ VISITING FARO

INFORMATION
Rua da Misericórdia 8 – 12
Tel. 289 803 604

PARKING
There is free parking on Largo de São Francisco in the south of the city at the Centro Histórico.

SHOPPING
There are many small shops in the pedestrian zone around Rua de Santo António. In Forum Algarve – its architecture has won prizes – at the edge of town on the road to the airport everything is available under one roof; it is open until late in the evening.

EXCURSIONS
Formosamar
Clube Naval Building
Marina de Faro
Tel. 918 720 002
www.formosamar.pt
Trips in traditional fishing boats along the Ria Formosa and to the Ilha Deserta.

Ilha Deserta
In the summer boats leave from the landing at the Porta Nova (by the old city wall)
Tel. 918 779 155, www.ilha-deserta.com

Ilha de Faro
In the summer boats leave from the landing at the Porta Nova.

GOING OUT
In the side streets off Rua Conselheiro Bivar there are any number of pubs and bars.

WHERE TO EAT
▶ Moderate
① *A Taska*
Rua do Alportel 38, tel. 289 824 739
Good selection of fish dishes. The specialty is »xarém«, maize mash, served for example with mussels.

② *Restaurante Faro e Benfica*
Doca de Faro, tel. 289 821 422
Restaurant at the yacht harbour with a beautiful view of the sea. Large selection of fish and seafood.

north side of the cathedral is unusual. It is not one unified surface but consists of three side chapels, of which the middle one even has a dome.

The church was rebuilt in the 18th century and the light character of its interior, which almost resembles a hall church although it consists of a nave and two aisles, is remarkable. On each side of the nave three delicate and barely noticeable columns separate it from the aisles. The choir is covered by a coffered, barrel-vaulted ceiling. In the Capela de Santo Lenho on the right next to the altar António Pereira da Silva, bishop of the Algarve from 1704 until 1715, had his last resting place built. The side walls of the cathedral are asymmetrical, with four chapels on the one side and three on the other, all of which have completely different sizes. The azulejo wall coverings of the chapels mainly date from the 18th century. In the choir loft above the entrance there is a Baroque organ, painted by Francisco Cordeiro between 1716 and 1751 and completely restored only a few years ago. In the front chapel on the left there is a small organ made in 1762.

③ *Cidade Velha*
Rua Domingues Guieiro 19
Tel. 289 827 145
Homely restaurant somewhat hidden behind the cathedral. Traditional Algarve cooking.

▶ **Budget**
④ *Chelsea*
Rua D. Francisco Gomes 28
Attractive and centrally located. Fish, meat and international dishes.

⑤ *Fim do Mundo*
Rua Vasco da Gama 53
Tel. 289 826 299
A large menu and a good selection of typical Portuguese dishes at the »end of the world«.

WHERE TO STAY
▶ **Mid-range**
① *Hotel Eva*
Avenida da República 1
Tel. 289 001 000
Fax 289 001 002
www.tdhotels.pt

Solid, modern hotel, centrally located right on the yacht harbour; it doesn't look like much on the outside, but its 140 rooms are comfortable and pleasantly furnished. There is also a pool with sun lounges on the roof.

▶ **Budget**
② *Hotel Sol Algarve*
Rua Infante D. Henrique 52
Tel. 289 895 700
Fax 289 895 703
www.residencialalgarve.com
Recommended, relatively new bed & breakfast in a quiet street in the town centre – the rooms are small, plain and tidy.

③ *Residencial Madalena*
Rua Conselheiro Bivar 109
Tel. 289 805 806
www.residencialmadalena.com
Family-run, friendly and typically Portuguese pension with plain rooms in various sizes and furnishings.

The **ascent of the bell tower** of the cathedral is rewarding for its magnificent view of the old quarter and the lagoon area. There is also an exhibition of sacred art and a small capela dos ossos (bone chapel). Opening times: 10am – 6.30pm, in the winter months 10am – 5pm. Sometimes it is possible to go into the church itself be-

Faro Map

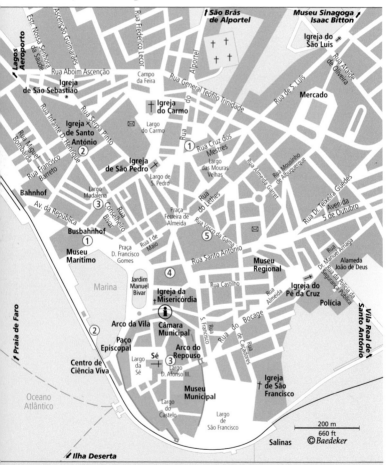

Where to eat
① A Taska
② Faro e Benfica
③ Cidade Velha
④ Chelsea
⑤ Fim do Mundo

Where to stay
① Hotel Eva
② Hotel Sol Algarve
③ Residencial Madalena

fore 10am without paying admission. Otherwise buy a ticket for the tower, the bone chapel and the church itself.

From the Largo da Sé walk via the south-west corner to the Arco da Porta Nova, the second of the remaining gates in the old city wall. It was built in 1630 and restored in 1992. The Arco da Porta Nova leads directly to the water. Boats leave from here on trips into the Ria Formosa lagoon, to the Ilha Deserta and to Praia de Faro. From Largo da Sé a side trip through the arch at the end of Rua do Arco is worthwhile. There is a small lookout at the end of the courtyard.

Arco da Porta Nova

East of the cathedral is the Praça Afonso III. On a lawn n the middle of this square stands a monument to the king, under whose rule the Arabs were driven out of Faro and other Algarve cities.
On the south side is the relatively plain façade of the former monastery of the Order of Saint Clare, Nossa Senhora da Assunção, which was founded in 1518 by Dona Leonor, the third wife of Manuel I, and completed in 1561 to plans by Diogo Pires. The two-storey little cloister is very pretty. The Museu Municipal is housed in the part of

Museu Municipal

Faro cathedral with Gothic, Renaissance and Baroque elements, and the original bell tower

the building around the cloister. Finds from Roman times – including an **Oceanus mosaic** from the 2nd or 3rd century – and utensils from everyday life from the Moorish period are on display here. A fragment with a Phoenician inscription is interesting testimony to the presence of Phoenician traders on Portugal's southern coast. A section of the museum devoted to paintings exhibits mainly Renaissance, Mannerist and Baroque works. Opening times: Tue – Fri 10am – 7pm (winter until 6pm), Sat, Sun 11.30am – 6pm (winter 10.30am until 5pm)

Arco do Repouso

Only a few steps to the east stands the Arco do Repouso. According to tradition **Afonso III** is supposed to have rested here for the first time after conquering Faro (*repouso*, rest). A prayer chapel was built into the beautifully restored gateway. Afonso can be seen on several tile pictures mounted on the city wall outside the gate, including one scene of the city conquest.

Igreja de São Francisco

Rua D. Teresa and Rua de Caçadores lead to the Igreja de São Francisco on Largo de São Francisco, which is used as a parking lot now. Igreja de São Francisco dates originally from the 17th century and was remodelled after the earthquake. The church is only open during mass, when azulejo paintings with scenes from the life of St Francis can be seen. There is also a tile painting of the coronation of Mary.

Museu Regional do Algarve

To learn about **everyday life in the Algarve** before the onset of tourism and what this region looked like in the early 20th century, visit the small Museu Regional do Algarve on the busy Praça da Liberdade. It exhibits collections of old tools and implements, including a donkey cart that was used by an *aguadeiro*, a water carrier. There are also exact replicas of rooms of Algarve houses. The photographs of towns and landscapes are especially interesting – it is impossible to recognize the sights from today's perspective. Moreover there are photos of Algarvios at work in the salt works, fields, fishing, weaving baskets and transporting water. Opening times: Mon – Fri 9am – 12.30pm, 2pm – 5.30pm

Alameda João de Deus

The walk to Alameda João de Deus is worthwhile for a break in a quiet place. This park with its flower beds, tall trees, pool and basketball court is extremely pretty. Little kiosks sell refreshments. The park is named after the probably most famous Portuguese educator; countless kindergartens were established using his model, which is related to the Montessori method.

Praça de Dom Francisco Gomes

The Praça de Dom Francisco Gomes, located right by the harbour, is marked by heavy traffic. The obelisk was erected in 1910 in honour of the diplomat Ferreira d'Almeida, who was born in Faro in 1847; while serving as navy minister he built a naval college and did much to advance the fishing industry.

The Jardim Manuel Bivar, bordering on the south, is quieter. The gardens with flower beds, palms and jacaranda trees are a favourite place for older Faroese to read, write, take a nap or enjoy some people-watching.

Jardim Manuel Bivar

On the east side of the park stands the Igreja da Misericórdia, a church that was originally built in the 14th century, destroyed by the earthquake in 1755 and rebuilt a short time later.

Igreja da Misericórdia

The Museu Marítimo Almirante Ramalho Ortigão on the north-west corner of the harbour basin houses an appealing hodgepodge of **articles related to the sea**. Various ship models – from a Portuguese caravel to a steamship – are on display, as well as a small collection of seashells; there is also information on various methods of catching sardines, cod and squid. Opening times: Mon – Fri 9.30am – noon and 2.30pm – 5pm

Museu Marítimo

The Centro Ciência Viva on the southern end of the harbour basin introduces children and young people to the world of the natural sci-

Centro Ciência Viva do Algarve

Not hectic but friendly – the pedestrian zone in Faro

ences. Various physical and chemical processes can be observed while performing experiments. Space exploration is one of the focal points. Opening times: July 15 – Aug 31 Tue – Sun 3.30pm – 11.30pm, rest of the year Tue – Fri 10am – 5pm, Sat – Sun 11am – 6pm

Igreja de São Pedro

The Igreja de São Pedro is located on the small square of the same name in the northern part of the city centre. It was built in the 16th century to replace a chapel dedicated to St Peter when a new congregation was formed in the course of urban development in this part of Faro. A figure of São Pedro is integrated into the pretty Renaissance doorway. The church choir has a barrel-vaulted ceiling. In the first chapel on the right aisle is an azulejo painting that was reconstructed after the earthquake.

Igreja do Carmo, Capela dos Ossos

North of the Igreja de São Pedro is the broad Largo do Carmo with the Igreja do Carmo, a Baroque church flanked by two low bell towers that dates from 1719. The rebellion against occupation by Napoleon's troops was planned at an assembly that took place in this

The Faro marina at sunset: Jardim Manuel Bivar and the Centro Histórico with Arco da Vila in the background

Portuguese national colours in the streets of Faro

church in June 1808. The talha dourada around the high altar and on the side altars give the church interior its atmosphere. The sacristy is plainer with various figures of Christ in small wooden niches. A look at the wooden ceiling of the sacristy is also worthwhile: it consists of 24 panels painted with different motifs.

Go through the small cemetery to get to the **Capela dos Ossos (bone chapel)**, which was dedicated in 1816 and which is known far beyond Faro. The vaulted ceiling and walls are »decorated« with bones and skulls of the dead. The chapel was built by monks, and the human bones are from earlier graves in the cemetery. Opening hours: ⏱ Mon – Fri 10am – 1pm and 3pm – 6pm (in winter until 5pm), Sat 10am – 1pm, in winter also on Sun during services

In Rua Leão Penedo on the north-eastern edge of the city centre there is a Jewish cemetery which was restored in 1992 on the initiative of Isaac Bitton, a Portuguese Jew who moved to the USA in 1959. A museum on Jewish culture and history in the Algarve was attached in 2007, which is run by the Faro Jewish Heritage Centre. Exhibits include articles from the two synagogues that used to exist in Faro. A copy of the first book ever printed in Portugal is on display: a Hebrew Pentateuch printed in 1487 by Samuel Gacon. Opening hours: Mon–Fri 9.30am – 12.30pm and 2pm – 5pm (tours: tel. ⏱ 925 071 509, 282 416 710)

Museu Sinagoga Isaac Bitton

Around Faro

✳
Praia de Faro

Faro's local beach is the Praia de Faro on Ilha de Faro about 10km/ 6mi from the centre by car. Take the road to the airport. A narrow bridge leads to the lagoon island with a sandy beach which extends east and west for miles. Buses also run to the beach from the city centre; in the summer there are also boats.

Ilha Deserta

The Ilha Deserta, also called Ilha Barreta, is a **spit of land** beyond the lagoon islands. Boats run from Faro to the unoccupied island. They leave from the landing near the Porta Nova in the old quarter.

Lagoa

E 5

Conselho: Lagoa   **Population:** 18,500

Lagoa is known as a place for shopping – on the edge of town, especially along the N 125, there are several large shopping centres. It is much quieter in the town centre north of the highway. A side trip to the market hall on the Praça da República in the morning hours is worthwhile.

Lagoa is located about 5km/3mi north of the beach resort Carvoeiro, 8km/5mi east of Portimão and 8km/5mi south of Silves. Two important traffic arteries – the N 125 and the N 124 – intersect here.

Not much is known about the town's history. The name already gives reason to speculate: Lagoa means »lagoon« or »inland lake«.

Lagoa is known as the **centre of the most important winegrowing region of the Algarve**. This region generally produces relatively heavy **red wines**. Examples are the dry Algar Seco, the sweet Algar Doce and Aguardente Afonso III, which is stored in oak barrels and drunk as an aperitif. Lighter vintage wines are sold under the label Lagoa; young table wines are available under the name Porches.

> ! **Baedeker TIP**
>
> **Wine tasting**
> Algarve is not a region usually associated with wine – but get ready for a surprise. Wines from the Lagoa region in the Algarve are best tasted in a winery: Adega Cooperativa de Lagoa at the edge of town on the N 125; tel. 282 342 181.

What to See in Lagoa

Igreja Matriz

In the Igreja Matriz, whose main façade dates from the 19th century, there is a figure of Nossa Senhora da Luz by the most important Portuguese Baroque sculptor, Machado de Castro.

The monument on the church square planted with jacaranda and araucaria trees commemorates the soldiers who were killed in the colonial wars in Guinea, Mozambique and Angola.

Not far from here rises the Torre-Mirante, the bell tower of the former Convento de São José. In the monastery there is a **gallery** which shows rotating exhibitions; there are often **concerts** in the main hall.

Torre-Mirante

Around Lagoa

Estômbar is a rural town nicely located 3km/2mi west of Lagoa on an elevation. José Joaquim de Sousa Reis was born here in 1797; he went down in history under the name Remexido (►Famous People). He led a group of monarchists that terrorized many places in the Algarve and southern Alentejo during the Liberal Wars in the early 19th century.
The church of Estômbar is a bit higher up in an attractive location. It has a Baroque façade with a Manueline doorway preserved from the 16th century.
On the N 125 between Estômbar and Lagoa is the **Slide and Splash** water park. Opening times: daily 10am until 5pm.

Estômbar

⊕

✷ Lagos

C/D 5

Conselho: Lagos   **Population:** 18,000

A town centre that has kept its original looks and atmosphere, wonderful coves framed by bizarre rock formations and endless sandy beaches have made Lagos one of the most popular tourist centres in the Rocky Algarve.

Lagos does not just live from tourism. Many local people can be seen in the bustling town centre going about their daily business; they hardly let the international tourists bother them.
Lagos, located on the western edge of a wide bay (Baía de Lagos), is about 40km/25mi from Cabo de São Vicente. The N 125, which is in part a four-lane road, is a quick link to Faro about 90km/55mi away – and with it the international airport. Moreover the railway line begins in Lagos and runs along the entire coast to the Spanish border at Vila Real de Santo António.

Lagos is one of the most historic cities in the Algarve. The Phoenicians established an important trading post here in the early 1st millennium BC. Greeks and Carthaginians also used the ideal anchorage in the wide bay. In Roman times, from the 2nd century BC, the city was called **Lacóbriga**. The Arabs named it Zawaya, which means well

History

or lake, and gave the settlement sturdy walls. In 1189 Lagos was conquered by Portuguese troops who were supported by German and English crusaders and led by Sancho I; two years later the Arabs took it back.

During the reign of Afonso III in the mid-13th century the city was finally taken by the Portuguese. Since then it has been called Lagos, which comes from Portuguese *lago*, lake. The city walls were renewed in the 13th century and again in the 14th century under Afonso IV as a protection against the Arabs.

Lagos' actual golden age was in the 15th and early 16th century, when it was the port of departure and **centre of the Portuguese voyages of discovery and conquest**. Numerous shipyards built the famous Portuguese caravels, whose construction was designed in nearby Sagres under Henry the Navigator. These conquests and the new trading opportunities made Lagos very wealthy. The trade in human beings began at this time, with the first slave auction taking place in Lagos in 1444.

While Lagos was made the capital of the Algarve province in 1577, the region became less and less important, especially during the 60 years in which Spain ruled Portugal in the 16th and 17th centuries.

Lagos' location on the water was decisive for its history

In 1755 the great earthquake caused extensive damage. A year later Faro became the capital of the Algarve. It was only when tourism began to develop in the second half of the 20th century that Lagos was awakened from its enchanted sleep.

Lagos is prepared for tourism, but the city has also been able to maintain a congenial life of its own. Parts of the medieval wall still border the old city centre. A walk through the side streets away from the main thoroughfares of the city centre is also worthwhile. Here Lagos is neither picturesque nor quaint, but simply a residential town. A small area around Praça Gil Eanes and Praça da República in the centre has been converted into a pedestrian zone. There are many small shops and any number of restaurants and cafés with outdoor seating.

Tourist city with a congenial life of its own

What to See in Lagos

The ideal place to start exploring Lagos is the centrally located Praça Gil Eanes. After a detour northwards to the Igreja de São Sebastião, go south through the pedestrian zone to Praça da República. From there a detour to the waterfront and the Ponta da Bandeira fortress is convenient. Then visit the famous Igreja de Santo António and Museu Municipal before continuing westwards to the city wall. It pays to step through the city gates just to feel the completely different atmosphere outside the city walls. Then stroll through the narrow, quiet streets of the west part of the old quarter back to the starting point of the tour. Finish the walk around Lagos with a stroll down Avenida dos Descobrimentos. The palm-lined street along the harbour channel leads past the fishing port; further north cross the Ribeira de Bensafrim via a drawbridge to the marina. There are cafés and restaurants here, so it's possible to linger awhile and enjoy the harbour air.

Walking tour

 DON'T MISS

■ Praça Gil Eanes with the statue of the legendary King Sebastião
■ Slave market – slaves were put on display and sold here
■ Praça da República with the famous monument to Henry the Navigator
■ Museu Municipal has interesting exhibits and curiosities
■ Igreja de Santo António: a superb example of Portuguese *talha dourada*

Praça Gil Eanes, named after the seafarer who was born in Lagos (►Famous People), is one of the two main squares. In the middle is a famous statue of the »longed-for« king **Dom Sebastião** (►Famous People). The statue was created in the 1970s by the Portuguese sculptor **João Cutileiro**.
The east side of the square is bordered by the Lagos city hall, with the main post office a little farther. Morning visitors should not miss the market hall that was built in 1924 on the promenade.

Praça Gil Eanes

▶ VISITING LAGOS

INFORMATION
Turismo
Praça Gil Eanes
Tel. 282 763 031

PARKING
With luck there are parking spaces along Avenida dos Descobrimentos at the waterfront; otherwise right at the city gates west of the old quarter, for instance at the western gate on Rua Infante de Sagres.

BOATING EXCURSIONS
In Lagos boats leave for Ponta da Piedade and go along the rocky coast to various grottoes, or out to sea for dolphin watching.

GOING OUT
There are plenty of bars and pubs in Lagos, most of them in the old quarter; but the bars at the marina also stay open until late.
Zanzibar in Rua 25 de Abril in the middle of the old quarter is recommended; there is good jazz at Stevie Ray's (Rua Senhora da Graça 9).
In the Centro Cultural in Rua Lançarote de Freitas in the city centre there is a selection of cultural events.

WHERE TO EAT
▶ Moderate/Inexpensive
① *Dom Henrique*
Rua 25 de Abril 75
Tel. 282 087 000
Typical Portuguese cooking, but there are also international dishes on the menu.

② *O Alberto*
Largo Convento Sra. da Glória
Tel. 282 769 387
Centrally located but a little outside the city walls. Mostly Portuguese guests. There is a good wine list.

Baedeker recommendation

③ *Adega da Marina*
Avenida dos Descobrimentos 35
Tel. 282 764 284
The atmosphere leaves something to be desired, as does the range of choice on the menu. But the food is good and comes in large quantities. Popular among the locals, too.

WHERE TO STAY
▶ Mid-range
① *Villa Monte d'Oiro*
Tel. 282 770 079
Fax 282 782 047
www.sonelhotels.com
North-west of Lagos – outside town but not too far: a pretty design hotel with 17 rooms, garden, swimming pool and a small hotel bar.

▶ Mid-range/Budget
② *Hotel Marina Rio*
Avenida dos Descobrimentos
Tel. 282 780 830
www.marinario.com
Cosy family hotel with tidy rooms, some with a view of the marina.

▶ Budget
③ *Hotel Lagosmar*
Rua Dr. Faria e Silva 13
Tel. 282 763 523, 282 241 154
www.lagosmar.com
Comfortable, clean hotel, centrally located, but very quiet. The rooms are small, with modern furnishings. Beautiful roof terrace.

From Praça Gil Eanes walk through the arch and across Praça Luís de Camões to Igreja de São Sebastião a little further north. Steps go up to the pretty church square. The building of the church began in the 14th century but significant changes were made later. The church was heavily damaged in the earthquake of 1755. The Renaissance doors with the Portuguese crown have been preserved. Inside columns with beautiful capitals divide the nave from the aisles. The crucifix to the left of the altar is supposed to have been taken to **Alcácer Quibir** in 1578; it was one of the few remains that were brought back to Portugal from the devastating battle in which King Sebastião lost his life. The statue of Nossa Senhora da Glória in one of the side chapels is from a stranded ship. There is a small bone chapel behind the side entrance.

Igreja de São Sebastião

Praça da República on the southern end of the pedestrian zone is the other central square. The square opens towards the harbour channel.

Praça da República

Evening illumination: historic centre of Lagos

Henry the Navigator is enthroned on a stone pediment – looking towards the water. The monument was erected in 1960 to commemorate the 500th anniversary of his death (►Baedeker Special, p. 66).

Delegação da Alfândega
Black African slaves were put up for auction for the first time beneath the arcades of the Delegação da Alfândega (customs house) in 1444, on the north side of the square. They were tied up under the arcades and initially put on show as a kind of curiosity, only to be sold later (►Baedeker Special, p.204).

Lagos Map

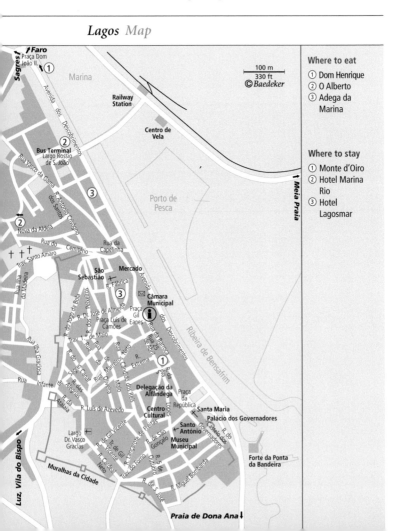

Where to eat
① Dom Henrique
② O Alberto
③ Adega da Marina

Where to stay
① Monte d'Oiro
② Hotel Marina Rio
③ Hotel Lagosmar

100 m
330 ft
©Baedeker

Faro
Praça Dom João II.
Sagres
Marina
Avenida dos Descobrimentos
Railway Station
Centro de Vela
Bus Terminal
Largo Rossio de S. João
Rua Vasco da Gama
Porto de Pesca
R. António Crisógno dos Santos
Nova da Aldeia
Rua do Cemitério
Rua da Capelinha
São Sebastião
Mercado
R. Fábrica
Câmara Municipal
Praça Gil Eanes
Praça Luís de Camões
Trav. 1.º de Maio
R. Dr. José de Almeida
R. Extrema
Delegação da Alfândega
Praça da República
Centro Cultural
Santa Maria
Palácio dos Governadores
Santo António
Museu Municipal
R. Luís de Azevedo
Largo Dr. Vasco Gracias
Muralhas da Cidade
R. de Gil Vicente
R. Miguel Bombarda
Forte da Ponta da Bandeira
Ribeira de Bensafrim
Meia Praia
Luz, Vila do Bispo
Praia de Dona Ana

On the south side of the square stands the Igreja de Santa Maria, on the site of an older church dating from the 14th century. It was rebuilt after the earthquake of 1755. **Henry the Navigator** was buried in the earlier church in 1460; his body was later re-interred in the Capela do Fundador in Batalha.

Igreja de
Santa Maria

On Avenida dos Descobrimentos, the Avenue of Discoveries, which runs parallel to the harbour channel, parts of the old city wall can be seen. In one place in the defensive wall a **Manueline window** has been preserved; it belonged to the former governor's palace; King Sebastião is supposed to have heard his last mass from there before sailing for North Africa. There is a monument commemorating **Gil Eanes**, who set sail from the harbour of his birthplace Lagos in 1434 and was the first European to sail around Cape Bojador.

Avenida dos
Descobrimentos

The Ponta da Bandeira fortress was built in the 17th century in order to protect the harbour. A narrow drawbridge gives access to the inte-

Forte da Ponta
da Bandeira

Coffee and the latest news

A HORSE FOR TEN PEOPLE

1444 is an infamous year in the history of Portugal: slaves were sold for the first time, in Lagos. The Portuguese had just discovered the mouth of the Senegal River and met black Africans there for the first time. As proof of their landing and more or less as a souvenir from this region of Africa, several local inhabitants were forced to make the undignified journey to Portugal.

The first black slaves were more likely just put on display in 1444 in Lagos, rather than being exploited as a profitable business venture. It was unfortunate for the Africans that they proved to be especially resilient. They were expected to do every kind of work imaginable. At that time the Algarve was sparsely populated and there was a demand for additional labour. The Portuguese expansion had caused a labour drain: many Portuguese went to newly discovered countries as traders, others joined the explorers as sailors or were killed on the high seas.

Profitable business

Slavery quickly proved to be an extraordinarily lucrative business. Besides the spice trade it was Portugal's **main source of income** for a long time. In the 16th century the country financed one third of its sea travel and expansion to Africa, Asia and America by trading in human beings. Anyone who needed labour went to Lagos to Praça da República. Slaves were acquired here through barter. Ten people, for example, were traded for one horse. The **barter value** fluctuated according to demand and »quality«. Christians cost more than pagans. Before black Africans were offered for sale in Lagos, they had already suffered devastating journeys. After being captured they were transported in overloaded ships under inhuman conditions. One captive in four died on the sea journey. **English Quakers** were the first to protest publicly against the brutality of this commerce. Many Jesuits in Portugal followed suit, but slave trading was not banned until the 19th century.

Slaves were put on display and then sold under these arcades

rior, where there is an exhibition dedicated to the **age of discovery**. ⊙
Opening times: Tue – Sun 9.30am – 12.30pm and 2pm – 5pm

The colourfully jumbled collection in the Museu Municipal is fun to see. From the church there is also access to the Igreja de Santo António. Along with an azulejo collection and a few sacred objects, there is a small archaeological department with excavation finds from the Neolithic, Bronze and Iron Ages. There are a few Roman finds, including a bust of the emperor Gallienus, which was found in Milreu, also pottery, vessels and oil lamps from the Arab period. Also on display are items from the history of Lagos and all sorts of folk art: pottery, craft work and the typical chimneys of the region. Opening times: Tue – Sun 9.30am – 12.30pm and 2pm – 5pm

Museu Municipal

⊙

The Baroque chapel of Santo António is one of the most impressive churches in the Algarve (entrance via the Museu Municipal). It was built as the regimental church for troops stationed in Lagos whose patron saint was St Anthony. No one knows exactly when it was established, but it is assumed that the church was built under the rule of João V between 1706 and 1750. After the earthquake it was reconstructed in 1769 using old plans.
The interior is designed in **typical Portuguese Baroque style** and almost completely decorated in talha dourada. The altar wall is especially elaborate. On the high altar is a figure of Santo António with an officer's sash, command staff and carrying the infant Jesus. The side walls of the church are also covered with talha dourada above the blue and white azulejo base. The tile paintings depict scenes from the life of St Anthony, including the healing of a blind man and restoring of a foot that was cut off. The wooden cherubs and figures below the corbels, which seem to be bearing the weight of the pilasters, are worth a closer look. Above the gilded magnificence a barrel-vaulted ceiling bears the Portuguese coat of arms and crown. Before leaving take a look at the underside of the gallery: three virtues – faithfulness, hope and charity – look on the visitors from the midst of all the gold.

★
Igreja de Santo António

A visit to the cultural centre is recommended for anyone interested in modern art. In addition to exhibitions of contemporary art, the centre stages theatre, dance and concerts. There is also a cafeteria. Opening times: Mon – Sat noon – 8pm (www.centroculturaldelagos.wordpress.com)

Centro Cultural

⊙

Around Lagos

An alternative to the rocky bays south and west of Lagos, which are crowded during the high season, is Meia Praia north-east of the city. The sandy beach follows the gentle curve of Baía de Lagos for several miles.

Meia Praia

Get to Meia Praia by walking past the Lagos railway station or take the small bus that runs to all the local beaches about once every hour. There are also small boats that leave from Avenida dos Descobrimentos via Ribeira da Bensafrim.

✳ Beaches

In the south of the town are two small beaches, **Praia do Camilo** and the famous **Praia de Dona Ana** with little rocky islands opposite. Praia de Dona Ana is said to be the most beautiful of all the bays in the vicinity, but during peak season it is very busy. Steps go down from Praia de Dona Ana, which is divided into two smaller coves by a promontory. During high tide it is impossible to get from one to the other without getting wet feet. Above Praia de Dona Ana there are various large hotels. A few kiosks and restaurants serve food and drinks to the sunbathers.

✳ ✳ Ponta da Piedade

From Praia de Dona Ana it is just 2km/1.2mi south by car or on foot to Ponta da Piedade – a path runs right along the top of the cliff in places. These are probably the loveliest **rock formations on the Al-**

Ponta da Piedade: a spectacular rocky setting best explored by boat

garve coast. They can be seen on land, but the water is an even better vantage point. Boats go from Lagos to Ponta da Piedade and in peak season also from Praia de Dona Ana.

Ponta da Piedade is a superb promontory at the southern end of the Baía de Lagos, with steep cliffs going straight down into the sea. At their highest point the cliffs are 20m/65ft high. There is a profusion of rocky outcrops, single crags and tors, natural arches and gateways, and together they create a bizarre and wonderful fantasy landscape. A lighthouse guides ships passing in and out of the Lagos bay. Steps lead down to the water from the lighthouse. Boat tours through the rock formations leave from here as well.

West of Ponta da Piedade lies Praia do Porto de Mós with a few restaurants and beach cafés, a broad sheltered bay with little surf and good conditions for water sports. Towards Ponta da Piedade there are tiny coves that can only be reached by boat, so they are mostly deserted.

Praia do Porto de Mós

Luz is a former fishing village, about 5km/3mi west of Lagos, which has developed into a tourist resort. The municipal beach, the lovely Praia de Luz, is good for water sports: surfing, waterskiing, diving and pedaloes.

Luz

Zoo Lagos is an animal park 10km/6mi north-west of Lagos (from Lagos take the N 120 towards Aljezur, in Bensafrim turn off to the left towards Barão de São João, after a few miles the road to the zoo is on the left). A great variety of birds, monkeys, sheep, goats, donkeys and llamas can be seen on the lawns. In the ponds there are reptiles and hippos; plant lovers can admire many varieties. Opening times: daily 10am – 7pm, Oct 1 – Mar 31 until 5pm

Zoo Lagos

⊙

The village of Odiáxere, 6km/3.5mi north of Lagos, has suffered greatly from the traffic on the busy N 125, which passes right through its centre. But leave the highway behind, and the rural atmosphere of times gone by appears. The pretty village church still has the Manueline main portal from the previous church.

Odiáxere

In Odiáxere a road branches off north from the N 125 to the Barragem da Bravura reservoir or Barragem de Odiáxere. The road first leads through meadows and orange groves for about 10km/6mi and later onto a plateau through a sea of white and yellow rockroses. It gets more mountainous towards the end of the drive and the reservoir appears suddenly surrounded by wide eucalyptus forests. Barragem da Bravura is one of a series of reservoirs that Salazar built in Portugal in the later 1950s; while they are very popular among the Portuguese as recreation sites, tourists do not find them very attractive. There is a beautiful lookout and a small restaurant. Barragem da Bravura is not suitable for swimming or water sports.

Barragem da Bravura

★ Loulé

G 5

Conselho: Loulé   **Population:** 20,000

There are good reasons to head for Loulé, a pretty little town 15km/9mi north-west of Faro: There is a loud, bustling market in the market hall in the mornings, and a stroll through the narrow old streets with little galleries and cafés rounds off the day.

History

Some Portuguese historians assume that the town was founded by the Carthaginians in the year 404 BC, while others think that it was founded in Roman times. Under the Arabs Loulé was called Ulyá, which turned into Laulé and later Loulé. According to legend the name comes from a **laurel tree** which is supposed to have stood near the fortress and was immortalized in the city coat of arms. In 1249 Loulé was conquered by Portuguese troops under Dom Paio Peres Correia. The most recent important event in its history: Loulé was given a town charter in 1988.

Pleasant rural town

Loulé – a busy centre in the Algarve hinterland – is an attractive little town, with almost metropolitan avenues and squares and a pretty historic centre full of nooks and crannies. At times the smart, white-washed houses make the old parts of the town look like **stage sets**. The streets around the Praça da República, Largo Gago Coutinho and Avenida José da Costa Mealha appear more modern and lively. There are numerous shops in the pedestrian zone along Rua 5 de Outubro.

What to See in Loulé

Walking tour

A short tour through Loulé could begin at Largo Bernardo Lopes, go past the fortification walls and further south through the old city streets to Igreja Matriz de São Clemente. From here walk along Rua Engenheiro Duarte Pacheco and Avenida Marçal Pacheco to Igreja da Misericórdia and – after a short detour to the remains of Convento da Graça – to the market hall. Afterwards do not miss the pilgrim chapel Nossa Senhora da Piedade, which stands a short distance outside Loulé to the west on a hill where it can be seen for miles around.

Castelo/Museu Municipal

The ancient castle probably dates back to Moorish times. Only a few sections of castle wall remain, marking the centre of the earlier settlement. Stone steps lead up onto the remaining walls. From here there is a beautiful view of Loulé and the surroundings as far as the sea.

The former residential part of the castle now houses a department of the municipal museum. Along with archaeological finds **farming equipment** is on display. A traditional Algarve kitchen is also dis-

Loulé Map

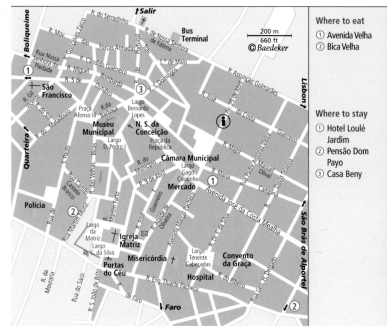

played in one room. Opening times: Mon – Fri 9am – 5.30pm, Sat 10am – 2pm.

Next to it is the tastefully restored Convento do Espírito Santo. The monastery was founded in the late 17th century, severely damaged by the earthquake of 1755 and dissolved in 1836. Today it serves as a cultural centre which shows rotating exhibitions.

Convento do Espírito Santo

Opposite the monastery is the plain façade of the Ermida de Nossa Senhora da Conceição. This chapel was built in the mid-17th century in gratitude for the restoration of independence from Spain. It is closed most of the time, but should it be open a look at the 18th-century **altar decorated with talha dourada**. At the same time the interior walls were covered with tile pictures, which show scenes from the life of the Virgin Mary.

Ermida de Nossa Senhora da Conceição

Loulé's main church is in the historic centre, between Largo da Silva and Largo da Matriz. Its origins go back to the second half of the 13th century, and it was probably commissioned by the archbishop of Braga in northern Portugal. Parts of the church were destroyed by the earthquake of 1755; further quakes in 1856 and 1969 caused

Igreja Matriz de São Clemente

! *Baedeker* TIP

Miradouro

The little garden of the Igreja Matriz is an inviting place to take a break: tall shady palm trees and colourful flowers. There is also a nice view of the newer part of town.

more damage. Inside the **pretty capitals** on the columns stand out especially. A few side chapels were added in the 16th century, including one dedicated to São Brás with a Manueline pointed arch, and one dedicated to Nossa Senhora da Consolação, which has **Manueline cross-ribbed vaulting**.

Portas do Céu South of the church leave the historic city centre through an old city gate, the Portas do Céu (heaven's gate). A small chapel, the Portas do Céu chapel, was built into the arch.

Igreja da Misericórdia From here follow Rua Engenheiro Duarte Pacheco and Avenida Marçal Pacheco to the Igreja da Misericórdia. The **Manueline doors**, which are reached via broad steps with a granite cross, stand out clearly from the façade. Heavy stone-carved ropes surround the finely worked door frames.

Convento da Graça Only a small remnant of the former Convento da Graça on Largo Tenente Cabeçadas has been preserved, but it is still impressive: a relatively well-preserved Gothic doorway arch stands between modern houses.

✱ Mercado The market hall on busy Largo Gago Coutinho was built in **neo-Moorish style**. There is a market here every day, and the bordering streets are also full of life. Fruit, vegetables, fish and poultry are sold in the market.

Igreja de São Francisco Igreja de São Francisco outside the old city centre is known for its tabernacle in the form of a pelican.

Around Loulé

✱ Capela de Nossa Senhora da Piedade 2km/1.2mi west of Loulé, above the road to Boliqueime, is the 16th-century Capela de Nossa Senhora da Piedade. A **pilgrim route** goes up the hill. At the top the first thing to be seen is an old Renaissance chapel in which a statue of the Senhora da Piedade is kept. The chapel is always open and the people of Loulé often come on weekdays to visit the **city's patron saint**.
Next to the old chapel a large, brilliantly white domed church was built, where masses are held for the pilgrims. From the front of the church there is an excellent view of the hilly Algarve landscape to the north and the great expanse of sea to the south.

Querença A good 10km/6mi north-east of Loulé in a sparsely populated region lies the village of Querença. The landscape is already bleaker here

⏵ VISITING LOULÉ

INFORMATION
Rua 25 de Abril, 9
8100-506 Loulé
Tel. 289 463 900

SHOPPING
Market
A stroll through the market hall is worthwhile in the morning; mostly food items are on sale here. A nice shopping street, which has been converted to a pedestrian zone shaded by sun sails, is Rua 5 de Outobro. It has both small, elegant shops as well as stores for normal, everyday items.

WHERE TO EAT
▶ Moderate
① *Avenida Velha*
Avenida José C. Mealha 13
Tel. 289 416 474
Friendly service, good Portuguese cuisine.

② *Bica Velha*
Rua Martim Moniz 17
Tel. 289 463 376
Upmarket; rustic decor.

WHERE TO STAY
▶ Mid-range/Budget

Baedeker recommendation

① *Hotel Loulé Jardim*
Praça Manuel de Arriaga
8100-665 Loulé
Tel. 289 413 094, 289 242 729
Mobile 968 691 167
www.loulejardimhotel.com
Very pleasant hotel with 52 rooms in a lovely old town house

▶ Budget
② *Pensão Dom Payo*
Rua Dr. F. Sá Carneiro
Tel. 289 414 422, fax 289 416 453
Well-kept guesthouse, modern fittings and furniture, with 26 rooms

③ *Casa Beny*
Rua São Domingos 13
Tel. 289 417 702
Private rooms, well kept with nice fittings and furniture, bath and TV, central location

---

since the more fertile parts of the Algarve lie towards the south. Around Querença there are forests, great expanses of rockroses line the road and on many hilltops there is only macchia growth. The road leads up to the old city centre located on a hill and appears to end on the church square. With a little luck the church, which goes back to the 16th century, will be open: it has a pretty baptismal font and images of saints by various local artists. The restaurants on the wide church square serve tasty food and are especially busy on the weekends.

The Benémola spring near Querença is nice to visit. To get there leave Querença towards Aldeia da Tor. A footpath (distance to the spring c 4km/2.5mi) branches off from the road and soon afterwards

Fonte Benémola

Neo-Moorish, beautiful and busy in the mornings: the market hall in Loulé

a gravel road for cars leads into the spring area with its lush vegetation. There is a picnic site there.

Olhão

Conselho: Olhão   **Population:** 27,000

As far as atmosphere goes Olhão is probably the most bizarre town on the Algarve coast. Olhão has a life of its own, which has nothing to do with the tourist-dominated life on the Algarve coast.

East of Faro the area is largely untouched by tourism to this day. The most important industry in the lagoon region of the Ria Formosa is **fishing**. In the early morning the fishermen rattle to the harbour on their mopeds, and after the work is done they recuperate over coffee and schnapps in the breakfast bars. The poverty and lack of social services can't be overlooked. Olhão might not appeal at first sight, but look again and you will find the authentic and unique vitality of the town fascinating.

▶ VISITING OLHÃO

INFORMATION
Largo Sebastião Martins Mestre 6 A
Tel. 289 713 936

PARKING
With luck, parking spaces can be found on Avenida da República; otherwise down by the water on Avenida 5 de Outubro or a little further east on Avenida das Forças Armadas at the harbour.

SHOPPING
There are numerous little shops in the pedestrian zone, where you can shop quite cheaply.
Every Saturday a large market is set up around the market halls down by the water, where shoppers find not only fresh food but also everything from music cassettes to clothes, flowers, dried fruit and toys.

WHERE TO EAT
▶ **Moderate/Inexpensive**
① *O Tamboril*
Avenida 5 de Outubro 160
Tel. 289 714 625
On the menu here are good fish and mussel dishes, prepared in a manner typical for the region.

WHERE TO STAY
▶ **Budget**
① *Pensão Bicuar*
Rua Vasco da Gama 5
Tel. 289 714 816
www.pension-bicuar.com
Pleasant guesthouse in the centre of town. There is a good view of Olhão from the roof terrace.

② *Pensão Bela Vista*
Rua Teófilo Braga 65, tel. 289 702 538
This small, renovated guesthouse with nine rooms is located in the centre of the old town.

The fishing harbour on the eastern edge of town is the largest in the whole region; in the district of Faro, only Portimão has a comparable turnover. Sardines and tuna are the main catch in Olhão, and they are processed there immediately. Ships also leave from here to fish on the high seas off the coast of North Africa and in the Arctic Ocean.

History The city is young compared to others in the Algarve. It grew out of a 14th-century fishing settlement. At that time there were numerous **fresh-water springs** in the region around Olhão. They were called *olhos* (eyes), which is where the town's name comes from. Because of these springs many sailors and fishermen stopped at the village to replenish their supplies of fresh water. The water carrier, or *aguadeiro*, was a typical Olhão occupation for a long time.

One spectacular operation by several fishermen has gone down in Portuguese history. The citizens of Olhão had excelled in the battle to gain independence from Napoleon's troops in the early 19th century: after the French were driven out a group of fishermen from Ol-

Olhão Map

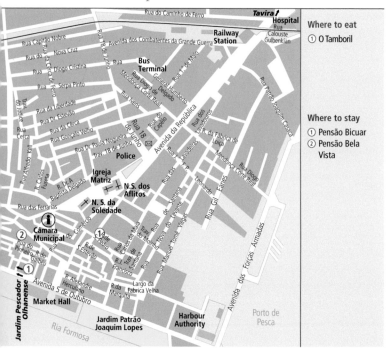

Where to eat
① O Tamboril

Where to stay
① Pensão Bicuar
② Pensão Bela Vista

hão set out in a small fishing boat called *O Bom Sucesso* (Good Success) across the Atlantic to Brazil to bring the news to the royal family, who had fled there. For this deed João VI gave the village the title **Olhão da Restauração** (Olhão of the Restoration).

Olhão flourished in the middle of the 19th century because of the expanding fishing and fish-processing industry. The port became more and more important. Since the town is dependent for the most part on fishing and fish processing, the decline of this industry in the past decades has hit it particularly hard.

Almost North African Olhão is different from other Algarve towns both in appearance and in atmosphere. It is said from time to time that Olhão bears many similarities to the towns of North Africa. This impression stems primarily from its characteristic white, cubic, flat-roofed houses. The fishing quarter in particular, located down by the sea, consists of two or three-storey **cubic houses** of this kind, arranged in a maze-like pattern. All the houses are similar, but none is exactly the same as any other. All have one feature in common, their **açoteias**, flat roofs. On almost every roof there is a small turret from which, it is said, the wives of the fishermen look out for their husbands' boats. The

North African influence on the architecture can be traced back to the trade between Olhão and North African coastal towns; the construction methods used there were effective in Olhão because of the similarity in climate.

What to See in Olhão

There is not a great deal to see in Olhão; its attraction lies in its atmosphere. Those wishing to take a look at the town's buildings are best advised to follow the main thoroughfare, Avenida da República, in the direction of the sea – past the parish church and the Capela de Nossa Senhora dos Aflitos, then further on through the pedestrian zone to the two market halls and the promenade.

Walking tour

Construction of the Igreja Matriz, funded by the town's fishermen, began in the late 17th century: the foundation stone was laid in 1698. The connection between the church and fishing as well as sea-faring still exists today: until recently there was a **red navigational light** on the main façade facing the water, visible in the evening from the lagoon to help the fishermen get their bearings. Meanwhile the

Igreja Matriz de Nossa Senhora do Rosário

Olhão at night: the lights are reflected in the polished mosaic paving

buildings in the town have become taller, and the red light has been placed on the top of the church.

The interior of the barrel-vaulted church makes a rather sober impression; the Baroque high altar decorated with talha dourada is the only striking feature. On no account should visitors miss the ascent of the church tower, from which there is a magnificent view over the roofs of Olhão out to the lagoon and the open sea.

Capela de Nossa Senhora dos Aflitos At the back of the Igreja Matriz is the Capela de Nossa Senhora dos Aflitos. The chapel consists of a room which is open on one side – although fitted with bars – and lined with tiles. Candles burn constantly, flowers are on display and **votive offerings** such as waxen arms, legs, feet and heads are stacked up. In stormy weather in winter, the wives of fishermen go to the popular little chapel to pray for their husbands.

Museu da Cidade On the Praça da Restauração next to the Igreja Matriz there is a small museum with a nicely presented exhibition of archaeological finds, art and handicraft items. Visitors can also learn something about fishing and seafaring here. Opening times: Tue – Fri 10am – 12.30pm and 2pm – 5.30pm, Sat 10am – 1pm

Rua do Comércio Rua do Comércio, the main street, is a pedestrian zone and shopping area. The shops are simple; some of them are very cheap.

The long Avenida 5 de Outubro runs parallel to the shoreline. Coming from the town centre, the two **market halls** are straight ahead, and between them a passageway leads directly to the lagoon. The large market halls each have four corner turrets, in which there are **little shops and cafés**. A large open-air market takes place around these halls on Saturdays.

! **Baedeker TIP**

Mild summer nights in Olhão
There is activity around the market halls in the summer until late at night. Sit outside and enjoy watching the lighthouse blink from the islands across the lagoon.

East of the market halls stretches the **Jardim Patrão Joaquim Lopes**, where visitors can sit down on the benches and enjoy the view of the tidal flats. Ducks and geese enjoy the carefully fenced-in pond and a monument commemorates Patrão, who was born in Olhão and after whom the park was named. A little further outside the town is the jetty from which ships sail to the islands of Culatra and Armona. To the west of the market there is a small yacht harbour.

Porto The actual port of Olhão begins east of the landing. Smaller fishing boats tie up near the landing. Then a little further on lies the big fishing harbour, which is bordered by several fish processing plants.

Around Olhão

Since 1987 a 60km/35mi-long section of coastline covering 18,400ha/45,500 acres between Faro and Manta Rota has been a nature reserve: the Parque Natural da Ria Formosa. The plant and animal world in the lagoon area with its extensive **dunes** and **salt meadows** is unique. The **bird world** is especially well represented with many rare species, and in the winter months birds come from northern Europe to spend the winter while others stop on their way from or to North Africa. More than 200 different species have been observed in the conservation area.

★
**Parque Natural
da Ria Formosa/
Quinta de Marim**

A visit to the information centre of the Ria Formosa, the **Quinta de Marim**, about 1km/0.5mi east of Olhão's harbour, near the campsites is definitely worthwhile. Take some time to explore the grounds of the Quinta de Marim on foot. Small informative signs give interesting information on the lagoon area of the Ria Formosa and its plant and animal life, as well as about ecological issues and nature conservation in general.

The walk leads down to the water, where a **tide mill** (*moinho de maré*) is still standing. The first mill of this kind already existed in the 12th century in France; in Portugal they were introduced in the late 13th century. The *moinho de maré* on the grounds of the Quinta de Marim was built in 1885 and used until 1970. It is one of the last remaining tide mills. In the east of the area, the ruins of **Roman salt works** were found. Beyond this are areas that were used for farming. A *nora*, a well that goes back to the Arab culture, has been preserved here. Opening times: Quinta de Marim: Mon–Fri 9am–12.30pm and 2pm–5.30pm ⏱

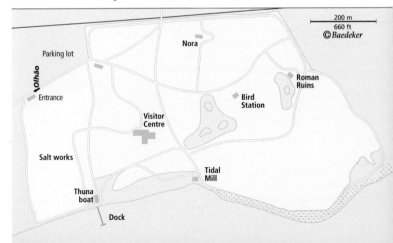

Quinta de Marim Plan

200 m
660 ft
© *Baedeker*

Nora

Parking lot

Olhão

Roman
Ruins

Entrance

Bird
Station

Visitor
Centre

Salt works

Tidal
Mill

Thuna
boat

Dock

At home in the water: the cão de água, the Portuguese water dog, has been saved from extinction

LIKE A FISH IN WATER

It looks like a poodle, only smaller. In the past Portuguese water dogs were reliable helpers and companions for fishermen – for example in Olhão. They were used on the high seas to drive swarms of fish into the nets. Later they entered the *Guinness Book of Records* as one of the oldest and rarest dog breeds in the world. These bundles of energy were saved from extinction at the last minute. Now they are bred all over the world and sold at high prices.

A *cão de água* looks like and is often confused with a poodle. The **cão de água português** with short floppy ears, a long tail and long wavy or curly hair all over – mostly cut short at the back – is not a poodle, but is considered to be the ancestor of poodles. It has several characteristics that make it extremely well adapted to water: unlike »normal« dogs it can swim with all four legs; it has **webbed feet**, can close off its throat and dive up to 3m/10ft deep with an open mouth; and the hair on its chest becomes matted in sea water to protect it from the cold.

Fishermen's helper

Portuguese water dogs really are **excellent swimmers and divers**. With these abilities they were able to help fishermen along the coast, and especially in the Algarve, for centuries. They were always ready to throw themselves into the waves: without being commanded to do so they drove fish into the nets, prevented them from escaping or from freeing themselves from hooks, or caught escaped fish. Or they dived into the water and retrieved equipment that had fallen overboard; they **saved the lives of people who had fallen overboard**; as tireless swimmers they carried messages between boats or to land, and were agile enough to climb back into boats. If a dog refused to jump into the water the crew knew why: dangerous enemies were nearby – sharks! On land too the very muscular water dogs prove themselves to be **attentive**

friends that carefully watch the boat and property of their »family«. They are highly intelligent, can see very well and have a remarkable sense of smell.

Unknown origin

The water dog is the official **Portuguese national dog**, one of the oldest and rarest breeds in the world, but its origin is unknown. Maybe they came to Portugal in the 5th century with the Goths, or maybe the Moors brought them. The Romans already reported when they occupied the Iberian peninsula about a »canis piscator«, a dog that caught fish. In Rome there was a dog at that time whose hair was trimmed like a lion's mane, which was called »canis leo«. In 1297 a monk wrote in his diary that a dog had saved the life of a drowning fisherman.

Preserved from extinction

When the fishing boats and nets got bigger and bigger, and technology advanced, this loyal servant was no longer needed. The old breed would certainly have become extinct had the Portuguese shipowner **Vasco Bensaúde** not come to the aid of water dogs. He began to breed the poodle looka-like in the 1930s, which proved to be difficult – and in 1981 the Portuguese water dog appeared in the *Guinness Book of Records* as the rarest breed of dogs in the world. Today the cão de água português is not used for fishing anymore, but as a tracker, as a lifeguard, to sniff out drugs and as a therapy dog.

Anyone interested in buying one can expect to join a long waiting list. The cão de água português is a good family dog, and one of the breed found a prominent new home: the family of Barack Obama. The dogs are friendly with a cheerful, sometimes spirited, but always **kind character**. They are intelligent animals, which fit well into families and make good watchdogs. While this breed with its stern expression, penetrating and watchful look and controlled walk can be stubborn and proud, it is reliably obedient and very good with children.

Culatra, Armona ✳ Ships sail to both of the islands in the lagoon from Olhão: from June to September several times a day, in winter somewhat less often. On Culatra island the ships put into the harbours at Culatra and Farol, and another ship goes to Armona in the east, at the island's western tip. The landing is near Avenida 5 de Outubro near the harbour. Both of the islands in the lagoon are flat dune islands with very good beaches. There are hardly any residents, but a few restaurants and cafés. There is a lighthouse west of Culatra.

Fuzeta Fuzeta is a fishing village about 8km/5mi east of Olhão. Its location is somewhat elevated and there is a wide view of the mud flats and the island of Armona. The little village is not especially pretty but makes a lively and natural impression. The cube-shaped houses are similar to those in Olhão. The entire harbour area along the water has been nicely designed. Small boats leave here for Armona in the summer. On the northern edge of town the typically Portuguese cemetery, with graves shaped like houses and arranged in little streets, is worth visiting.

Moncarapacho North of Olhão there is beautiful landscape with orchards. Moncarapacho is a somewhat larger but typical village of this area, located about 8km/5mi north-east of Olhão. There are two churches here: one is the parish church with a beautiful Renaissance doorway; the other, the wonderful Santo Cristo chapel, a gem completely clad in azulejos, is nearby. A small outdoor museum with an archaeological collection is attached. Opening times: Mon – Fri 11am – 5pm

Serra de Monte Figo North of Moncarapacho lies the Serra de Monte Figo, which rises to 410m/1350ft at the peak São Miguel. A narrow lane leads up the mountain and there is a beautiful view of the eastern Algarve coast when the weather is clear.

Portimão

D 5

Conselho: Portimão   **Population:** 30,000

In Portimão, the second-largest town in the Algarve, it is obvious that changes have taken place. While tourism ignored it for a long time, this centre of industry and commerce has now developed into an attractive place for shopping.

For decades Portimão was the **centre of Portuguese sardine fishing** and highly subsidized processing. Until the mid-1970s more than 70 trawlers regularly set off for the fishing grounds from Portimão, and fish were processed in a total of 61 factories. After the end of Salazar dictatorship the subsidies were reduced considerably. Today few residents of Portimão still make a living from fishing.

▶ VISITING PORTIMÃO

INFORMATION
Avenida Zeca Afonso
Tel. 282 470 732

SHOPPING
There are good shops in the streets north of Largo 1° de Dezembro.

BOATING EXCURSIONS
Information and bookings down by the water: trips to the grottoes on the coast, also trips up the Rio Arade to Silves (water level permitting). Book trips on the Santa Bernarda at the boat south of the city centre.

WHERE TO EAT
▶ Moderate
① *O Mané*
Rua Damião L. F. Castro 1
Tel. 282 423 496
Popular, centrally located cervejaria. The specialty is carne de porco à Alentejana and carapauzinhos fritos, small grilled sardines with rice mixed with beans.

② *Restaurante Forte e Feio*
Largo da Barca – Zona Ribeirinha
Tel. 282 413 809
One of the many restaurants in this quarter in which grilled fish is served.

③ *Marisqueira Carvi*
Rua Direita 34

Tel. 234 417 912
As it should be in a marisqueira: it serves good seafood.

WHERE TO STAY
▶ Mid-range
Hotel Casabela
Ferragudo, Vale de Areia
Tel. 282 490 650
www.hotel-casabela.com Beautiful hotel with 53 rooms some distance from the town near the beach; hardly any planned activities on offer, more a place for those seeking peace and quiet.

▶ Mid-range/Budget
① *Hotel Globo*
Avenida 5 de Outubro 26
Tel. 282 405 030
www.hoteisalgarvesol.pt
Respectable town hotel with 62 rooms. Centrally located and rather noisy.

▶ Budget
② *Pensão Arabi*
Praça Manuel Teixeira Gomes 13
Tel. 282 423 334
Bed & breakfast (16 rooms) on a busy square on the banks of the Rio Arade.

A stroll through the partially traffic-free city centre – north-west of the Praça Manuel Teixeira Gomes shops line the streets – is rewarding for tourists too. Then visit the spacious squares along the banks of the Rio Arade, which flows into the sea here, to experience Portuguese everyday life. Near ►Praia da Rocha a bit further south a marina was built with the aim of making the town more attractive for tourists.

History Portimão originated as a Phoenician trading post. Greeks and Carthaginians also came to the mouth of the Arade River. Tradition records two names for the site in Roman times: Portus Magnus and Portus Hanibali, though no-one knows which one is correct. Portimão was already an important fishing port under the Arabs. In 1242 it was conquered by Christian knights, just like the two neighbouring towns, Silves and Alvor. In the late 15th century Count Gonçalo Castelo Branco had sturdy walls built around the city, which had been granted to him in 1476 by Afonso V for honourable military service. The significance of the harbour in Portimão grew during the voyages of discovery and conquest that took place in the 15th and 16th centuries. **Shipbuilding** broke all records, and wood for the caravels was cut in the nearby Monchique mountains. In 1487 Bartolomeu Dias sailed from here and was the first European to round the Cape of Good Hope. The discovery of a sea route to India and the resulting upswing in commerce brought riches to Portimão. It also whetted appetites: in the 16th and 17th centuries Portimão suffered various **attacks by pirates**. Fortaleza de São João and on the other side of the Arade estuary Fortaleza de Santa Catarina were built to guard the entrance to the harbour.

Just as in many other Algarve cities, the earthquake of 1755 caused extensive damage in Portimão. The city only recovered slowly from the catastrophe. A quick economic upswing began in the middle of the 19th century with the onset of the fishing industry.

Fisherman in the Portimão harbour on the shores of the Rio Arade

Portimão Map

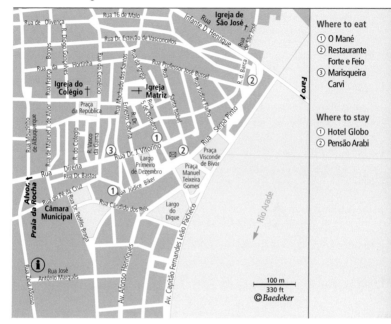

Where to eat
① O Mané
② Restaurante Forte e Feio
③ Marisqueira Carvi

Where to stay
① Hotel Globo
② Pensão Arabi

100 m
330 ft
© Baedeker

Portimão is a very lively town with unspoilt daily life that has not been affected much by tourism, but in which guests from all over the world do play a role. Since the **fishing harbour** was moved to the opposite **eastern Arade riverbanks** Portimão has hardly any port atmosphere. It is almost impossible to imagine how great a role fishing once played in this city. Only on the western banks of the Rio Arade near the old road bridge can a little of the old fishing atmosphere be felt. There are a few modest family-run restaurants here where sardines are grilled on large charcoal grills. Further to the south the pleasant riverbank with spacious open spaces is a good area to linger in local cafés. In the bustling centre the buildings are taller than in other Algarve towns, and the streets are hopelessly congested in the afternoons – in short: this is a proper little town with many facets to explore.

Impressions of the city

What to See in Portimão

From the river promenade walk toward Largo 1° de Dezembro and then north toward Igreja Matriz. From here it is only a few steps to the Praça da República. Finish off with a stroll back to the river and then north along the promenade to the area around the old road bridge.

Walking tour

Praça Visconde de Bívar	Praça Visconde de Bívar, located by the riverside, is set out as a pretty little park. From here there is a pleasant view over the Arade to the opposite bank and the town of Ferragudo.
Praça Manuel Teixeira Gomes	Adjacent to the south lies Praça Manuel Teixeira Gomes, the tourist centre of Portimão. There are a few cafés, including the popular Casa Inglesa, the favourite café of many local people and tourists.
Largo 1° de Dezembro	The right-angled Largo 1° de Dezembro has been made into a small park. Its special feature are ten benches with azulejo pictures on which important events in **Portuguese history** are represented. These include the conquest of Ceuta on 21 August 1415, the discovery of Brazil by Pedro Álvares Cabral on 24 April 1500, the restoration of independence from Spain in 1640 and the declaration of the republic in 1910.
Museu Municipal ⊙	Further south along the river is the **former Feu cannery**, now the home of the Museu Municipal. The interesting exhibitions are devoted to fishing and fish processing. Opening times: Tue 2.30pm–6pm, Wed–Sun 10am–6pm, July, August Tue 7.30pm–11pm, Wed–Sun 3pm–11pm
Santa Bernarda	Nearby the Santa Bernarda is moored. Excursions along the coast are available on this two-masted ship.
Igreja Matriz	North of Largo 1° de Dezembro towers the Igreja Matriz. Before the earthquake in 1755, a 14th-century church stood here, and the Gothic portal, which can be seen clearly in the newly designed façade, is still preserved from this precursor. The small, meanwhile very weathered capitals showing various heads are of note. In the interior there are depictions of saints, some of which come from the destroyed church.
Praça da República	The Igreja do Colégio on the north side of the square used to be part of a Jesuit college. It originated in the 17th century and was rebuilt after the earthquake.
Sardine grills	The area along the riverbanks below the old road bridge has a special ambience. The brick chimneys of several sardine grills are the sign of restaurants – a few old-established ones and a few modern ones along the river – where sardines are served.

Around Portimão

Praia da Rocha	The tourist hotspot ▶Praia da Rocha is a neighbouring town to the south of Portimão, right on the coast.

A delight to the eye: the picturesque fishing village Ferragudo →

Opposite Portimão on the other side of the Rio Arade lies the fishing ✱
village of Ferragudo, a popular subject for postcards because of its
picturesque location. Up in the village stands a pretty church as well   **Ferragudo**
as the Fortaleza de São João, built in 1622 to protect the entrance to
the river. Today the fort is in private ownership.

In picturesque Ferragudo it is easy to think that the **old Algarve** is
alive: alleys lined with fishermen's houses, a few simple guesthouses
and bars and all in all a very pleasant atmosphere. But here too many
apartment complexes have been built lately around the old town
centre and a new marina is planned just outside Ferragudo on the
Arade. When seen from Ferragudo, Praia da Rocha and its skyline,
located opposite, is an eyesore that gives a clear picture of the current situation along this popular Portuguese coast.

South of Ferragudo lies the wide Praia Grande. A breakwater at the   **Praia Grande**
mouth of the Rio Arade ensures that it is safe to swim here. On the
other hand the water quality in the estuary of the Arade is not the
best.

South of Praia Grande there are other coves suitable for swimming,   **Praia de**
with Praia de Caneiros making the best impression. It is possible to   **Caneiros**
swim in the open Atlantic Ocean here in front of a pretty backdrop
of rock cliffs.

Praia da Rocha

   D 5

Conselho: Portimão   **Population:** 4000

**With its faceless apartment and hotel buildings, Praia da Rocha is
as one of the absolute blots on the landscape of the Algarve. Today, nothing remains of the flair of the stylish seaside resort that
Praia da Rocha must have been in the first half of the 20th
century.**

In administrative terms, the holiday town of Praia da Rocha is a sub-
urb of the seaport ▶Portimão 3km/2mi to the north. Its appearance
and atmosphere are as depressing as those of Quarteira and Armação
de Pêra. There is a good tourist infrastructure here, with facilities for
sport and recreation and numerous restaurants, cafés and bars.
Nightlife is important in Praia da Rocha – for this reason the coastal
road is even closed to motorized vehicles at night. There is also a casino. The excellent wide sandy beach that extends to the Rio Arade
estuary is the reason for the explosion in construction. To the west

← *Almost a bit surreal: a single crag juts out of the flat sandy beach –
typical of the coast by Praia da Rocha*

▶ VISITING PRAIA DA ROCHA

INFORMATION
Avenida Tomás Cabreira
Tel. 282 419 132

WHERE TO EAT
▶ **Moderate**
Falésia
Avenida Tomás Cabreira
Tel. 282 412 917
Pleasant restaurant with a nice terrace.

Safari
Rua António Feu 8
Tel. 282 423 540
The specialities here are seafood and African dishes.

WHERE TO STAY
▶ **Luxury**
Hotel Algarve Casino
Av. Tomás Cabreira
Tel. 282 402 000
Fax 282 402 099
www.solverde.pt
Old-established luxury hotel on the promenade with 220 rooms. Nicely furnished, excellent service, playground, casino.

▶ **Mid-range**
Hotel Bela Vista
Av. Tomás Cabreira
Tel. 282 450 480
Fax 282 415 369
www.hotelbelavista.net
A traditional Algarve hotel. The painstakingly renovated building on the promenade with 14 rooms exudes atmosphere. Good service and amenities.

The charming Hotel Bela Vista

there is a series of quiet coves, mostly separated from each other by rocky crags and tors. The boat tours along the coast to Praia dos Três Irmãos are enjoyable.

Promenade for tourists Above the approximately 2km/1.2mi-long and almost 100m/330ft-wide main beach runs Avenida Tomás Cabreira, lined with hotels, restaurants, cafés, boutiques and shops. At the east end of the Avenida the Fortaleza de Santa Catarina, a 17th-century fortification, stands guard over the mouth of the Rio Arade. There is also a pleasant café on the terrace within the walls. From here there is a nice view over to Ferragudo (▶Portimão) and the **marina** directly below the fort. With room for 620 boats the marina is one of the largest in Portugal; a shopping centre and apartment blocks have been built

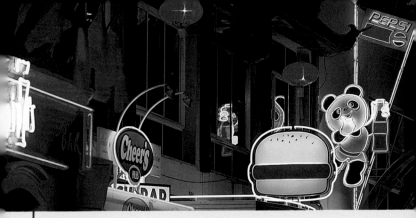
Nightlife in Praia da Rocha

along the edge. From the western end of Av. Tomás Cabreira there is a beautiful view over the cliffs of Praia da Rocha.

Around Praia da Rocha

The next beach to the west of Praia da Rocha is Praia do Vau. While the interior has also been developed here, it still seems practically quaint in comparison to Praia da Rocha. **Praia do Vau**

Quarteira

G 5

Conselho: Loulé   **Population:** 14,000

Quarteira is one of the places that got the Algarve its bad reputation. Like Armação de Pêra and Praia da Rocha, Quarteira is a monotonous city of high-rises.

Located 15km/9mi west of Faro, this tourist centre has long sandy beaches and a wide range of entertainment and recreational activities, which makes holidays in Quarteira attractive for some. The town lives for tourism. The interior is built up as far as the N 125 and there are holiday complexes further north as well. The only compensation is the beach. Accommodation right on the coastal road Avenida Infante de Sagres

 **QUARTEIRA**

INFORMATION
Praça do Mar
Tel. 289 389 209

WHERE TO EAT
▶ **Moderate**
O Romeu
Rua Gonçalo Velho 40
Tel. 289 313 990
Known for good fish specialties.

with a view of the open sea has its charms, but if the room is on the next street inland there is not much to compensate. There are, however, a few nice beach cafés on the coastal road at the edge of town.

Water park The Aquashow Family Park on the N 396, which runs north-east from Quarteira, is a good place for families to visit. Opening times: June, Sept daily 10am – 6pm, July until 6.30pm, Aug until 7pm

★ Sagres

B 5

Conselho: Vila do Bispo   **Population:** 2000

Sagres' fame is primarily rooted in history. Located in the far south-west of the Algarve, the town played an important part in the Portuguese ocean voyages of the 15th and 16th centuries. Even today, the whole region profits from this historic role.

In the extreme south-west, the raw climate makes for sparse vegetation

Tourism has only been moderately developed. Though there are some hotels and private lodgings in and around Sagres, so far the tourist infrastructure is in no way comparable to that in holiday destinations further east. But anyone looking for a quiet holiday and a somewhat fresher climate and natural conditions with deserted sandy coves will be happy here. There is a usually strong west wind on all the beaches and no shelter from it.

Europe's south-western outpost

Both Sagres and **Cabo de São Vicente** 5km/3mi away, the southwesternmost point of the European mainland, are situated on a rocky plateau that drops off abruptly at the coast as a cliff 150m/500ft high. The plateau is divided into two parts: one part is south of Sagres and ends at Ponta de Sagres, while the other part is further north-west and drops off to the Atlantic at Cabo de São Vicente. Between these two points lies the bay of Beliche (Belixe), a relatively sheltered anchorage. Further to the east beyond Ponta de Sagres, Sagres Bay offers excellent shelter, especially from north winds.

Sagres has a long **history**: archaeological investigations have shown that the southwesternmost region of Europe was already settled in the Stone Age. Traces of grave sites from the 3rd millennium BC have been found, which are of Iberian or Celtiberian origin.

Sagres Map

Where to eat
① Vila Velha
② A Tasca

Where to stay
① Pousada do Infante
② Memmo Baleeira Hotel

The Greek geographer and historian Strabo meant Cabo de São Vicente when he wrote about the »**holy mountains**«. Pliny the Elder also wrote that this are was known by the Romans as **Promontorium Sacrum** (holy promontory). The Romans believed that this isolated place must have been the seat of the gods. When the region was settled under the Arabs, too, there was a religious site here. The Portuguese in the end made the place a major centre of European history (►Baedeker Special, p. 232).

The modest houses of Sagres are scattered across a barren, windy plateau. Visitors will search in vain for a proper town centre. The main street ends at the busy fishing harbour.

Collection of modest houses

▶ VISITING SAGRES

INFORMATION
Turismo de Sagres
Rua Comandante Matoso
Tel. 282 624 873

EXCURSIONS
Hiking is possible in the unspoilt landscape of the Costa Vicentina. In Sagres harbour (Porto da Baleeira) various excursions are offered: trips along the coast by ship, fishing and deep sea fishing trips. There is also a diving school in the harbour.

WHERE TO EAT
▶ **Moderate**
① *Vila Velha*
Estrada Pousada
Tel. 282 624 063
A very pleasant, well-run restaurant serving excellent fish and meat dishes.

② *A Tasca*
Porto da Baleeira

Tel. 282 624 177
A restaurant that is popular among the locals for its delicious seafood and fish.

WHERE TO STAY
▶ **Mid-range/Luxury**
① *Pousada do Infante*
Tel. 282 620 240
Fax 282 624 225
www.pousadas.pt
Modern pousada in a marvellous location above the Praia da Mareta with a view of the cliffs on the coast.

▶ **Mid-range**
② *Memmo Baleeira Hotel*
Baleeira
Tel. 282 624 212
Fax 282 624 425
www.memmobaleeira.com
Pleasant hotel in a nice location above the harbour.

✳ Ponta de Sagres / Fortaleza de Sagres

A road leads from Sagres in a southerly direction to the Ponta de Sagres 2km/1.2mi away, on which stands the Fortaleza de Sagres. The fortress is considered to be the **centre of Portugal's history of discovery and conquest** in the 15th and 16th centuries. It is assumed that there was a research centre inside the fortress during the time of Henry the Navigator (▶Famous People), which provided the theoretical basis for sailing the world's seas. Within the fortress only scant remains from the time of Henry the Navigator have been preserved. The present fortress walls, which are among the most impressive in all of Portugal, date from 1793.

The Fortaleza is presently being restored, so viewing will be limited for some time. After passing through the massive gate visitors see what is popularly called a *rosa dos ventos* (wind rose) on the left; it has a diameter of 43m/140ft and was assembled from stones. It was buried and covered with grass for centuries, and only found by acci-

São Bartolomeu de Messines and Surroundings

The Igreja Matriz goes back to a previous church from the 14th cen- **Igreja Matriz**
tury. The current church was built in the 16th century, and in the
18th century it was extensively remodelled. Only the Baroque main
façade from the year 1716, which is made of red sandstone, is remarkable. The **entrance is framed by two spiral columns** – a rarity
in the Algarve. The interior is worth a look for its columns, which
are reminiscent of early Manueline stone rope columns. Some of the
side chapels still have Manueline ceilings. The little marble pulpit is
pretty; the marble was quarried in the area.

Some distance outside the town to the north-west stands the small **Ermida de São**
Ermida de São Pedro. It is usually closed and its architecture is not **Pedro**
very noteworthy, but its location on a small hill is impressive.

About 15km/9mi north-west of São Bartolomeu de Messines lies São **São Marcos da**
Marcos da Serra, where a church crowns the highest point of the vil- **Serra**
lage. In the heat of the day the streets are deserted, but in the early
morning or late afternoon a visit will leave an impression of rural life
in the Algarve.

*A classic rural scene: horse and cart in front of the parish church
in São Bartolomeu de Messines*

São Brás de Alportel

H 5

Conselho: São Brás de Alportel   **Population:** 10,000

São Brás de Alportel lives mainly from agriculture. There is some tourism, but of a quieter more rural kind. In the early 20th century São Brás de Alportel was a popular place for holidays for people from cities because of its dry, mild climate.

The pretty rural town, 17km/10mi north of Faro, where the N 2 crosses the N 270, nestles in hilly landscape. Not far to the north the ▶ Serra do Caldeirão rise up to 500m/1650ft. About 2km/1.2mi north there is a wonderful view of the foothills from a pousada.

History Archaeologists found traces from Roman times in the São Brás de Alportel region. It is assumed that there was an Arab city named Xanabus or Xanabras more or less on the site of the present town. The earliest written documentation is from 1517. A small chapel dedicated to St Blaise is mentioned, around which a few houses had been built. As the earthquake of 1755 caused extensive damage to the town, most of the buildings date from a later period.

! **Baedeker TIP**

Easter festivities

Easter is celebrated elaborately in São Brás de Alportel. After the Easter Sunday mass a procession moves through streets decorated with carpets of flowers. All participants – men only! – carry artistic flower batons that are awarded prizes in a big festival in the afternoon.

São Brás de Alportel is a **typical, pleasant Algarve town** with no tall buildings. Largo de São Sebastião is the town centre; it is the intersection of the N 270 and the N 2, and so quite busy. Avenida da Liberdade with its shops, cafés, a local cinema and a gallery is also lively. The part of town south-east of Largo de São Sebastião towards the church is a quiet and attractive residential area.

What to See in São Brás de Alportel

Igreja Matriz Follow Rua Gago Coutinho from Largo de São Sebastião to the Igreja Matriz de São Brás de Alportel to the edge of town; unfortunately it is usually only open during a mass, but the pretty church square has a **beautiful view of the gently rolling garden landscape**. In the 15th century the first chapel was built here, and was dedicated to São Brás. It was expanded and remodelled several times. Francisco Gomes do Avelar, at that time the bishop of the Algarve, initiated the reconstruction in 1792 after severe damage during the earthquake in 1755. The church has a nave and two aisles, each with a barrel vault, separated by relatively delicate columns. The depiction of the Trinity on the left in the choir is a mid-20th century copy of an early 18th-century painting, which was made in Rome and given to the church of São Brás de Alportel in 1991. In the front of the left aisle there is a neo-classical altar made of marble; its design and the material used make it a rarity for this region. It was probably designed by the Italian architect Francisco Xavier Fabri, who was very active in the Algarve after the earthquake.

After the seat of the bishop was moved from Silves to Faro in the 16th century, São Brás de Alportel was chosen as the site of the bishop's summer residence. Simão de Gama and António Pereira da Silva, two bishops who were in office in the late 17th and early 18th centuries, took the initiative to build here. Today only reconstructions of parts of the **former bishop's palace** can be seen; they were rebuilt in the first decades of the 20th century. Part of the building houses a school.

SÃO BRÁS

INFORMATION
Largo de São Sebastião 23
Tel. 289 843 165

WHERE TO STAY
▶ **Budget**
Estalagem Sequeira
Rua Dr. Evaristo S. Gago 9
Tel./fax 289 843 444
Centrally located, modest guesthouse. 32 en-suite rooms with TV. The house has a restaurant.

In Rua Dr José Dias Sancho – on the left going towards Tavira – the Museu do Trajo occupies the villa of a former cork manufacturer. The luxurious 19th-century furnishings have been preserved. There are rotating exhibitions on the subjects of clothing, furnishing and customs of the Algarve people. A permanent exhibition includes old agricultural implements like cork presses and cooking pans for cork, blacksmith's tools, coaches and donkey carts. No-one who is interested in the **rural Algarve** of past times should miss this museum. A cultural centre is attached. Opening times: Mon – Fri 10am – 1pm and 2pm – 5pm, Sat, Sun 2pm – 5pm

✷
Museu do Trajo

✷ ✷ Serra de Monchique

D/E 3/4

Conselho: Monchique   **Elevation:** up to 902m/2900ft

The Serra de Monchique extends like a protective wall in the north-west of the Algarve, holding back cool Atlantic influences on the weather and in this way ensuring a coastal climate that is North African in character.

! *Baedeker* TIP

**The most beautiful routes
through the Serra**

From the coast drive via the N 124 and the N 266, a beautiful road that leads directly to Monchique. A quieter route further east runs through beautiful scenery above the Ribeira de Odelouca to Alferce. Finally there is another route that passes through an untouched area: the N 267, which branches off from N 266 and then crosses the Serra de Monchique east to west.

The Serra de Monchique is charming hilly country. Its highest peaks, **Fóia** and **Picota**, reach 902m/2959ft and 774m/2539ft respectively. Eucalyptus, cork oaks, firs and mimosas grow on the slopes and gradually give way to low shrubs and rhododendrons further up – a varied and lush flora which in the last few years has suffered from more and more **fires in both forested and open areas**. In the orchards, which adjoin the Serra in the direction of the coast to the south, lemons, figs, almonds and olives thrive.

Geologically the mountain massif rests on the slate bedrock of the region. Thanks to the low permeability of the ground, precipitation collects in streams and rivulets and is transported to the coast. Due to volcanism there are several hot springs.

What to See in Serra de Monchique

Monchique   The small hill town of Monchique (458m/1503ft) located on the slopes of the Serra de Monchique is the region's principal residential area with around 10,000 inhabitants . Monchique is traditionally a manufacturing centre for craft objects like textiles, basketry, wood carving and ceramics. The Serra de Monchique is known for *medronho*, a high-alcohol spirit made from the fruit of the strawberry tree.

Monchique nestles picturesquely on the slopes of the mountain. Steep streets and alleys run through the centre of the town. Everywhere there are views of the surrounding mountains. The town caters mainly to day-trippers and has many cafés and restaurants. The centrally located but not especially attractive Largo dos Chorões is the focal point of life in Monchique. The modern fountain at its centre represents a *nora*, a component of the irrigation system introduced by the Arabs to the Algarve.

A narrow street runs up to the **Igreja Matriz**. The 16th-century Manueline church door with five rays stands out. The tile frieze inside is made of new azulejos and depicts a traditional *ponta de diamante* design, which was very popular in Portugal in the 17th century. The figure of Nossa Senhora da Conceição on the high altar is attributed to the popular Portuguese Baroque sculptor Machado de Castro.

The neglected **ruins of the Convento de Nossa Senhora do Desterro** are less rewarding than the walk there. Follow the walking signs depicting a camera and binoculars through town: outside Monchique the path is cobbled and leads through tall trees. After an uphill walk

Typical small Algarve house on the slopes of the Serra de Monchique

of about 15 minutes the monastery ruins surrounded by old cork oaks appear. From here there is a wonderful view of Monchique. With a little luck people who live nearby in a small house will give a tour of the ruins; the remnants of monastery and church walls are still quite impressive.

The drive to the summit of the Fóia, at 902m/2959ft the highest peak of the Serra de Monchique, is extremely worthwhile. From Monchique a winding road leads through beautiful landscape in several serpentine curves up the south slopes of the mountain. The road first passes pretty houses and tourist cafés. Stop briefly at the *miradouro* (lookout) with a small well: there is a very wide view of the whole coastal strip of the Algarve. Portimão is located right below; to the west lies the **Cabo de São Vicente** and the west coast of the Algarve, and on clears days **Faro** can be seen to the east. Further up the vegetation becomes sparser – rockroses and rhododendrons predominate, herds of sheep and goats graze in the valleys. After a wide bend, the **Alentejo** to the north suddenly comes into view.

✱ ✱
Fóia

The barren peak is relatively inhospitable: beneath a veritable forest of aerials are bases of the Portuguese telecoms company, the radio station RDP and the air force. There is however a café and a souvenir shop for day-trippers.

Monchique owes its fame to the Caldas de Monchique, the **warm springs** (caldas) 6km/4mi further south. The water that bubbles here is bottled and sold all over Portugal.

✱
Caldas de Monchique

▶ VISITING SERRA DE MONCHIQUE

INFORMATION
Monchique
Largo São Sebastião
Tel. 282 911 189

SHOPPING
Tiles, wickerwork and wooden articles are sold in Monchique. A typical product is the curule chair, a wooden folding stool.

HIKING
Various companies and individuals offer hiking holidays in the Serra de Monchique. Enquire at travel agents.

**WHERE TO STAY /
WHERE TO EAT**
▶ **Mid-range**
*Estalagem Abrigo
da Montanha*
Estrada de Fóia, Corte Pereira
Tel. 282 912 131, fax 282 913 660
www.abrigodamontanha.com

Very well-kept, pleasant hotel located slightly outside Monchique on the road up to Fóia, the highest mountain of the Serra de Monchique.

*Villa Termal das
Caldas de Monchique*
Caldas de Monchique
8550-232 Monchique
Tel. 282 910 910, fax 282 910 990
www.monchiquetermas.com
Spa hotel complex with a large spa programme. The complex includes three smaller hotels, an estalagem (guesthouse), an apartment building and the restaurant 1692.

Albergaria do Lageado
Tel. 282 912 616
Fax 282 911 310
www.albergariadolageado.com
Comfortable, reliable guesthouse with 19 rooms in the idyllic centre of the village of Caldas de Monchique.

The springs, which are said to help with rheumatism and liver, urinary tract and intestinal complaints, and with chronic respiratory illness, were known to the Romans. They built a thermal bath named **Mons Cicus**. The most famous patient to take the waters at Caldas de Monchique was **King João II** (▶Famous People) , but his stay in the year 1495 did not have the desired effect, and the king died a short time later.

The tiny town centre is located in a narrow valley under tall, shady trees. Villas and cottages built around 1900 give Caldas de Monchique a special charm. The Fundação Oriente also recognized this and bought the thermal baths in 1994; they have been completely restored. Guests of the spa and other visitors can stay in two pretty hotels, a guesthouse or an apartment building. Those with less time should at least stop in a café or restaurant on the shady square in the town centre and soak up the charming atmosphere. It only takes a few steps to reach lush vegetation. Follow the course of a stream uphill through the woods to a picnic site, beyond which the woods become quieter.

The charming Caldas de Monchique, where the hot springs of the Serra flow

Right on the N 266 south of Caldas de Monchique is an old mine, now open to the public. The home of the former mine owner accommodates a small but interesting museum. Opening hours: daily 10am – 7pm, in the winter until 5pm

Parque da Mina

✷ Serra do Caldeirão

Conselhos: Loulé, Tavira, Alcoutim, São Brás de Alportel, Almodôvar   **Elevation:** up to 589m/1932ft

To explore the Serra do Caldeirão, be prepared for a time-consuming drive. The narrow winding roads only allow slow progress, but it's worth the effort: time seems to have stood still in the remote villages and hamlets of this region, which has hardly been touched by tourism .

The ranges of the Serra do Caldeirão continue from the Serra de Monchique to the east; in the north they extend as far as the Alentejo, in the east to the Guadiana. The landscape of the area is less pretty than that of the Serra de Monchique. The vegetation is sparser; dry, rocky areas alternate with woods and fields. The gently rolling hills reach 589m/1932ft at the **Pelados** peak. In many villages life goes on in the traditional way; ceramics, basketry and other handicrafts are produced painstakingly by hand.

Drive through the Serra do Caldeirão

São Brás de Alportel
In order to have some time for stops, begin this trip as early as possible, because driving is slow on the winding roads. The starting point for this drive through the eastern Serra do Caldeirão is ▶São Brás de Alportel. Follow the winding N 2 northwards to Barranco Velho and then turn off on the N 124 eastwards.

Cachopo
The N 124 runs through beautiful mountain and forest scenery with only few settlements, reaching Cachopo after 20km/13mi. Hardly any guests find their way to this remote Algarve village.

Vaqueiros
A road that is hardly ever used leads eastwards from Cachopo. A few scattered houses appear on the right or left of the road. After 12km/7mi turn off left to Vaqueiros. The most noticeable building in the village is the 16th-century church, which was renovated in the 18th century. Inside it is worth looking at the pretty side altars with their paintings.

Copper mine
Follow the road a bit further to Martim Longo. Where a track turns off to the right, follow the signs »Parque Mineiro Cova dos Mouros«

*There are plenty of secluded places in the Serra do Caldeirão –
for those who like being alone*

to get to the grounds of an old copper mine. The roughly 3km/2mi-long track runs above the Ribeiro da Foupana and offers good views of the river valley. The mine shafts in this area were already exhausted 2700 years ago, but only rediscovered in 1865. The oldest mine is 30m/100ft deep. Parque Mineiro Cova dos Mouros, which was established here to attract visitors to the mine, is no longer open regularly. Information tel. 289 999 229, 281 498 505.

Continue through the barren, sun-dried landscape to Martim Longo. This region already hints at conditions in the Alentejo. Not only at midday are the streets of the village of 1700 residents deserted. In the parish church the remains of wall paintings from the 16th century can be seen.

Martim Longo

The N 124 connects Martim Longo with ►Alcoutim 30km/18mi further to the east. In the village of Giões, 2km/1.2mi north of the road, some pretty pictures of saints, including a Nossa Senhora that holds *relíquias* from the 16th century, are to be seen in the 16th-century parish church.

Giões

To return to the coast it is best to drive from ►Alcoutim along the banks of the Rio Guadiana, then via the N 122 to ►Castro Marim and ►Vila Real de Santo António.

Return to the coast

Silves

E 4

Conselho: Silves   **Population:** 10,800

Silves is an attractive destination for a trip into the Algarve hinterland. The little town lies in beautiful landscape in the southern foothills of the Serra de Monchique. Only a few historic buildings testify to its former greatness: in the Arab period Silves was the capital of the Algarve.

The town spreads over a hill on the right banks of the Rio Arade and can be seen from far off. This area was probably already settled by Celtiberians. It is known that the Phoenicians considered it to be a suitable **river port**. The Carthaginians and later also the Romans appreciated the location. In the 8th century Arabs – it is assumed that they were of Yemenite and Egyptian origin – took over control of Silves and named it **Xelb**. It soon became the **capital city of the**

History

✔ DON'T MISS

- Fortress above the city centre with cisterns from Moorish times
- Cathedral: built on the site of a mosque and severely damaged by the earthquake
- Archaeological museum: many finds from Moorish times

▶ VISITING SILVES

INFORMATION

Posto de Turismo
E.N. 124 – Avenida Marginal
Tel. 910 762 385
On the riverbank near the market hall

Posto de Turismo Municipal
Praça do Municipio
8300-184 Silves

WHERE TO EAT

▶ Expensive

① *Marisqueira »O Rui«*
Rua Comandante Vilarinho 23/25
Tel. 282 442 682
Nice eatery with good Portuguese food; the menu offers plenty of fish and shellfish.

▶ Moderate

② *Casa Velha de Silves*
Rua 25 de Abril
Tel. 282 445 491
Very good food and excellent service.

③ *Café Inglês*
Below the castle
Tel. 282 442 585
Very nice café and restaurant.

WHERE TO STAY

▶ Mid-range/Budget

① *Hotel Colina dos Mouros*
Pocinho Santo
Tel. 282 440 420
www.colinhahotels.com
A very pleasant Portuguese hotel on the south side of the river. Some of the rooms at the back have a splendid view of Silves's old town with the castle. It is rather loud on the street side.

▶ Budget

② *Quinta da Figueirinha*
Tel. 282 440 700
Fax 282 440 709
www.qdf.pt
Quinta in the middle of the countryside under friendly management. Several holiday flats and rooms for rent.

③ *Quinta do Rio*
Santo Estevão
Tel. 282 445 528
quintariocountryinn.home.sapo.pt
The Quinta do Rio lies north-east of Silves in the countryside: very pleasant »turismo rural« accommodation.

province Al-Gharb, which belonged to the Emirate and later Caliphate of Córdoba. Xelb is said to have had about 40,000 inhabitants at that time. Historians, jurists, philosophers, poets and musicians gave the city a reputation far and wide. The glory of Xelb was sung and declaimed in poetry; it was said to have been more beautiful than Granada. Troops of the Portuguese king Sancho I conquered Xelb in 1189. Famous crusaders like Richard the Lionheart and Emperor Frederick Barbarossa, who had allied themselves with Portugal, took part in the military campaign. Immediately after the conquest a Flemish priest was installed as bishop. Two years later the Arabs re-

Silves Map

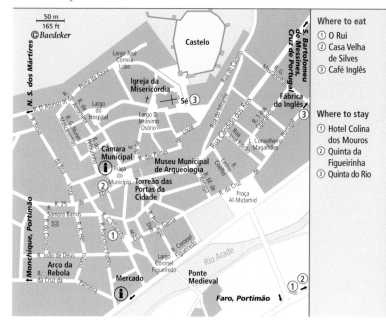

Where to eat
① O Rui
② Casa Velha de Silves
③ Café Inglês

Where to stay
① Hotel Colina dos Mouros
② Quinta da Figueirinha
③ Quinta do Rio

gained control for a short time. It was only under the leadership of the grand master of the Order of the Knights of Santiago, Dom Paio Peres Correia, that Xelb was finally conquered in 1242; the Portuguese renamed it Silves.

Economic decline in the region began with the withdrawal of the Arabs. The town flourished again briefly in the early 16th century, during the time of the Portuguese voyages of discovery and conquest, when ships laden with **pepper** and other goods sailed up to Silves via the **Rio Arade**. However, the silting up of the Rio Arade put an end to its prosperity as a port.

In 1577 the seat of the bishop was moved from Silves to Faro; Lagos became the capital of the province Algarve. The 1755 earthquake destroyed most of the architectural testimony to the cultural and economic blossoming of the city. Silves sank into insignificance.

Silves shows grandeur at the Praça do Município; the cathedral and the crenellated castle clearly bring the town's former glory to mind. In recent years the authorities in Silves have made obvious efforts at beautifying the town. Rua Elias García and some smaller streets nearby have been converted into an attractive pedestrian zone with small shops and street cafés. Near the bridge over the Rio Arade a park with benches, trees and fountains was laid out.

What to See in Silves

Begin a tour through Silves at the Praça do Município, and walk up-hill to the cathedral and castle. In the old quarter there is also an interesting archaeological museum. After a visit relax in one of the cafés nearby; Café Inglês at the castle or a simple café on the Praça do Município are recommended. A look at the famous Cruz de Portugal at the eastern edge of town is also worthwhile. Finally don't miss walking down to the Rio Arade.

Walking tour

The dominant structure on the square is the town hall, the câmara municipal, a tall building fronted by an arcaded walk. The **Torreão das Portas da Cidade**, a former watchtower and city gate on the eastern corner of the square that was once integrated into the city wall, is impressive. On the other side of the town hall, to the west, the course of the old city wall can still be seen. Near the former city gate is a so-called *pelourinho*, the pillory of Silves, which like the tower is made of the red sandstone typical of this region.

Praça do Município

The cathedral of Silves was built in the Gothic style in the 13th century **on the site of a former mosque** after the Portuguese conquered the city. It was altered several times in the following centuries. Silves was the episcopal see for more than 300 years, from 1242 until 1577, and thus the main church of the Algarve.

★ Sé

The **earthquake** of 1755 destroyed the main part of the church, but the crossing and choir were spared, as can be seen inside. Gothic elements, which survived the earthquake more or less undamaged or were restored, are recognizable outside as well. The massive **doorway with a pointed arch** of yellow sandstone stands out clearly from the façade. Note the heads of humans and animals above the arch. The Gothic pinnacles contrast strangely with the Baroque decorations at the top of the façade. When walking around the outside of the church, note the elongated **Gothic windows** on the southern transept and the choir. The choir was built using red sandstone from the Monchique mountains.

The different styles are especially clear inside: Most of the church nave was rebuilt after the earthquake with red sandstone, which harmonizes quite well with the undamaged parts. The sandstone columns are very plain with especially sober capitals, but their basic form relates to the remaining Gothic capitals with simple plant decoration at the crossing. The purely Gothic crossing and the choir with cross-ribbed vaulting are unique in the Algarve. The Portuguese coat of arms is on one of the capstones in the choir. The grave slab for King João II is set into the floor of the choir, but his remains were taken to the monastery church of Batalha in 1499. In the left transept

← *Inside the cathedral of Silves: the choir was one of the few examples of Gothic architecture in the Algarve to survive the earthquake of 1755*

⏱ and the choir there are graves of crusaders and bishops. Opening times: Mon – Fri 9am – 1pm, 3pm – 6pm, Sat 9am – 1pm

Igreja da Misericórdia

The Igreja da Misericórdia was built in the 16th century. On the side facing the cathedral a **Manueline window frame** from this time is still visible. The main doorway is in the neo-classical style. Inside paintings from the 17th century have been preserved. The work on the high altar was done by a well-known Algarve amateur painter in the 19th century.

★★ Castelo

Visible from a great distance, the mighty red sandstone Moorish castle towers over the town, crowned by battlements. There were probably fortifications on this site already in Phoenician, Celtiberian and in Roman times. The complex, which dates from the Arab period, gained its present appearance from restoration work in 1940. There is a monument to the Portuguese king **Sancho I**, who conquered Xelb for the first time in 1189.

Archaeological excavations in the inner courtyard exposed parts of the Moorish castle, so that visitors have an impression of its layout. **Cisterns** and **underground storerooms** were also found. The good storage facilities and water supply meant that the Arabs were able to withstand a long siege. The Cisterna Grande, the large cistern, was built in the 13th century and served as Silves' main water reservoir until the 20th century. On the castle grounds there is also an old mine shaft where Arabs and before them the Romans mined copper. In the broad courtyard there are trees and shrubs, some of them imported from overseas by the Portuguese: jacaranda trees with blue blossoms and pepper trees from Brazil, cedars from Bolivia, Japanese loquats with their yellow fruits and Canarian date palms. During a comprehensive renovation of the courtyard modern touches were added to contrast with the old features. A stroll along the circular wall offers beautiful views of Silves and the surrounding
⏱ countryside. Opening times: daily 9am – 5.30pm

Museu Municipal de Arqueologia

Museu Municipal de Arqueologia is located in Rua das Portas de Loulé. A large private home stood here before the earthquake, and during excavations utensils for everyday use were found in large numbers. The finds in the museum mainly come from Silves, Loulé and São Bartolomeu de Messines.

A tour through the museum – signs and descriptions are in Portuguese – goes through the archaeological collection in chronological order with exhibits from the Palaeolithic, Neolithic, Bronze and Iron Ages. Then come Roman finds, many remains from the Arab period and finally excavation finds from after 1189 or 1242, i.e. from Portuguese culture. There is also a **cistern** from the 12th or 13th century that was integrated into the museum building. Stairs run around the inside of the 18m/60ft-deep shaft. As the water level sank it was possible to go down to the lower level. Another survival from the Arab period is the city wall, which can be seen through the glass front of the museum. Opening times: Mon – Sat 9am until 5.30pm

Fábrica do Inglês

In the eastern part of the town centre there are the grounds of a former cork factory. The cork industry traditionally played a role in the region around Silves; there were several smaller and larger cork factories here. The factory, which was originally in English ownership (hence the name »Fábrica do Inglês«), was founded in 1894. Until the mid-1990s corks mainly for port bottles were made and stored here.

Relax and enjoy: café in the old city of Silves below the cathedral

CORK – NOT JUST ANOTHER PLUG

There was a revolution in European drinking in the 17th century. First chocolate came from Central America, then coffee from Arabia, finally tea from China. The consumption of spirits spread after the Dutch developed the art of distilling. Beer with hops lasted longer and the cities finally got clean water – from pipes as Roman times. But no one had found a way yet to make wine keep. ...

Ever since Roman times, wine had been stored in **wooden casks**, which had two disadvantages: the wine's bouquet disappeared during lengthy storage in wood, and after the casks were tapped the wine quickly lost its character. At the beginning of the 17th century **glass bottles** were introduced, but only to bring wine up from the cellar. Then it was discovered that wine could age safely and that it kept better in a neutral, airtight glass bottle closed with a cork. At that time bottles were very convex and could only be stored standing up, which made the cork dry and allowed air to get into the bottle. In the late 18th century slimmer bottles were developed in which wine could be

stored lying down – in this way the wine kept the cork moist and the seal remained airtight. In the early 18th century port bottles were still shaped like round carafes; they have had their present shape since 1812.

Every nine years

With 55% of the world's volume, Portugal **is the leading producer of cork**. Portugal has been exporting corks for over 200 years; about 30 million corks are produced daily in Portugal, 500 million champagne corks per year. Portugal's 70 million cork oaks grow mainly in the Ribatejo, the Alentejo and the Algarve. The trees grow to a height of 6 – 10m/ 20 – 33ft and have an average lifespan of 150 years. The cork oak, or *sobreiro*, can only be peeled the first time when it is **at least twenty years old**. Cork, which is the bark of the tree, can only be harvested in the hot summer months when the tree's metabolism is at its most intense and the bark can be peeled off more easily. However, the inner bark, from which the cork grows, should not be damaged in the process. It takes **at least nine years** until the tree has formed new cork and can be peeled again. A number is written on the tree trunk after the harvest: a »5« means for instance that the tree was peeled in 2005, and its cork cannot be harvested again before 2014.

Versatile

After the harvest the cork bark is stacked, dried for three months and then sent to **cork factories** to be processed. In order to eliminate bugs and to remove mineral salts and tannins, the cork is boiled first. Boiling causes the cells to expand, which makes the cork elastic and supple. Then the bark is pressed, dried, sliced and sorted according to how it will be used. Since cork is long-lasting, light, elastic, impermeable for gas and water, non-inflammable and does not conduct electricity, it has **many uses**: for coasters, gaskets, life-savers, insulation, insoles, wall cover-ings, buoys for fishing nets etc. But the most important product is still bottle corks. Bottles can be sealed ideally with cork because of tiny suction cups in the cork walls and because of its strong natural ability to expand. Putrefactive agents cannot penetrate it. Since cork has no taste or smell, contains no toxigens and does not change, it is perfectly suited for storing wine. Winegrowers world-wide agree that **there is no material more suitable to their purposes** – even if synthetic corks are becoming more and more of a threat to cork produc-ers.

Cork is becoming rare

Although cork is a renewable raw material, it still should not be thrown away – for several reasons. The large amount of resin in cork means that **poisonous gases** are released when **cork is burned**. Moreover the natural renewal of cork in Portugal is no longer to be taken for granted: the many **eucalyptus trees** that were planted for the paper industry draw water out of the ground. Cork groves near eucalyptus plantations are often completely dried out deep under ground; **there is not enough water** for growth and the ecological balance is permanently damaged. So this ver-satile raw material could become even more expensive in the future.

✷

Cruz de Portugal

When leaving town in the direction of São Bartolomeu de Messines the famous Cruz de Portugal, which was made around 1500 out of white limestone, can be seen. This sacred sculpture is an example of a **Manueline way cross** that is unique for the Algarve. Christ on the cross is depicted on the front side; on the back a Pietà is shown. The year 1025 carved into the base of the cross is a riddle for historians. It is assumed that the lower part dates from the Arab period.

Ermida de Nossa Senhora dos Mártires

The Ermida de Nossa Senhora dos Mártires north-west of the Praça do Município originated in a 12th-century structure, built when Silves was first conquered by crusaders under Sancho I. The fighters who fell in the battle for the city were laid to rest in the chapel. The second chapel on this site was built in the Manueline period, fell victim to the earthquake and rebuilt after 1755. The grave inside is probably that of a bishop of the 13th or 14th century.

Arco da Rebola

In Rua da Cruz da Palmeira the remains of an originally Arab city gate have been preserved on one building. It was presumably still an entrance to the city during Portuguese times.

Ponte

The pretty bridge across the Rio Arade stands on the site of a bridge from Roman times. Today's bridge was built in the Middle Ages and reinforced in later years.

The Rio Arade is a peaceful river here, and turtles can be seen occasionally on its banks. When there is enough water, boats make the trip to Portimão and back during the high season.

Mercado

In the market hall down near the bridge there is lots of activity on weekday mornings.

Around Silves

Barragem do Funcho

Rio Arade is dammed up a few miles north-east of Silves at Barragem do Funcho. The giant water reservoir is a popular **local recreation area** for the Portuguese. Some water sports are also possible here. Tourists generally do not find the reservoir attractive, but the drive on the narrow road along the southern shore offers great views.

Sítio das Fontes

An idyllic place for picnicking, strolling or just relaxing is the Sítio das Fontes, a picturesque area of springs 5km/3mi south-west of Silves. From the N 124 in Silves-Gare a road branches off to the west towards Estômbar and runs through pretty orchard landscape. Follow the signs to the right to the Sítio das Fontes, then drive a dirt track for about 500m/1650ft. From the parking area it takes just a few minutes to walk to the picnic grounds with olive trees in picturesque landscape. Narrow paths lead to the limestone springs that well up out of the ground. There are several freshwater ponds. This is a popular spot at weekends, but it is quieter here during the week.

★ Tavira

K 5

Conselho: Tavira   **Population:** 10,000

Tavira is one of the prettiest towns in the Algarve. It is picturesquely situated on the banks of the Rio Gilão. Tavira is often called »Little Venice«, a somewhat daring comparison, though when its typical hipped roofs are reflected in the still waters of the river it is a delightful place.

The town is located in the south-east of the Algarve, only about 20km/13mi from the Spanish border. It is built on both banks of the Rio Gilão (also called Rio Séqua), which flows into the Atlantic here. Tavira itself is not adjacent to the open sea, but lies close to the Ria Formosa lagoon. Just to the south-west of the town is the Ilha de Tavira, an island in the lagoon primarily characterized by its sand dunes. The expansive orchards – mainly oranges and lemons – in

 ## VISITING TAVIRA

INFORMATION
Praça de República 5
Tel. 281 322 511

WHERE TO EAT
► Moderate
③ *Beira Rio*
Rua Borda d'Água da Asséca
Beautiful location a short distance from the river. Well-cooked international dishes, good Portuguese wines

► Moderate/Inexpensive
① *Bica*
Rua Almirante Cándido dos Reis 24
Tel. 281 323 843
Old-established typical restaurant in the centre of town, always busy. The house specialties are cataplana and various good grilled dishes.

② *Ponto de Encontro*
Praça Dr. António Padinha 39
Tel. 281 323 730
Simple local restaurant with a homely atmosphere specializing in fish.

WHERE TO STAY
► Luxury/Mid-range
① *Hotel Vila Galé Albacora*
Quatro Águas
Tel. 281 380 800
Fax 281 380 850
www.vilagale.pt
A little way outside Tavira, directly by the sea. Located in a former tuna fishing station.

► Mid-range/Budget
② *Hotel Porta Nova*
Rua António Pinheiro
Tel. 281 329 700
Fax 281 324 215
www.varandoteis.com
Nice, comfortable hotel; the rooms have splendid views of Tavira.

► Budget
③ *Princesa do Gilão*
Rua Borda d'Água Aguiar 10-12
Tel. 281 325 171
Small, simple and well-kept guesthouse on the banks of the river.

Tavira's hinterland fill the air with aromatic scents during the spring blossom.

Fishing plays a key role in Tavira – the town was once the centre for tuna fishing off the Algarve coast – as does salt extraction. At the mouth of the Rio Gilão there are some salt flats. In spite of the glorious sandy beaches in the neighbourhood, tourism is not yet as important in Tavira as in many places further west along the Algarve coast. The first large hotels in the area have only just been built – and have not spoiled the landscape.

History   When exactly Tavira was established has not yet been clarified. The town probably goes back to an Iberian settlement in the 2nd millennium BC and it is assumed that the Phoenicians also had a trading post here. When the Romans came they found a settlement at the mouth of the Rio Gilão named **Balsa** and adopted the name. The present name Tavira comes from **Tabira**, which is what the Arabs called it. Tavira was an important harbour in Arab times and well into the Middle Ages. In 1242 the Portuguese under Dom Paio Peres Correia conquered Tavira – according to tradition seven Portuguese knights were murdered by Arabs despite a ceasefire, so the Portuguese took the city by force. During the early colonial period Portuguese forces in North Africa were supported from Tavira because of its proximity to the coast of Morocco. The harbour lost its role after the North African colonies were given up; the harbour basin also silted up. Spain's rule over Portugal between 1580 and 1640 and a plague epidemic in 1645–46 sealed the decline. Finally the earthquake of 1755 destroyed large parts of the city. Since then Tavira has not been an important place.

Built in a harmo-nious and unified style   Since the town had to be completely rebuilt after an earthquake, few buildings are less than 250 years old, but their uniformity gives the town a very harmonious look. One typical feature of Tavira is are **hipped roofs** of many older houses. This shape has since been adopted by modern architects. It is interesting to compare neighbouring Olhão, where the houses are cube-shaped and the manner of construction is completely different.

What to See in Tavira

Walking tour   Tavira should be toured at leisure to take in the atmosphere. Anyone wanting to see a few sights while touring the town could begin at the centrally located Praça da República and first look at the south-western part of the centre. The Igreja da Misericórdia, the castle and Igreja de Santa Maria do Castelo can be visited. Then cross the river on the old Roman bridge and stroll through the pretty residential lanes and alleys of the quieter part of town on the other side of the

Tavira – the Algarve's »Little Venice« →

Tavira at sunset: the park along the river is illuminated at night

river. The view from the road along the riverbank road Rua Jacques Pessoa to the other side of the town is wonderful. Several restaurants or cafés on the riverbank provide a break.

Praça da República

The centre of Tavira is the Praça da República on the right bank of the river. Next to the square on the east is a park with flowers and trees. Beyond the park on the south-east is Tavira's former **market hall**, which was built in 1887, and is no longer actually a market. After it was restored shops and eateries moved in. Small bars and cafés have wonderful seating right next to the river.

Ponte Romana

In recent years many bridges have been built across the Rio Gilão. For centuries there was only the one, the seven-arched bridge north of the Praça da República. The bridge goes back to Roman times, and the **Roman road** connecting Faro and Mértola used to lead across it. Today's bridge, which is a footbridge, is a reconstruction built in the 17th century.

✳
Igreja da Misericórdia

The narrow Rua da Galeria leads off Rua da Liberdade to the Igreja da Misericórdia. Right next to the church stands the Arco da Misericórdia, the remnant of a city gate from Arab times.

In spite of rebuilding undertaken in 1755 after the earthquake, the church, which originally dates from 1541, remains one of the finest examples of ecclesiastical **Renaissance architecture** in the Algarve. Details of the façade are interesting: in the middle of the door under a canopy is the Senhora da Misericórdia, the lady of mercy, who is supported by angels. To the left are the crown and coat of arms or Portugal, to the right is Tavira's coat of arms with a seven-arched bridge, a Portuguese king with a crown and an Arab king with a turban.

Inside the blue and white azulejo pictures with elaborate frames and the gilded high altar catch the eye. Again there is the Portuguese crown and under the canopy the coat of arms. The capitals are worth a closer look: some of them have masks on them. The organ on the loft is unusual – organs are rare in Algarve churches.

Tavira Map

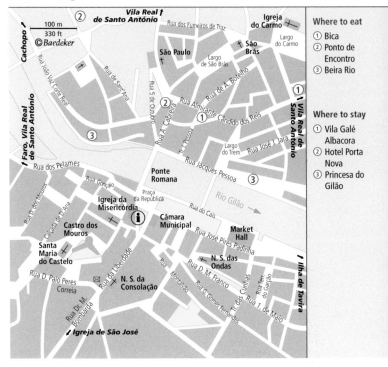

The castle, which stands above the town centre, is entered via Travessa da Fonte. The castle was originally built by the Romans and was taken over by the Moors. It was also rebuilt when Dom Dinis I conquered the town for the Portuguese, but nowadays all that remains of the fortification are a few walls. Part of the castle grounds have been landscaped as a pretty garden, which is privately owned but still open to the public.

There is a great view of Tavira and the Rio Gilão from the garden and the castle walls. Opening times: Mon – Fri 8am – noon, 1pm – 5pm, Sat, Sun 9am until 7pm (in the winter until 5pm)

★
Castro dos Mouros

☾

Next to the castle garden is the church of Santa Maria do Castelo. It was built by the Portuguese on the site of a mosque. The original structure dates from the 13th century and was completely reconstructed according to the original plans after the earthquake. Of the Gothic church only the entrances have remained, along with the furnishings in some of the side chapels and the arches over the side altars.

★
Igreja de Santa Maria do Castelo

In the choir of the church are the tombs of Dom Paio Peres Correia and **seven Portuguese knights** who were killed by the Moors in 1242 in spite of a truce having been agreed, upon which the city was attacked and taken by Christian troops. The second side chapel still has Manueline ceiling decorations.

Water tower / A visit to the *câmara obscura* in the water tower is a real pleasure.
Câmara obscura The câmara obscura makes it possible to observe Tavira from a
🕓 hidden vantage point. Opening times: June – Sept 10am – 8pm, Oct – May until 6pm

Palácio da A visit to the Palácio da Galeria a short distance behind the church
Galeria Igreja da Misericórdia is also worthwhile; it shows rotating exhibitions.

Igreja de The church Igreja de São José on Praça Zacarias Guerreiro, south-
São José east of the city centre, has an interesting floor plan. It is octagonal with sides of unequal length. The high altar is decorated with trompe-l'oeil painting. Two side chapels are of Gothic and Manueline origin respectively.

Praça Cross the Rio Gilão via the old bridge and follow Rua 5 de Outubro
Dr Padinha to Praça Dr Padinha, a very pretty square bordered by flowerbeds and trees. On the square is the **Igreja de São Paulo**, originally a Renaissance church, with beautiful painting from the 15th and 16th centuries.

Largo de A square with an equally pleasant atmosphere is Largo de São Brás
São Brás with a few Judas trees. The little Capela de São Brás on the northeast end of the square has a pleasantly austere façade.

Igreja do Carmo Not far to the north-east of Largo de São Brás is the very sober Largo do Carmo. The former Carmelite monastery with the Igreja do Carmo is located here. The church was built in the 18th century and is known for the carving work inside as well as the elaborately decorated 18th-century choir stalls.

Around Tavira

✳
Ilha de Tavira The Ilha de Tavira lies off the coast to the south-west of Tavira and can be reached by boat during the high season. The **ferry** sets out from the road leading along the shore a little way beyond the market hall; another quay is located outside town near the mouth of the river at Quatro Águas. Boats leave from here for the island all year round. There is a narrow pedestrian bridge to the islands a little further west at Santa Luzia (Pedras d'El Rei). The Ilha de Tavira has a long sandy beach and shallow dunes. The surf is not that strong, so the beach is well suited for children).

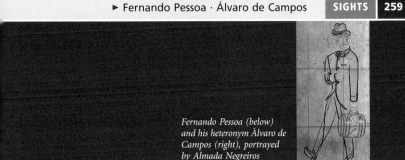

Fernando Pessoa (below) and his heteronym Àlvaro de Campos (right), portrayed by Almada Negreiros

BORN IN TAVIRA

Even though he never existed, he was born on 15 October 1890 in Tavira. He wore a monocle, was tall, thin and always slightly stooped. He was described as having a temper and even as having no feelings. Álvaro de Campos was not a pseudonym, no character from a novel, not even a person who was deliberately invented – Álvaro de Campos was a heteronym.

And it was one of several in whose existence the poet Fernando Pessoa clothed himself or divided himself up or multiplied himself. Much thought has been given to the heteronyms of the most famous Portuguese writer of the 20th century. Pessoa spent his childhood in South Africa, where he grew up bilingual, and he wrote poetry at that time already. One possibility, it is claimed, is that Pessoa tended to be lonely, and with his heteronyms he created a **circle of friends** for himself. The most important of them, next to Álvaro de Campos, were the bucolic poet Alberto Caeiro and Ricardo Reis, a doctor from Porto who wrote neo-classical poetry. Bernardo Soares was a half-heteronym that always appeared when Fernando Pessoa was tired and sleepy. Each one of them had a specific character, a certain appearance, birth date, birthplace and more: Pessoa even had **horoscopes** made for them. Álvaro de Campos came from a Jewish family. After attending secondary school he trained as a **ship-building engineer** in Glasgow. He took a long voyage to the orient. In 1914 he returned and lived in Lisbon, where he devoted much time to **doing nothing**, and the rest of it to writing poetry. He was an adherent of »non-Aristotelian aesthetics« and wrote his **poetry** in this spirit. The heteronyms were in close dialogue with each other, and they held discussions with Pessoa as well. It is known that Álvaro de Campos associated with **avant-garde circles in Lisbon** who stirred up the citizens. He is supposed to have got along well with Alberto Caeiro, and even dedicated writings to him. He was still closer to the poet Fernando Pessoa. Their affinity was so strong that Álvaro de Campos died in 1935, the same year that Pessoa died.

Santa Luzia Santa Luzia, 2km/1.2mi west of Tavira, is a somewhat developed fishing village. The local fishers specialize in catching squid. To do this they lower ceramic pots attached to ropes into the water. Since squid like darkness they are easy to catch in these jars.

Colourful fishing boats are tied up in the channel in the mud flats, and Ilha de Tavira lies beyond them. On the western edge of Santa Luzia near the holiday resort Pedras d'El-Rei a **bridge** leads across to the island. The beach at Barril can be reached either on foot or with a small **island train**.

Luz de Tavira Luz de Tavira is located 5km/3mi west of Tavira on the busy N 125. Igreja Matriz on the through road dates from the 16th century and was one of the few churches to survive the 1755 earthquake almost undamaged; it is an impressive example of Renaissance architecture on the Algarve. A few Manueline elements such as the pretty **side door** and the baptismal font have been preserved on the building. The azulejo decoration in the main chapel was made in

> ## ! *Baedeker* TIP
>
> ### Marisqueira Fialho
> A very popular restaurant right on the lagoon, south of the Torre de Aires, which serves very good seafood. Tel. 281 961 222

the 15th century in Seville. 2km/1.2mi south-west of Luz de Tavira near the coast there are the remains of a medieval watchtower (Torre de Aires or Torre de Ares). The drive here is more rewarding than the destination itself: the road goes past a small hamlet of typical Algarve cottages and then directly along the edge of the lagoon.

Cabanas 6km/3.5mi east of Tavira lies Cabanas, a holiday resort in the region east of Tavira, where tourism is flourishing. The holidaymakers, most of whom stay in bungalow villages, appreciate the broad, mostly deserted sandy beach on an offshore sandbank that is reached by boat from the village.

Cabanas caters for visitors with several new cafés and restaurants along the new promenade. There is a pretty path from here along the water to Fábria or Cacela Velha (►Vila Real de Santo António).

Vila do Bispo

B 5

Conselho: Vila do Bispo   **Population:** 3500

This village in the extreme south-west of the Algarve is an insignificant place in itself, but is the seat of the regional administration under which once-mighty Sagres falls. Far away from the bustle of the touristy Algarve coast, Vila do Bispo really is almost »at the end of the world«.

The »end of the world«: Costa Vicentina near Vila do Bispo

In the Middle Ages the village was called Santa Maria do Cabo; the name shows its relationship to Cabo de São Vicente 10km/6mi away. Later it was given to the bishop of Faro as a gift, which explains its present name: Vila do Bispo (city of the bishop).
Vila do Bispo is a quiet rural village without any special features. The village church, which was built in the late 18th century, is pretty. The interior is richly decorated with blue 18th-century azulejos and gilded woodcarvings.

Around Vila do Bispo

Some of the destinations round about are more interesting than Vilo do Bispo itself, especially ▶Sagres and Cabo de São Vicente.

Sagres

2km/1.2mi east of Vila do Bispo lies the village of Raposeira; it is remembered for the fact that Henry the Navigator is supposed to have lived here in the Casa do Infante. There is a small village church with a Manueline doorway.

Raposeira

On the N 125 between Raposeira and Vila do Bispo in the middle of a field north of the road (visible from the road) stands the chapel in which Henry the Navigator is said to have prayed. A visitor centre is being built. This, the oldest church in the Algarve, was built in the 13th century with an early Gothic door and a simple rosette window over the entrance. The capitals on the columns inside, decorated with human and animal heads, are especially pretty. Despite the

★
**Ermida de
Nossa Senhora
de Guadalupe**

nearby N 125, this place always radiates a very special atmosphere. There are changing exhibitions on display in the information centre nearby. Opening times: May – Sept Tue – Sun 10.30am – 1pm and 2pm – 6pm, Oct – April Tue – Sun 9.30am – 1pm and 2pm – 5pm

Beaches Via Raposeira there is access to the beaches **Praia de Ingrina** and **Praia do Zavial** 4km/2.5mi to the south; these are small sandy coves that have hardly been used by tourists.

Salema In Salema, 8km/5mi east of Vila do Bispo, tourism has been dominant for some time already, but the old village, which consists of little more than a single street, has not changed much. Large hotels and apartment buildings have been built around the old town centre, but there is still some distinctly individual accommodation. Praia da Figueira further to the west (access via Figueira) is quieter than the municipal beach.

Burgau Burgau 12km/7mi east of Vila do Bispo has to an extent kept its old character. The town sprawls along the edge of a cliff above a relatively narrow cove. There is modest accommodation in Burgau and a great variety of eateries.

Vilamoura

G 5

Conselho: Loulé

The holiday resort Vilamoura was built in the 1970s and 1980s around a marina that was ultra-modern at that time. The »Moorish village«, which was planned on the drawing board, is an exclusive holiday destination with a great variety of luxurious accommodation and numerous recreational activities.

There are several golf courses close by, as well as countless tennis courts and horse riding, and of course all sorts of water sports can be enjoyed. Along with many bars and nightclubs a casino also entertains the guests. If this is not enough, Quarteira is nearby and Albufeira only 10km/6mi to the west.

On the drawing board Vilamoura's houses are spread out over a broad green area. It is clear that the planning was done on a drawing board; nothing grew up spontaneously. Systematically organized areas with pretty, low apartment buildings are interspersed with high rises that are not lined up in a row but stand isolated. The buildings line broad streets that are semicircular or horseshoe-shaped so that all sense or orientation is lost immediately. Fortunately city maps are posted everywhere that help people get around this city without a centre.

What to See in Vilamoura

The most likely place to call a town centre in Vilamoura is the marina, which is known for its international clientele. It was built in the 1970s, and is one of the largest and best-equipped yacht harbours in Europe. There is room for almost 1000 boats – from luxurious yachts to simple dinghies. Restaurants and cafés line up along the harbour promenade.

Marina

The Phoenicians probably found this section of the coast a good place to drop anchor. A Roman settlement between the 1st and 5th centuries AD has been documented. There must have been a harbour on a lagoon here, from which they sailed into the open sea. The remains of a patrician house, several smaller houses, baths, wells and water reservoirs have been found. Interesting mosaics from the 3rd century AD were preserved. The excavation finds are on display in a small adjacent museum. Traces of later cultures have also been found, so it is known that the Visigoths used the area between the 5th and 8th centuries and the Arabs from the 8th to the 11th centuries. Opening times: daily 9.30am – 12.30pm and 2pm – 6pm, in the winter half year until 5pm

**Cerro da Vila
Estação
Arqueológica**

Sunset at the yacht harbour of Vilamoura

⏵ VISITING VILAMOURA

WHERE TO EAT

▶ Moderate

Akvavit
Marina de Vilamoura
Tel. 289 380 712
www.restaurante-akvavit.com
Fish and seafood are specialties;
extensive wine list.

WHERE TO STAY

▶ Mid-range
Hotel Dom Pedro Marina
Avenida Tivoli Lote H 4
Tel. 289 300 780, fax 289 381 001

www.dompedro.com
Hotel with 150 rooms; popular with
Portuguese guests. Relatively moderate prices, tastefully furnished rooms,
near the beach.

▶ Mid-range/Budget
Cegonha Country Club
Tel. 289 300 850
www.cegonhacountryclub.com
Quietly located west of Vilamoura
with seven apartments of different
sizes. Breakfast can be ordered
separately.

Family Golf Park Anyone looking for a diversion can go to the interesting crazy-golf
course Family Golf Park for fun golf in a »Roman« ambience. Open-
ⓞ ing times: Feb – May and Nov daily 10am – 6pm, June until 10pm,
July – mid-Sept until midnight, mid-Sept until late Oct until 7pm.

Vila Real de Santo António

L 4

Conselho: Vila Real de Santo António   **Population:** 11,000

**Vila Real de Santo António is located deep in the south-east of
Portugal on the Guadiana River. The small border town is a popular destination for day trippers – including many from Spain – who
like to wander through the bustling centre with its shops looking
for bargains.**

Vila Real de Santo António is connected to its Spanish counterpart
Ayamonte on the opposite bank by means of a regular ferry service,
although the ferry has been declining in importance since a motorway bridge was built across the river a few miles to the north. A trip
down the Guadiana from Vila Real is enjoyable. The city is the ter-
minus of the railway line, which comes from Lagos and runs along
the Algarve coast.

History Vila Real de Santo António is still young: it was completely rebuilt in
1774 after the older town **Santo António da Arenilha** was destroyed
by **disastrous floods** in the early 18th century. Santo António da

▶ VISITING VILA REAL DE SANTO ANTÓNIO

INFORMATION
Avenida Marginal, Monte Gordo
Tel. 281 544 495

EXCURSIONS
Guadiana Tour
Rui and Bettina Gaspar do Rosário
8950-418 Castro Marim
Tel. 281 956 634
Mobile 968 831 553, 965 648 189
www.guadianatour.com
Various tours, including boat tours on
the Guadiana from Vila Real de Santo
António up to Alcoutim and back.

ENTERTAINMENT
The place for night life in the region is
Monte Gordo. There is also a casino
there.

WHERE TO EAT
▶ Moderate
Caves de Guadiana
Avenida da República 89
Tel. 281 544 498
Excellent Portuguese cuisine makes
the Caves de Guadiana highly popular
with the locals, too.

WHERE TO STAY
▶ Mid-range
Hotel Casablanca
8900 Monte Gordo
Praceta Casablanca
Tel. 281 511 444
Fax 081 511 999
www.casablancainn.pt
Small but stylish hotel in the centre of
Monte Gordo, somewhat removed
from the bustling promenades. About
40 rooms, some with a view of the sea.
There are patios around the building,
the furnishings are pleasant, and the
service very good. No organized
entertainment or sport but a guarantee of quiet relaxation.

▶ Budget
Hotel Apolo
Av. dos Bombeiros Portugueses
8900 Vila Real de Santo António
Tel. 281 512 448
Simple but pleasant and well-kept
hotel with 42 rooms.

Arenilha was a fishing town and also a defensive post against attacks
from North Africa. The small locality had fortifications; some of the
towers remained until the 19th century. Vila Real de Santo António
is not a reconstruction of this earlier town, as under the Marquês de
Pombal (▶Famous People), who was a minister under José I, **a completely new city was built** in only five months. The new town was
settled by fishermen from Aveiro on the Portuguese west coast, who
had to give up fishing there when the town was cut off from the
ocean after a storm. Other people came from various regions of the
Algarve, including the nearby Monte Gordo. The resettlement took
place under massive pressure by the government. Within a short
time an economic upswing began with the help of government subsidies. In 1777 Vila Real de Santo António already had about 5000 inhabitants.

Praça do Marquês do Pombal – the focus of the grid-like city centre

Small, square city plan

The town centre alongside the river has a distinctively uniform appearance. The highly regular layout of the town was the work of the Marquês de Pombal (▶Famous People), who had previously rebuilt the lower quarter of Lisbon, Baixa, after the Portuguese capital was largely destroyed by the disastrous earthquake of 1755. Like Baixa in Lisbon, the centre of Vila Real de Santo António was conceived on **a chequerboard pattern** – a principle of urban planning that was already employed in Greece in the 5th century BC. Since the town had to be completely rebuilt, a concept like this one could be put to use. It suited Marquês de Pombal's world view, too, since he was Portugal's most important proponent of enlightened absolutism. The basic principle was a rational appearance of sober clarity and functionality. The historical centre is sometimes called the **Pombaline Centre** after the Marquês de Pombal. The most important planners and architects were Reinaldo dos Santos, Ramão de Sousa and Carlos Mardel; the latter was also involved in the rebuilding of the centre of Lisbon.

What to See in Vila Real de Santo António

Praça do Marquês de Pombal

The centre of Vila Real de Santo António is the Praça do Marquês de Pombal. The spacious square was paved in 1879 with star-shaped paving stones. The rays start at the obelisk in the middle, which has the crown and armillary sphere at the top. It was built in 1775 for **José I**, who carried out many educational and agricultural reforms during his reign. The square is bordered by low, relatively uniform houses. The sobriety is relieved by pretty orange trees, which fill the square with their scent in spring, and a few street-side cafés.

On the north side of Praça do Marquês de Pombal the line of houses is interrupted by the Igreja Paroquial. The church, which was also built in the 18th century, was completely renovated in 1949. The tiled baptistery is worth a look.

Igreja Paroquial

Not far to the west of Praça do Marquês de Pombal the market hall was converted into an arts centre. Rotating exhibitions are held here. The small Museu Manuel Cabanas has also moved into this building. It displays woodcarvings and etchings by the artist Manuel Cabanas (1879 – 1969).

Centro Cultural Antonio Aleixo

Avenida da República runs along the bank of the Guadiana. There are benches for relaxing and enjoying the view of the yacht harbour and across the river to the opposite side and on to Ayamonte.

Avenida da República

Around Vila Real de Santo António

Monte Gordo, the neighbour to the west of Vila Real de Santo António, is the only really unattractive **tourist centre** east of Faro. As is

Monte Gordo

Cacela Velha: view of the lagoon island from the church square

usually the case in the central Algarve coast, large hotels and apartment buildings were built right on the Atlantic coast in this former fishing village. There is a beautiful beach right in town and in both directions from the town. Holidaymakers will find a **good tourist infrastructure** with many shops, restaurants, bars, discos and a casino.

Manta Rota is a small, somewhat unstructured looking village some 10km/6mi west of Vila Real de Santo António. The lagoon system of the Ria Formosa ends here and thus Manta Rota is right on the open sea. The endless beach, which stretches toward the east as far as Monte Gordo, is excellent; its best-known section is the fabulous Praia Verde, which is bordered by a pine wood.

Manta Rota

Another 5km/3mi to the west lies the tiny hamlet Cacela Velha in an extremely charming location above the coastline. Cacela Velha was once an important place. Today it consists of only a few houses, but appears quite natural and complete. It was probably founded by the Phoenicians. The **church square** is unusually beautiful and offers a view of the mud flats, the off-shore islands and beyond them the open sea. The 16th-century church has a pretty Renaissance main door and a Gothic side door. Many day-trippers come here, but there are still only a few restaurants.

✱
Cacela Velha

← *Beach holiday on the Algarve coast – recreation guaranteed!*

INDEX

PHOTO CREDITS

LIST OF MAPS AND ILLUSTRATIONS

PUBLISHER'S INFORMATION

Illustrations etc: 153 illustrations, 19 maps and diagrams, one map
Text: Dr. Eva Missler, Achim Bourner (Special p. 216/217)
Baedeker editorial team: Dr. Eva Missler; English edition: John Sykes
Translation: Barbara Schmidt-Runkel
Cartography: Franz Huber, Munich; MAIRDUMONT/Falk Verlag, Ostfildern (map)
3D illustrations: jangled nerves, Stuttgart
Design: independent Medien-Design, Munich; Kathrin Schemel

Editor-in-chief: Rainer Eisenschmid, Baedeker Ostfildern

1st edition 2012
Based on Baedeker Allianz Reiseführer »Algarve« 7. Auflage 2012

Copyright: Karl Baedeker Verlag, Ostfildern
Publication rights: MAIRDUMONT GmbH & Co; Ostfildern

Printed in China